EASTER IN THE EARLY CHURCH

An Anthology of Jewish and Early Christian Texts

*Selected, Annotated, and Introduced
by*

Raniero Cantalamessa

Revised and Augmented by the Author

*Newly Translated from the Sources
and Edited with Further Annotations
by*
James M. Quigley, S.J.
and
Joseph T. Lienhard, S.J.

D1343039

A Liturgical Press Book

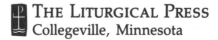

THE LITURGICAL PRESS
Collegeville, Minnesota

Cover design by Ann Blattner.
Icon: Crucifixion, School of Dionisij (15th century), Tretjakov Gallery, Moscow.

The original Italian edition, with texts in Greek and Latin, was published under the title *La Pasqua nella Chiesa antica* at Turin by the Società Editrice Internazionale in 1978 in the series "Traditio Christiana" edited by André Benoit, Franco Bolgiani, John Gordon Davies, and Willi Rordorf. A French translation by Françoise Morard, *La Pâque dans l'Église ancienne*, and a German translation by Annemarie Spoerri, *Ostern in der alten Kirche*, were published by Peter Lang at Berne in 1980 and 1981 respectively.

2	3	4	5	6	7	8	9

Library of Congress Cataloging-in-Publication Data

Pasqua nella Chiesa antica. English.
    Easter in the early church : an anthology of Jewish and early Christian texts / selected, annotated, and introduced by Raniero Cantalamessa ; revised and augmented by the author ; newly translated from the sources and edited with further annotations by James M. Quigley and Joseph T. Lienhard.
        p.   cm.
    Translation, without the original Greek and Latin texts, of:
La Pasqua nella Chiesa antica.
    Includes bibliographical references and indexes.
    ISBN 0-8146-2164-3
    1. Easter—History of doctrines—Early church, ca. 30-600—Sources.
I. Cantalamessa, Raniero. II. Quigley, James M., d. 1988.
III. Lienhard, Joseph T. IV. Title.
BV55.P2713   1993
263'.93'09015—dc20   92-43999
                                                      CIP

Contents

Sources for the History of the Paschal Controversy
of the Second Century

Greek Writers

Syrian Writers

Acknowledgments

The author and The Liturgical Press are grateful to the following publishers for the use of the copyrighted texts noted below:

Tanakh, edition of 1985; pp. 100–102; Exodus 12:1-28, and p. 300, Deuteronomy 16:1-10 by permission of the Jewish Publication Society, Philadelphia, Pennsylvania.

Reprinted by permission of the publishers and the Loeb Classical Library from Eusebius of Caesarea, *Ecclesiastical History,* vol. 2, pp. 235–237 (42 lines); Josephus, vol. 4, p. 301 (12 lines); Philo, vol. 7, pp. 395–397 (23 lines), Cambridge, Massachusetts: Harvard University Press.

St. Dionysius of Alexandria, tr. C. L. Feltoe, pp. 76–81 (51 lines), Macmillan Publishing Co., New York.

"Fathers of the Church," vol. 6, Justin Martyr, tr. Thomas B. Falls, pp. 208–209, 319–320 (29 lines); "Fathers of the Church," vol. 40, Tertullian, tr. Emily Joseph Daly, p. 174 (33 lines); "Fathers of the Church," vol. 64, Cyril of Jerusalem, tr. Leo McCauley and Anthony A. Stephenson, pp. 37–38 (23 lines) by permission of The Catholic University of America Press, Washington, D.C.

Melito of Sardis, *On the Pascha,* tr. Stuart George Hall, pp. 3–7, 23–25, 35–37, 39, 57–59 (131 lines); *Didascalia Apostolorum,* tr. R. H. Connolly, pp. 187–192 (13 lines) by permission of Oxford University Press, Oxford, United Kingdom.

New Holy Week Book, 1986, pp. 94–96: The Easter proclamation, *Exultet* by permission of Burns & Oates Ltd., Tunbridge Wells, Kent, United Kingdom.

Pp. 134–139, 141–142 from *Egeria's Travels,* J. Wilkinson, Warminster, 1981 by permission of Aris & Phillips Ltd., Warminster, England.

The quotations from Matthew 26:20-21, 26-29; Mark 14:17-18, 22-25; Luke 22:14-20; John 19:31-37, and 1 Corinthians 5:7-8 contained herein are from the Revised Standard Version Bible, Catholic Edition, copyright 1966 by the Division of Christian Education of the National Council of Churches of Christ in the United States of America. Used by permission. All rights reserved.

"Ancient Christian Writers," vol. 16, *Irenaeus,* tr. Joseph P. Smith, p. 64 (11 lines); vol. 40, *Paulinus of Nola,* tr. P. G. Walsh, p. 272 (11 lines), Paulist Press, New York.

Translators' Preface

In making an English edition of *La Pasqua nella Chiesa antica*, I could not be content with simply translating the author's translations of ancient texts. Nor could I simply gather existing English translations; for very many of the works excerpted in this book have never been translated into English, and in those that have, literal accuracy was often sacrificed to smooth style and English idiom, whereas, for our purposes, the reverse should be the case. Consequently I have, in most cases, made a fresh translation from the source—in the light of Father Cantalamessa's Italian version, of course, and with the help of the available Latin, German, French, or English translations.

The Introduction summarizing the author's conclusions from his study of the sources has been translated faithfully from the Italian, but two paragraphs in the section on the Syrian tradition have been revised by the author and partly transferred to the notes on text 87.

This English edition does not reproduce the Greek and Latin texts which the original edition printed on the pages opposite their Italian translations. But it does preserve the Scripture references and some of the textual variants and conjectures that were printed under the Greek and Latin texts. Hence it was necessary to recast all the annotations. The references to Scripture, if they are not too long, have been put in parentheses in the texts, and the significant textual variants have been incorporated into the single body of notes.

The author was under pressure to make his notes as brief as possible, and so, not only was he very economical with words, but he also frequently packed several notes into one. At the risk of misstating or missing some nuances of his thought, I have "unpacked" many of these compendious notes, pointing out the precise relevance of passages cited from patristic and modern sources and attaching each note or comment to the word in the text to which it belongs. With the author's approval I have added here and there an explanatory note of my own, but, lest he be blamed for my mistakes, I have marked my notes "(Tr.)."

All the references, whether to ancient or to modern works, have been verified. References have also been supplemented, both by including more recently published critical editions of the sources and by noting English translations of studies originally published in German, French, or Italian. Bibliographical information is often redundant rather than concise, for the sake of the beginning student and for those whose access to books through computers requires precise titles and exact spellings.

The material quoted in texts 7, 39, 50, 56, and 87 has been extended slightly in order to give the ancient authors' remarks on the Pascha more of a context and to allow them to speak for themselves rather than to have their ideas summarized in the notes. Text 89 has been replaced by a new text, and the author himself has added one new passage (text 141) and some references to recent studies, and has augmented the bibliography. The result is that the first English version of this highly-praised work is, at the same time, a thoroughly revised and augmented edition. We hope that as such it will be useful to advanced as well as to beginning students of patristic thought.

James M. Quigley, S.J.
August, 1988

Father James M. Quigley died on August 7, 1988. He had known for at least two years that his death was approaching. Three days before he died he was still working on his translation of Fr. Cantalamessa's book. Those who were members of his community in the last years of his life attest to his devotion to, and enthusiasm for, this project. Before his death, he asked me to finish the work of translation and editing and see the book through the press, a task I was more than happy to undertake. Most of the work is Father Quigley's. The translations of texts 117-122 and 128-141 are mine, as are the translation of the notes to those texts. These I have noted in their place, lest (in Fr. Quigley's own words) someone else should be blamed for my mistakes. I have also reviewed the whole manuscript, filling in lacunae that Fr. Quigley left and trying to make the style consistent. But Fr. Quigley was a careful scholar; there was little that needed correction. Lawrence J. Welch's assiduous proofreading further improved the manuscript. It has been a privilege for me to prepare Fr. Quigley's work for the publication it clearly merits.

Joseph T. Lienhard, S.J.
Fordham University
Easter, 1991

Note

Ancient authors often divided their works into books; modern editors have often added chapter divisions and section or sentence numbers. Accordingly "Eusebius, *Eccl. Hist.* 5, 23, 1" refers to his *Ecclesiastical History*, book 5, chapter 23, section 1. "Asterius, *Homily on Ps 5* 6, 4," however, refers to chapter 6, section 4, of Asterius' homily on Psalm 5. "PG 26, 1366 A" refers to *Patrologia Graeca*, vol. 26, column 1366, top of the column. In references to books of the Old and New Testaments, chapters are divided from verses by a colon—for example, "Jn 1:1." In allusions and implicit quotations from the Scriptures, and in quotations where the ancient author has added words of his own, only the words actually found in the Scripture are printed in italic type. Versions of the Bible are indicated by these abbreviations: LXX: Septuagint; OL: Old Latin, generally as edited by Pierre Sabatier; RSV: Revised Standard Version; Vg: Vulgate.

Introduction

I

There was a time in the life of the Church when Easter[1] was, in a way, everything—not only because it commemorated the whole history of salvation from the creation to the parousia, without having to share it with any other festival, but also because certain essential elements of the community's life took shape in the course of its celebrating Easter over the years: the liturgy, for instance, but also typological exegesis, catechesis, theology, and even some of the canonical Scriptures. In reference to this last item, it may be noted that some scholars have gone so far as to propose the celebration of the Pascha as the situation in which various New Testament writings (the Synoptic accounts of the Last Supper, the Fourth Gospel, 1 Corinthians, 1 Peter, Revelation) as well as some of the earliest patristic literature (Pseudo-Barnabas, Letter to Diognetus) took their shape or were actually composed.[2]

1. "Easter" will sometimes be used in this book to translate the Italian *Pasqua*. Usually, however, it seemed better to use the early Church's word *Pascha*. When the term is used to refer to the Jewish feast, it will usually be translated *Pesach* or "Passover." It should also be noted that in our sources the term *Pascha* sometimes denotes the paschal lamb rather than the feast, and sometimes it denotes both together. Moreover, when *Pascha* or "Passover" denotes the feast, it may be referring either to the supper on the first night or to the whole week of Unleavened Bread, which follows it. (Trans.)

2. See the studies by Schürmann, Ziener, Gaertner, Shepherd, Cross, Thornton, and Barnard noted in the bibliography. For an overview of the allusions to the Exodus and Pesach in the New Testament, see Le Déaut, *La nuit pascale*, 307–338. For the influence of the Pascha on the formation of theology, see Kretschmar, *RSR* 60 (1972) 287–323.

It is this very comprehensiveness of the early Easter that makes it so difficult to put together an anthology of texts on the subject. In the welter of meanings which have been given to the feast, which aspects should one select as most important? Which of them represent the authentic Christian tradition about Easter?

In order to avoid the appearance of arbitrariness, and at the same time to furnish a kind of key to the relevance of each text, I wish to list the interests which have guided my choice, or rather to list the aspects of the ancient Pascha which I have attempted to highlight. Each text, therefore, ought to be such as to illustrate one or more of the following subjects:

1. *Historical aspects.* Here belong conciliar decrees and all documents regarding the date of Easter—one of the liveliest problems in the life of the early Church.

2. *Ritual and liturgical aspects.* Here belong Easter liturgical legislation (canons and constitutions), formation of particular *genres* such as the *praeconium paschale*, concrete development of rites, genesis and development of the Easter cycle in its principal elements (Lent, Holy Week, Paschal triduum, Easter Vigil with initiation rites, Easter octave, Ascension Day, Pentecost). Alongside this progressive ritualization of the Pascha, we cite dissenting voices which, in the name of a purely interior and spiritual celebration, contest the very idea of a ritual Pascha made up of times and ceremonies.

3. *Spiritual and theological aspects.* These constitute the predominant interest of the anthology. The pertinent texts ought to reveal the patristic interpretation of the paschal mystery in its major facets and constituent dimensions. There are four of these:

a. The *historical* dimension, referring to the historical events commemorated in the feast.

b. The *sacramental* or *mystical* dimension, referring to the mystical (*in sacramento*) repetition in the believer of that passage from death to life that constitutes the inherent meaning of the historical events of the death and resurrection of Christ. This dimension is most intensely expressed in baptism and the Eucharist, but not only in them; for the paschal solemnity taken as a whole is itself a sacrament, the *paschale sacramentum*.

c. The *moral* and *spiritual* dimension, connected above all with the interpretation of the Pascha as *transitus*, that is, as detachment from evil, conversion to good, and progress in spiritual life, until the final *transitus* out of the body and out of the world.

d. The *eschatological* dimension, originally expressed in the vivid expectation of the coming of Christ, but gradually adapted to celebrating the presence of Christ among his own as a cultic anticipation of the parousia. Later it is expressed in individual eschatology as eagerness for the heavenly Pascha, and finally it takes the form of understanding the Pascha as an image and pledge of eternal life.

II

The view of the ancient Easter celebration outlined in the foregoing paragraphs is obviously systematic, but in the structural rather than in the dialectic sense. In historical actuality, as we know, Easter was not originally a fixed institution, everywhere the same; rather it was a living reality in continual development. These few pages of introduction are intended to sketch out the directions taken by this development in two dimensions: synchronic and diachronic. The former exhibits the diversity of ways in which different groups of Christians celebrated Easter at the same time; the latter, the historical evolution of the several traditions and of their common basis. From this analysis, summary as it might be, it is possible to gain some idea of the interior dynamic of the patristic Pascha.

If the monographs on the Pascha written in the last seventy years are evaluated from this point of view, it must be said that some of them have given great prominence to diversification but not enough to development, while others have reconstructed the development of Easter as a unit without paying enough attention to the variety of forms that it took.

The former path was followed by Carl Schmidt and Bernhard Lohse. To them we owe the theory that, at the beginning of Christianity, there were two Paschas, "radically different from each other in meaning." Lohse's conception was that the Quartodeciman Pascha of Asia Minor was based on the expectation of the parousia and included a fast of expiation for the crime of the Jews, whereas the Sunday Pascha of the Romans commemorated the historical events of the redemption.[3] Schmidt, however, thought of both paschal feasts as commemorations, the one of the passion, the other of the resurrection, and summed up his concept in the words *dort Passa, hier Ostern*.[4] That is to say, in Asia they kept a Christian Passover, and in Rome they kept Easter.

The second path was taken by Odo Casel, who popularized a certain method of investigating the paschal mystery of the early Church and made it almost classical. The essence of the paschal mystery is first established as passion and resurrection, death and life—or rather, passage from death to life, accomplished by Christ and after him by Christians. Then Casel demonstrates that both poles of the mystery are present in each of the two traditions, and this leads to the conclusion that we are dealing with what is theologically one and the same Pascha, in which Christ's passion and resurrection are given equal value. Having thus isolated the essence of the Christian Pascha, he masterfully traces the evolution from the primitive mystery-conception, founded in the dialectical unity of Pascha and *Pentêkostês*, up to the historicist conception, which emerged at the end of the fourth century and is based on the assignment of a distinct celebration to each event.[5]

This type of reconstruction, however, does not take fully into account either the tensions that, in the Bible, characterize the Pascha from its very beginnings, or the diverse forms that arise from such tensions and develop, each in a different way.[6] In other words, it does not take sufficiently into account the diversification of the traditions, and this is the reason why I intend to insist more on this aspect of the development in the attempt at synthesis that I sketch out here.

3. B. Lohse, 121.

4. C. Schmidt, 579.

5. Casel, *JLW* 14 (1934) 1–78.

6. Huber, in *Passa und Ostern*, often takes a position between Casel and B. Lohse, but his monograph, which is organized according to themes rather than historical phases, does not yield a historical outline of the development. It is, however, at present the fullest and best-documented study available of the ancient Pascha.

III

The diversification of the Pascha has its roots in the very origins of the institution. If we compare the two most characteristic paschal texts of the Old Testament, Exodus 12 and Deuteronomy 16 (texts 1a and 1b), we immediately notice differences with regard to the ritual aspect. In Exodus we have a ritual to be performed in every family, with the slaughter of a small animal such as nomadic shepherds would own; in Deuteronomy, on the other hand, we find a single sacrifice in the Temple in Jerusalem on behalf of all Israel, with the slaughter of bullocks as well as of sheep, that is, of cattle owned by a sedentary, agricultural people. But the texts also show a difference in the very meaning of the feast. In Exodus 12 we see the more archaic celebration, in which Pesach has an eminently theological meaning, that is, it recalls chiefly the saving act of God. It is *Pesah* because God *pasah* ("passed over," or "protected") the dwellings of the Israelites (Exod 12:23 and 27). In Deuteronomy 16, as in Exodus 13 and 14, we see the emergence of a new protagonist: humanity. To the ritual question of the son, "What does this ceremony mean?" the father from now on ought to answer, "With a strong hand the LORD caused us to go out from Egypt" (Exod 13:14; cf. Deut 16:1).

In this way the spiritual content of Pesach came to have two poles: (a) the immolation and eating of the lamb, connected with God's protecting and the Destroyer's passing over the houses of the Israelites, and (b) the exodus from Egypt, interpreted as a passing from slavery to freedom.

This primordial diversification was maintained and amplified after the return from the Babylonian exile. The rabbinic Judaism of Palestine preserved and accentuated the theological, ritual, and sacrificial character of Pesach (see texts 5 and 6), while the Hellenistic Judaism of the Diaspora, living far from the Temple, came to have a purely moral and spiritual conception of the feast, seeing it almost exclusively as humanity's passing from vice to virtue and from the world to God (texts 2 and 3).

The New Testament does not cancel out this bipolarity in the Pascha. We find it in the earliest mention of the Christian Pascha, in 1 Corinthians 5:7-8 (text 9). In characterizing the Pascha of the Church (*to pascha hêmôn*), Paul finds that, like the Pesach of the Jews, it has two levels of meaning: divine and human. On the divine level, the Pascha consists of sacrifice (*to pascha hêmôn etythê*), and this is henceforth realized in Christ (*to pascha hêmôn etythê Christos*, v. 7). On the human level, the Pascha consists of what Philo called the passage from vices to virtue, expressed by Paul as the turning away from the leaven of wickedness to the unleavened bread of purity (v. 8).

How did the institution of Passover get transplanted so quickly and cleanly from the Old to the New Testament, from Israel to the Church? The obvious basis for the transfer was a purely chronological datum: Christ had died (and risen) in Jerusalem during the celebration of a Jewish Pesach; indeed, John sets his death at the very hour when the paschal lambs were being sacrificed in the Temple. But this chronological datum all by itself would certainly not have been able to effect the great transformation of the Pesach unless there had been another, more powerful factor at work within it: the typological interpretation. The sacrificial death of Christ was seen as the realization of all the expectations and foreshadowings contained in the ancient Pesach. Melito of Sardis expresses this in language deliberately patterned on the Johannine language of the incarnation, as if to say that the paschal mystery is but the final act and logical conclusion of a process that began with the incarnation (text 20, § 7):

> The Law became the Word,
> the old became the new,
> . . . .
>
> the model became the reality,
> the lamb became the Son.

In the light of this event, the authors of the New Testament reinterpreted everything Jesus had done. This is precisely where the most original diversification of the Christian Pascha began: in the divers degrees and manners in which the several authors "paschalized" the life of Jesus, presenting it as the realization of the ancient Pesach. It was a gradual process, occupying the entire period of the formation of the Canon. The Synoptics "paschalize" the Eucharist: they see in it—that is, in the Last Supper—the moment at which the Pascha of Christ replaced the

Jewish one and the memorial of the Lord's death was superimposed on the memorial of the Exodus. Paul "paschalized" not only the Eucharist (1 Cor 11:23-26) but also baptism, seeing the latter as the antitype of the passage of the Red Sea (1 Cor 10:1-5). Finally, John "paschalized" the whole life of Christ, seeing in it the new Exodus of humankind accomplished by the new Moses, who gives the true manna (John 6) and makes the true water flow in the desert (John 4). And in the Fourth Gospel, all these correspondences culminate—not, as they do for the Synoptics, in the mystical immolation which took place in the Upper Room, but in the real immolation of the Lamb of God which took place on the cross (John 19:36; see text 8). This is Jesus' "hour," that is, the moment of his passing from this world to the Father (John 13:1).[7]

In one point, nevertheless, this "paschalization" of the story of Jesus remains incomplete: none of the evangelists applies it to the event of his resurrection. Absolute novelty that it is, the resurrection was the one element of the Christian Pascha which had not been prefigured in the Hebrew Pesach—even if its inseparability from the passion (and perhaps also its coincidence with the feast of the 'Omer'[8]) tended irresistibly from the very beginning to attract the resurrection, too, into the celebration of Pesach. In the New Testament, therefore, we do not as yet find the mystery of Christ completely equated with the paschal mystery. The ancient institution of Pesach did not suffice to express the entire Christian mystery as it is formulated, for example, in 1 Corinthians 15:3-8 and in Romans 4:25. The broadening of its meaning would come only later, in the time of the Church.

The tension between unity and diversity which we have sketched out up to this point passed from history into liturgy, from the Pascha of Christ to that of the Church. But when did this Pascha of the Church first appear? It would seem that, after the death and resurrection of Christ, the primitive Christian community continued for a while to "go up to the Temple" (Acts 3:1) and celebrate the Pesach with the other Jews. But the followers of Jesus

7. See Cantalamessa, *La Pasqua della nostra salvezza*, 71ff.

8. Van Goudoever, *Biblical Calendars*, 2nd ed., 168-169, 184, 190-191; Rordorf, *ThZ* 18 (1962) 167-189.

began to think of, and to experience, this yearly festival, no longer as the recalling of the events of the Exodus and as the expectation of the coming of the Messiah, but rather as the recalling of what had happened a few years before in Jerusalem at the time of Pesach, and as the expectation of the return of the Messiah. An interior detachment preceded the ritual one, and the Christian feast of Pesach was celebrated "in spirit and in truth" (John 4:23) in the privacy of the disciples' hearts before it became a rite and a feast in the proper sense. This development was not long in coming, however, and perhaps Paul is already referring to the distinctively Christian observance of Pesach when he exhorts his Corinthian converts to "celebrate the feast" (1 Cor 5:7). Thus the disciples celebrated the annual recurrence of Pesach with a feast of their own, and gradually recognized how radically new their observance was.

In its liturgical observance of the Pascha, the Church continued a process of diversification which was already present in the Old Testament. For too long, modern scholars have viewed the diversity of the earliest Christian Easter celebrations as the opposition between passion and resurrection or between commemoration and expectation. This has kept them from noticing other aspects of this diversity which, in my opinion, are more real and profound. Hence I wish to dwell on these other aspects, although I am aware that they are not the only ones and should not be absolutized.

IV

In the first place, until the third century, from the point of view of theological content, there exists an Easter tradition which is fundamentally uniform. From its place of origin and richest development it is known as the Asiatic. It is the tradition of a Christological Pascha, with historico-commemorative and eschatological content. What does this mean? That the feast of the Pascha has as its protagonist neither humanity nor even any longer the God of the Old Testament, but Christ. While commemorating the whole mystery of Christ—the mystery both "old and new" (text 20) which culminates in the saving event of the Cross and thus gives rise to the naive etymology *Pascha ex passione* (*Pascha* derived from *passio*, "suffering")—it also keeps alive the expectation of him.

On the historical and liturgical level (When should the fast be broken? On what day should the feast be celebrated?), for reasons and with a chronology that remain unclear, this theologically uniform tradition took two forms and was practiced in two different ways, with the result that the Church under Pope Victor was shaken by that "considerable controversy"[9] that, for the first time, brought it to the brink of a great schism. Naturally the choice of the anniversary of the passion rather than the anniversary of the resurrection as the date of the feast meant emphasizing one of the events more than the other. Still, the texts[10] clearly demonstrate that during this period, not only in Asia Minor but also in Gaul and Africa, at Rome, and even at Alexandria, the Pascha of itself commemorated primarily the passion of Christ—although, as Christine Mohrmann has shown,[11] in this age of persecution and martyrdom, the word *passio* is inseparably associated with the idea of victory and glory and hence with the idea of resurrection. Whether seen from the anniversary of the passion, as the Quartodecimans of Asia saw it, or from the Sunday of the resurrection, as the others did, the mystery of the Pascha changes its shape and perhaps its mood but not its content. The Christ whom the Quartodeciman Melito of Sardis contemplates during the paschal night is the Lord who, "having suffered for the one who was suffering, . . . rose from the dead, . . . and has carried humanity to the heights of heaven"; he is the Christ who proclaims himself to be personally "the Pascha of salvation" and "your resurrection" (text 24). On the other hand, Irenaeus, who celebrates the Sunday Pascha, affirms: "The name of this mystery is Suffering, the cause of liberation" (text 29). In all of this we find nothing to justify the phrase, *dort Passa, hier Ostern*.

It seems useful at this point to summarize what is known about the second-century controversy over the date of Easter—one of the most debated points of the whole ancient Pascha. (It is dealt with in texts 10 and 11.)

9. Eusebius, *Eccl. Hist.* 5, 23, 1.
10. For example, texts 16, 28, 29, 37, 45, 46, 95, and 98.
11. Mohrmann, *EL* 66 (1952) 41–42.

At the time of Polycrates of Ephesus and Pope Victor (around A.D. 195) the controversy concerned the date of the feast of Pascha or—what then came to the same thing—the hour at which the fast should be broken. For the Asiatics, as for the Jews, this date is the fourteenth of Nisan and the night following, on whichever day of the week it may fall; for the Romans and those in the West, however, it is the Sunday following the fourteenth of Nisan, on whichever day of the month this may fall. But modern scholars disagree about the situation before Victor's time—the situation described by Irenaeus in his letter to the bishop of Rome. What positions did Asia Minor and Rome take at the time of Polycarp and Anicetus in the middle of the second century? And what was the Roman practice before that time, under Pope Sixtus (A.D. 116–125)? The answer depends on how we interpret the antithesis *têrein* and *mê têrein* ("observe" and "not observe"), which is at the center of this whole discussion. Let me summarize the three principal theses on this subject, on the basis of the object to be understood with the verb *têrein*.

a. The traditional opinion, recently defended by B. Lohse, Nautin, and Mohrmann,[12] translates *têrein* as "observe the fourteenth of Nisan." In this view, the difference between Asiatics and Westerners is that the former celebrate the Pascha on the fourteenth of Nisan, the latter on the following Sunday. According to these authors, the Romans' practice of a Sunday Pascha goes back very far, perhaps to apostolic times.

b. Holl, Richard, and Huber[13] translate *têrein* as "observe the day of the Pascha," meaning "celebrate the feast of the Pascha." The difference in this case would be that, before Pope Soter, while the Pascha was a yearly feast in Asia, at Rome such a feast was unknown and there was only the weekly celebration of the resurrection of Christ. These authors believe that the Sunday Pascha as an annual feast originated after the settlement of a Gentile community in Jerusalem in A.D. 135 and did not arrive in Rome until shortly before the pontificate of Victor.

12. B. Lohse, 114–118; Nautin, *Lettres*, 79–84; Mohrmann, *VigChr* 16 (1962) 160–171.
13. Holl, 218ff.; Richard, *OrSyr* 6 (1961) 179–212 and *ZNW* 56 (1965) 260–282; Huber, 56ff.

c. Campenhausen,[14] taking up an old thesis of Theodor Zahn, translates *têrein* as "observe the paschal fast." He thinks that the difference between Asiatics and Romans before Victor does not concern the date of the Pascha (*Ostertermin*) but the fast which should precede the Pascha (*Osterfasten*). He holds that at Rome, in contrast to the rest of the Christian world, there was no paschal fast of any kind. (Irenaeus reminded Victor of the diversity of customs regarding the fast: text 10, ch. 24, §13.)

It is difficult to choose between these alternatives, but I regard the traditional position (a) as the most plausible, while conceding that the position of Campenhausen (c) must be taken seriously (but see text 10, note b).

V

On the conceptual level, the second great paschal tradition originates in Alexandria at the beginning of the third century with Clement and Origen (texts 33–43), who take up and christianize the moral and spiritual notion of the Pascha which had flourished in Hellenistic Judaism under the guidance of Philo. The key word in this tradition is not "passion" but "passage" (*diabasis*). It can be defined as an anthropological Pascha, in the sense that the protagonist of this passage is neither God nor Christ but human beings. In the new view unusual emphasis is given to the moral and spiritual content implied in the Exodus story and in the story of Christ, brought out point by point by means of a spiritual exegesis based on allegory. The whole life of the Christian and of the Church is an exodus from Egypt marked by various passages, beginning with the initial passing from unbelief to faith and ending with the final passing out of the world and out of the body. This is the beginning of three-stage typology (shadow, image, reality) and of the idea of a "third Pascha," that of heaven, which alone is true and definitive, because it is perfectly spiritual, without symbols or figures (see text 38).

What then is the historical and eschatological content of the Christian Pascha? If the Pascha is above all *humanity's* passing-over, clearly its major emphasis will not be on the past or the fu-

14. Campenhausen, *VigChr* 28 (1974) 114–138.

ture but on the present, the "time of the Church," in which alone this passing-over can take place. The saving events are certainly not denied: Origen is always appealing to them. Still, their importance is diminished, insofar as all of them are in some way symbolic—including even the Pascha of Christ, which is but a figure, albeit a clearer one than that of the Law (see text 71). A sign of this dehistoricization of the Pascha is the insistence on the idea of a continual Pascha at the cost of the anniversary festival, which refers much more explicitly to the historical event it commemorates. From this point of view, the Gnostic authors (texts 16–17) merely radicalize a tendency that is also present in the orthodox atmosphere of Alexandria. The actualization of the saving events is also achieved in the sacraments of the Church. Baptism and the Eucharist in fact occupy an extremely prominent position in this paschal catechesis, but in a way different from the rest of the tradition, since here they too are spiritualized. "For it is not to be thought . . . that corporeal things typify corporeal things; rather the corporeal things are types of spiritual realities" (text 38). What this rather obscure principle seems to mean is that the true eating of the flesh of the paschal lamb is not being content with receiving the Eucharist but rather nourishing oneself on the Word of God.

The eschatological tension does not disappear in this view of the Pascha, but, like the historical reference, it takes on a different cast. No longer is it the expectation of the coming of the Lord, but a moral and individual eschatology which finds its expression in "always passing over . . . from the affairs of this life to God and hastening towards his city" (text 43). But perhaps on this point one should speak not so much of eschatology as of anagogy, as Origen himself does (text 38 with note f).

VI

The two basic traditions about the Pascha which we have seen both embody a dialectic which is well-known in other areas of early Christian history as well: the dialectic between Asiatic and Alexandrian theology. Later Easter traditions, at least until Augustine, merely repeat and develop one of them—or, more frequently, combine the two. In this anthology we have tried to reconstruct the traditions corresponding to the three principal language-areas of the early Church: Greek, Syriac, and Latin. It is evident that even this distinction is too vague, since the double movement of formal diversification and historical development would have to be reconstructed within each of these three areas.

1. *The Traditions of the Greek Church*

At the risk of over-simplifying and over-schematizing, I believe it is possible to divide this tradition roughly according to its major centers. In Egyptian Alexandria the predominant influence is that of Origen. The historico-Christological and sacramental dimension (that is, the Pascha as commemoration of the saving event, actualized in the Eucharist) soon came to complete the moral and spiritual perspective, mainly with the help of Athanasius, who had Asiatic and anti-Gnostic training. Spiritually and liturgically, Eusebius of Caesarea also belongs to this school, even though, because of his knowledge of the ancient Easter traditions, he likes to combine Origen's Pascha-as-passage with the Asiatic tradition of Pascha-as-suffering (text 56, note a).

Lent was introduced at the time of Athanasius (text 60), but otherwise the liturgical structure, featuring Holy Week, Paschal Vigil, and Pentecost, simply continues that of the third century known already from Dionysius of Alexandria. The unitary character of the feast and of the mystery was maintained here longer than elsewhere (texts 78 and 81). The decision of Nicaea (see text 53) that the whole Church should adopt the Alexandrian way of reckoning the date of Easter provided the basis for the measure of uniformity in this matter which flowered briefly in the patristic era. The most important result of Nicaea for the theological development of Easter, however, is different: it was Nicaea that took the feast once and for all out of the Hebrew matrix. The struggle against those who wished to "keep the Pascha with the Jews," which occupies the whole of the fourth century, ended in fact by giving an unforeseen development to the weekly Pascha and thus to the Eucharist, to the extent of sometimes compromising the very significance of an annual solemnity. "Keeping the Pascha only once a year" becomes a synonym for Judaizing (see texts 74; 56, §7; and note on text 11).

For the Oriental Churches (those in Asia Minor and Palestine) on the *theological* level, it is very difficult to reconstruct a tradition as uniform as that of Alexandria, because every author is influenced more by his literary sources (which almost always include Origen) than by his surroundings. Thus, for example, in the Cappadocian Gregory of Nazianzus we find a conception of the Pascha that, on the theological level, is among the closest to Origen, while at the same time, as regards the liturgical order, it is among the most distant from the Alexandrian. The most frequent traces of the old conception of the Pascha as *memoria passionis* ("memorial of the passion") are certainly to be found in the milieux and authors known in the history of dogmas as Antiochene (texts 51, 74, 75, 82).

It is easier to identify an Oriental tradition different from the Alexandrian one on the *liturgical* level. Here is where the process of historicizing the paschal mystery and hence of breaking it up into distinct moments and feasts is most evident and appears to have been most rapid. For Asia Minor and Syria the process is known to us from the Cappadocian Fathers and the *Apostolic Constitutions*; for Jerusalem, from Egeria and the Armenian Lectionary. The predominant criterion here is no longer that of the mystery but that of the history: not to celebrate the whole mystery of Christ synthetically but to celebrate each event at the time—and, at Jerusalem, in the very place—of its original occurrence. This historicized Pascha quickly leads to the paschal cycle of feasts. In fact it is from this region that we have the first witnesses to the distinct feasts of the Descent into Hell on Holy Saturday (text 73), the Octave of Easter (texts 69, note d, and 116, §39), the Ascension, and Pentecost Sunday (text 116b, note a). The evolution is more visible than ever precisely in the two key terms *pascha* and *pentêkostês*: the former comes to mean ever more frequently the Sunday of the Resurrection, while the latter comes to refer to the feast of the Holy Spirit celebrated on the fiftieth day, according to a tendency which will be illustrated further on.

2. *The Syrian Tradition*

Our knowledge of the Syrian Christians' Easter presents a very special situation. It is known to us chiefly—and, at the beginning, exclusively—from liturgical and canonical sources: the *Didascalia* (texts 85–86), the *Testament of our Lord Jesus Christ*, and perhaps the *Canons of Hippolytus*. The result is that the Syrian Pascha is more abundantly documented for us in its ritual and liturgical aspects than in its theological content. All we really have for the latter is a work by Aphraates, some sermons and hymns by Saint Ephraem the Syrian, and two homilies by his nephew, the poet Cyrillonas. And yet, paradoxically, the few certainties we have about this tradition are in the area of theological content, while it remains practically impossible to tell how the feast was kept at this time, perhaps because the liturgical sources are composed of layers from successive stages of the tradition.

The Syrian Pascha is the direct heir of the Asiatic tradition of the Quartodecimans.[15] Its fourth-century exponents use the same two-stage typology (the figure foreshadows the reality) and the same anti-Jewish polemic (the Jews are blind to the meaning of their own scriptures) as did the second-century communities celebrating the Pascha on the same date as the Jews, and they feel the same need to distinguish their feast from the Jewish feast by its content. And, while celebrating the Pascha on Sunday (text 86 [5, 19, 1]), they still regard Friday, the day of the passion, as the most solemn day, and insist on its ideal correspondence with the fourteenth of the month on which the death of Jesus was thought to have occurred historically (text 86 [5, 18]; text 87, ch. 12). Where the Quartodecimans observed only one night, the Syrians extended the Pascha to include almost a week, but they still thought of it as a feast of the passion and death of Christ more than of the resurrection.

Theologically, however, the Syrian Pascha in the stage known to us—that is, in the fourth century—is in one respect quite distinct from the Quartodeciman. For it is, to a much greater extent than in any other tradition, a Eucharistic Pascha. This is typically expressed in the phrase, "to eat the Pascha." The Pascha of Christ was realized essentially in the Last Supper by means of the institution of the Eucharist—that is, in his mystical self-immolation, rather than on the Cross. It was in the Upper Room that Christ

---

15. For possible instances of direct dependence, see text 28, note a, and text 88, note b.

"did in truth what the Pascha foreshadowed" (text 87, ch. 6). This idea of mystic or Eucharistic immolation gave rise to that artificial way of counting the three days during which Christ had foretold he would be among the dead; for, according to Aphraates, Ephraem, and the *Didascalia*, this time began at the moment of the institution of the Eucharist, when Christ immolated himself (see text 87, ch. 7, with note h; and text 89, note b).

The mystic immolation, the Pascha of the Last Supper, however, is not independent of the real immolation, the Pascha of the Cross: Aphraates states that on the Pascha "we recall the crucifixion and the insults of the Savior" (text 87, ch. 8). Nor is there any separation between the two moments of the Pascha; indeed, according to Aphraates at least, the institution of the Eucharist and Christ's death occurred on the same day, the fourteenth—the former before sunrise, at cockcrow, and the latter in the afternoon, at the ninth hour (text 87, ch. 12).

Ephraem and Cyrillonas, who reflect the later Syrian tradition, have less to say about the chronology of the passion, but they have the same interiorized concept of the Pascha. The institution of the Eucharist constituted the Pascha of Christ; the celebration of the Eucharist today constitutes the Pascha of the Church. Here the typology is again in two stages: the type is contrasted with the truth, the transitory Pascha of Judaism with the definitive Pascha of Christ. Not only is the Old Testament Pascha set against the New, but above all, in the present, the Jewish Pascha is contrasted with that of the Church (text 90; cf. text 87, ch. 8). They never mention a "third Pascha," more perfect than the very Pascha of Christ—a notion dear to the Alexandrian tradition, as we have seen.

3. *The Latin Tradition*

The Latin theology of the Pascha is a clear instance of what has already been asserted: namely, that from the third century on, the authors only repeat, develop, or combine the two original traditions (the Asiatic and the Alexandrian). In fact, the development of the Pascha-concept in the West may be summarized, in extremely simplified outline, under the following heads:

a. Initial acceptance of the Asiatic tradition ("Pascha as suffering") and growth in the understanding of it until the second half of the fourth century.

b. The questioning of this concept when the West became aware of the Alexandrian tradition ("Pascha as passage").

c. Synthesis of both traditions and further development in the paschal theology of Augustine.

Now, to justify this historical reconstruction, let us briefly mention the main figures and their ideas.

Thanks to Irenaeus, who came from Asia Minor, as well as to Tertullian, Hippolytus, and Lactantius, who got their spiritual formation from authors of that region, the first paschal theology to take root in the West was the Asiatic—detached, of course, from the Quartodeciman praxis and adapted to the observance of Easter on Sunday. One of the proofs of this is the explanation, common to all these authors, that Pascha means *passio*. This explanation had a clear influence on the liturgical use of the term. Initially *Pascha*, in the strict sense, meant Good Friday, or else the interval between Christ's death and his resurrection. The vigil on Saturday night is the end of the Pascha and the beginning of the Pentecost. The latter appears in these authors at the same stage of evolution that it had in Asia Minor in the second century (as found, for instance, in the *Acts of Paul*). The growing prominence of the fiftieth day has not shattered the original unity of the fifty-day paschal period. *Pentêcostês* stands for a kind of sounding box for Easter joy (*laetissimum spatium*), in which to celebrate the full glorification of Christ, his spiritual presence (that is, his presence as Spirit) in the Church, and the expectation of his return (cf. text 93).

Gregory of Elvira, Priscillian, Chromatius of Aquileia, Filastrius of Brescia, and others show that towards the end of the fourth century this is still the prevailing attitude towards Easter in the West. No Latin author before this time translates *Pascha* with *transitus* ("passing over"). The feast is literally "the Pascha of the Lord" (Exod 12:11), a Christological Pascha, because the one who suffers, as Gregory of Elvira says (text 117), is Christ rather than the people. The vigil itself is a "vigil of the Lord" (Exod 12:42), because it commemorates Christ's sleeping in death, which became waking, i.e. life, for the whole world (cf. text 120). And so the Pascha is not so much the occasion for a moral discourse upon mortals as for a discourse about Christ and his redemptive work, and in particular about the mystery of the Cross. And in accord with this, the sacramental and mystical (especially the Eucharistic) aspect is emphasized.

Two things happened to make the West question this ancient and constant tradition. First, the Westerners again came into active contact with Greek theology, which at this time was essentially Alexandrian; and, second, the Latin translation of the Bible was revised according to the original texts. It was Ambrose who first inoculated Latin thinking with the moral and spiritual contents of the Alexandrian tradition connected with the translation of *Pascha* as *transitus*. The translation of *Pascha* as *passio* was too deeply rooted in Latin Christianity to be eliminated all at once, and Ambrose himself remains indebted to it in several ways. Nevertheless, the accent is henceforth no longer on Christ but on humanity, because it is human beings who now must pass from sin to virtue, from the world to God. The emphasis in typology tends to shift from the immolation of the lamb to the passage of the Red Sea, from Exodus 12 to Exodus 13–14. Consequently the paschal sacrament *par excellence* tends to be baptism rather than the Eucharist. In this change of thinking about Easter, Ambrose was aided and imitated by other saintly bishops of northern Italy such as Zeno of Verona, Maximus of Turin, and Gaudentius of Brescia.

Jerome, Hebrew text in hand, tried to rectify this anthropological, Philonic idea of *transitus* by pointing out that the original biblical meaning is theological: it is God who passes over.[16] The reaction of the Latin theologians defending the Pascha as *passio* was led by Ambrosiaster, who engages in polemics against Jerome and other innovators on this point.

This was the situation when Augustine came upon the scene. On the one hand, we had an archaic conception centering on

16. Text 114 with note a. Jerome posits the divine *transitus* as fundamental but does not fail to mention the human passage as well— *transitus noster*, to which he gives a moral or anagogical meaning (text 114 with note d).

Christ and the mystery of his death, but not easy to connect with the original biblical institution, once it was admittted that *Pascha* did not derive from *paschein*. On the other hand, in the translation of *Pascha* as *transitus*, we had a conception based on the original meaning of the name and of the institution, but no longer able to fill them with the new content of the Christ-event. What remained was a moral and spiritual Pascha (in Ambrose) or a theological one (in Jerome), but not a plainly Christological one, not a *Pascha Domini* ("Passover of the Lord") in the Christian sense. The essence of Augustine's contribution is that he solved this problem and achieved the difficult synthesis of the two ideas, Asiatic and Alexandrian, that lay at the heart of the Western Easter celebration. While sympathizing with the ancient conception of Pascha as passion (text 127 with note a), he accepted Jerome's correction. But he devalues the Old Testament and Philonic meanings of *transitus* ("passage of the people" and "passage of the soul") and confers on the word a new meaning which enables it to encompass the mystery of Christ. The Pascha is *Christ's* passing over from this world to the Father—an idea he finds in John 13:1. Upon it he builds his entire Easter catechesis, in which he equivalently defines Pascha as *transitus per passionem*, "passing over through the passion" (text 126). Such a definition does not represent a compromise between the two rival theories of the Pascha but rather a true synthesis. With it Augustine brings to term the process of Christianizing the ancient Pascha by giving full recognition to the paschal character, not only of Christ's sacrifice, but also of his resurrection (text 124 with note e). In sum, "the passion and resurrection of the Lord is the true Pascha."[17] This Pascha of Christ becomes the Pascha of the Church through faith in the Resurrection: "Through the passion the Lord passed from death to life, opening the way for us who believe in his resurrection, so that we too may pass from death to life" (text 126). The *beata passio*, as we see, keeps the central place it had in the archaic Latin tradition, but it is better integrated into the dynamism of the Pascha; for the latter no longer consists in a single event (the passion or the resurrection) but in a process, that is, in a passing through the passion towards the resurrection, from

17. Augustine, *De catechizandis rudibus* 23, 41, 3 (*CChr.SL* 46, 166).

death to life. This puts the sacramental and mystical dimension of the Pascha on a better foundation. Here too there was need to strike a better balance—for example, in the relation between this yearly Pascha (the *festum anniversarium*) and the daily Pascha, the Eucharist. The Asiatic tradition had so accentuated the former that it drew upon itself the (at first sight strange) accusation of celebrating the Pascha only once a year. The opposite is true of the Alexandrian tradition: it so insisted on the continual Pascha, and consequently on the weekly Pascha, that the very meaning of the *sollemnitas Paschae* was compromised. Augustine struck a balance that did justice to both. The Pascha of Christ continues on in the life of the Church, on two levels and with two different rhythms: a yearly rhythm represented by the feast of Easter, and a weekly and even daily rhythm constituted by the celebration of the Eucharist (texts 128 and 130). The *semel* ("once") is prolonged in both the *quotannis* ("each year") and the *quotiescumque* ("whenever"): history continues in the liturgy, and the event in the sacrament.

Augustine also gave a lucid formulation to the tridimensional structure of the Christian mystery (memory, presence, expectation), which was already operative in the tradition with varying degrees of clarity. Everything at Easter, even the joy, receives light from these three sources. For it is the joy indeed of the Church's present (text 129), the joy of those who live a good life and sing the Alleluia, but a joy also nourished by the memory of Christ's passion and resurrection as well as by the hope of the life to come (sermon Guelferbytanus 8, 2; *PLS* 2, 557).

Of course the Augustinian synthesis does not manage to include everything. Some of the vibrant moral and spiritual developments of the Pascha that well up from the typological and allegorical exegesis of Origen, for example, or of Ambrose, are missing from Augustine's writings, once the anti-Pelagian polemic had convinced him of man's inability to accomplish the passage from vices to virtue on his own initiative. Less vivid too is the grandiose cosmic vision of the Pascha as *renovatio vitae* ("renewal of life") and *renovatio in melius* ("renewal for the better"),[18] which is at

18. On the Pascha as *renovatio vitae*, see Augustine, letter 55, 5 (*CSEL* 34/2, 174–175). On *renovatio in melius*, see Gerhard B. Ladner, "Erneuerung," *RAC* 6, 260.

the root of the theology of the *O felix culpa!* ("O blessed fault!").

The synthesis worked out by Augustine nourishes late patristic thought and spills over into the Latin Middle Ages, as we see from the ever more frequent references to John 13:1. Nevertheless, the traditions that preceded Augustine were continued, in particular the ancient and dear tradition of the Pascha as *passio*, which persisted a long time, until it left some traces in practically every Western liturgy (see text 136, note a).

On the level of the liturgical order, we note the same tendency to parcel out the paschal mystery by commemorating different events on different days, though this differed from one region to another and in many cases proceeded less rapidly than in the East. In Chromatius of Aquileia the historical and mystical content of the Vigil appears still intact and unified and charged with eschatological tension. This is also the case with the community which gave birth to the famous paschal proclamation, the *Exsultet*. But already by Augustine's time, we see almost all of the Oriental innovations adopted in the West: the liturgicization of Holy Thursday, the double celebration of the passion (on Good Friday—but only on the level of readings and homily—and in the Paschal Vigil), the feast of the octave of Easter, and the feast of the Ascension on the fortieth day (*quadragesima*). It remains to be determined only whether this distribution of events in distinct celebrations always results in a true loss of meaning and intensity for the Paschal Vigil. The texts, even those few contained in this anthology, show that this certainly was not the case with Augustine.

VII

In the first centuries, as our sketch has shown, *Pascha* was inseparably connected with *Pentêcostês*. The two terms designate the same mystery, but as seen from opposite sides: that of the passion and that of the glorification. For this reason it would be very helpful to say something about the evolution of *Pentêcostês*, which has received only sporadic attention in this sketch up till now, and thus give a kind of counterproof of the evolution of *Pascha*. In this matter I believe two observations must be made to correct a certain oversimplification which has become prevalent in the reconstruction of the evolution of the meaning of *Pentêcostês*.

In regard to the "liturgical" development of the term (meaning the time period covered by the term *Pentêcostês*), it is not quite correct to regard this as a linear evolution in the sense of a progressive abandonment of the original "extended" meaning of *Pentêcostês* as a period of fifty days, in favor of the "restricted" meaning as the feast of the fiftieth day after the Pascha. At no point in its development did *Pentêcostês* have the extended meaning alone, just as at no point did it have the restricted meaning alone. In the second century the fiftieth day already appears as distinguished from the others, either by its character as the day concluding the period (see text 92, note b) or (later) by its link with the events of the ascension and the descent of the Holy Spirit (text 56, ch. 5, and text 61 with note). On the other hand, in the fifth century, the prevalence of the restricted meaning never obliterated the old extended meaning completely—not even in Augustine, for whom the *Pentêcostês* in spite of everything still remains "the fifty days," in which the Alleluia is sung and no one kneels.[19] What changes, therefore, is merely the relation between the two meanings, and this undergoes a clear and unmistakable evolution.

The second observation regards the "theological" development of *Pentêcostês*. This does not consist, as has sometimes been suggested, in the substitution of a historico-Trinitarian content (feast of the descent of the Holy Spirit[20]) for the original Christological one (celebrating Christ's "spiritual" presence among his disciples after the resurrection in an eschatological perspective,[21] together with his offering himself to the Father as the first fruits of

19. Augustine, letter 55, 32 (*CSEL* 34/2, 207). Nevertheless, for Augustine *Pentêcostês* usually means the *quinquagesima*, the fiftieth day—as, for example, in text 133.

20. Typologically linked to the Jewish feast of the bestowal of the Law or of the renewal of the Covenant: see Kretschmar, *ZKG* 66 (1954–1955) 209ff. Examples are found in texts 80 and 133.

21. On the Pentecost as anticipation of the kingdom, see text 47 with note c. For the interpretation of the Pentecost in an eschatological key, see Augustine, *Enarrationes in Psalmos* 148, 1 (*CChr.SL* 40, 2165–2166).

humanity[22]). A reference to the event of the descent of the Holy Spirit (that is, to the account in Acts 2) is operative in the Christian Pentecost as far back as the first documents (perhaps in Tertullian, certainly in Origen: see texts 43 and 93), just as the Christological and eschatological components are still present in the fourth-century feast of Pentecost, for example in Ambrose, Theophilus of Alexandria, and Basil the Great.[23] And so also in this case the evolution, at least in the patristic period, does not take the form of abandoning one meaning for another but of shifting the emphasis. It is understandable that the link between *Pascha* and *Pentêcostês* was sensibly stronger as long as the latter emphasized its Christological component by celebrating the resurrection prolonged in time, thus being a kind of long and joyous "day of the Lord"—as Athanasius calls it, the Great Sunday (text 30, note b; text 58).

22. Typologically linked to the Jewish Feast of Weeks and the sacrifice of first fruits: see Boeckh, *JLH* 5 (1960) 1ff.

23. See texts 47; 56, §4; 78; 81; 108; and, for Basil the Great, *On the Holy Spirit* 27, 66 (*PG* 32, 192B).

Texts in Translation

1a. Exodus 12:1-28: The Passover in Egypt and the Feast of Unleavened Bread

1. The LORD said to Moses and Aaron in the land of Egypt: 2. This month shall mark for you the beginning of the months; it shall be the first of the months of the year for you.   3. Speak to the whole community of Israel and say that on the tenth of this month each of them shall take a lamb to a family, a lamb to a household.ᵃ 4. But if the household is too small for a lamb, let him share one with a neighbor who dwells nearby, in proportion to the number of persons: you shall contribute for the lamb according to what each household will eat.   5. Your lamb shall be without blemish, a yearling male; you may take it from the sheep or from the goats.   6. You shall keep watch over it until the fourteenth day of this month; and all the assembled congregation of the Israelites shall slaughter it at twilight.   7. They shall take some of the blood and put it on the two doorposts and the lintel of the houses in which they are to eat it.   8. They shall eat the flesh that same night; they shall eat it roasted over the fire, with unleavened bread and with bitter herbs.   9. Do not eat any of it raw, or cooked in any way with water, but roasted—head, legs, and entrails—over the fire.   10. You shall not leave any of

25

it over until morning; if any of it is left until morning, you shall burn it.[b]

11. This is how you shall eat it: your loins girded, your sandals on your feet, and your staff in your hand; and you shall eat it hurriedly: it is a passover offering[c] to the LORD.[d] 12. For that night I will go through the land of Egypt and strike down every first-born in the land of Egypt, both man and beast; and I will mete out punishments to all the gods of Egypt, I the LORD. 13. And the blood on the houses where you are staying shall be a sign for you: when I see the blood I will pass over[e] you, so that no plague will destroy you when I strike the land of Egypt.

14. This day[f] shall be to you one of remembrance: you shall celebrate it as a festival to the LORD throughout the ages; you shall celebrate it as an institution for all time. 15. Seven days you shall eat unleavened bread; on the very first day you shall remove leaven from your houses, for whoever eats leavened bread from the first day to the seventh day, that person shall be cut off from Israel.

16. You shall celebrate a sacred occasion on the first day, and a sacred occasion on the seventh day; no work at all shall be done on them; only what every person is to eat, that alone may be prepared for you. 17. You shall observe the (feast of) Unleavened Bread, for on this very day I brought your ranks out of Egypt; you shall observe this day throughout the ages as an institution for all time. 18. In the first month, from the fourteenth day of the month at evening, you shall eat unleavened bread until the twenty-first day of the month at evening. 19. No leaven shall be found in your houses for seven days. For whoever eats what is leavened, that person shall be cut off from the community of Israel, whether he is a stranger or a citizen of the country. 20. You shall eat nothing leavened; in all your settlements you shall eat unleavened bread.

21. Moses then summoned all the elders of Israel and said to them, "Go, pick out lambs for your families, and slaughter the passover offering.[g] 22. Take a bunch of hyssop, dip it in the blood that is in the basin, and apply some of the blood that is in the basin to the lintel and to the two doorposts. None of you shall go outside the door of his house until morning. 23. For when the LORD goes through to smite the Egyptians, he will see

the blood on the lintel and the two doorposts, and the LORD will pass over[h] the door and not let the Destroyer enter and smite your home.

24. "You shall observe this as an institution for all time, for you and for your descendants.   25. And when you enter the land that the LORD will give you, as he has promised, you shall observe this rite.   26. And when your children ask you, 'What do you mean by this rite?'   27. you shall say, 'It is the passover sacrifice to the LORD,[h] because he passed over[e] the houses of the Israelites in Egypt when he smote the Egyptians, but saved our houses.' "

The people then bowed low in homage.   28. And the Israelites went and did so; just as the LORD had commanded Moses and Aaron, so they did.

1b. Deuteronomy 16:1-10: The Passover in the Promised Land and the Feast of Weeks

1. Observe the month of Abib and offer a passover sacrifice to the LORD your God, for it was in the month of Abib, at night, that the LORD your God freed you from Egypt.   2. You shall slaughter the passover sacrifice for the LORD your God, from the flock and the herd, in the place where the LORD will choose to establish his name.   3. You shall not eat anything leavened with it; for seven days thereafter you shall eat unleavened bread, bread of distress—for you departed from the land of Egypt hurriedly— so that you may remember the day of your departure from the land of Egypt as long as you live.   4. For seven days no leaven shall be found with you in all your territory, and none of the flesh of what you slaughter on the evening of the first day shall be left until morning.

5. You are not permitted to slaughter the passover sacrifice in any of the settlements that the LORD your God is giving you;   6. but at the place where the LORD your God will choose to establish his name, there alone shall you slaughter the passover sacrifice, in the evening, at sundown, the time of day when you departed from Egypt.   7. You shall cook and eat it at the place that the LORD your God will choose; and in the morning you may start

back on your journey home.   8. After eating unleavened bread six days, you shall hold a solemn gathering for the LORD your God on the seventh day: you shall do no work.

9. You shall count off seven weeks; start to count the seven weeks when the sickle is first put to the standing grain. 10. Then you shall observe the Feast of Weeks[a] for the LORD your God, offering your freewill contribution according as the LORD your God has blessed you.

2. PHILO OF ALEXANDRIA, *On the Special Laws* 2, 145–147

145. After the new moon comes the fourth feast, called the Crossing-Feast,[a] which the Hebrews in their native tongue call Pascha. In this festival many myriads of victims from noon till eventide are offered by the whole people, old and young alike, raised for that particular day to the dignity of the priesthood. For at other times the priests according to the ordinance of the Law carry out both the public sacrifices and those offered by private individuals. But on this occasion the whole nation performs the sacred rites and acts as priest with pure hands and complete immunity.[b]   146. The reason for this is as follows: the festival is a reminder and thank-offering for that great migration from Egypt which was made by more than two millions of men and women in obedience to the oracles vouchsafed to them[c]. . . .

147. But to those who are accustomed to turn literal facts into allegory,[d] the Crossing-Festival suggests the purification of the soul. They say that the lover of wisdom is occupied solely in crossing over from the body and the passions, each of which overwhelms him like a torrent, unless the rushing current be dammed and held back by the principles of virtue.[e]

3. PHILO OF ALEXANDRIA, *On the Preliminary Studies*, 106

This is the real meaning of the Pascha of the soul: the crossing over from every passion[a] and all the realm of sense to the "Tenth," namely, to the realm of mind and of God.[b] For we read: "On the tenth of this month let every man take a sheep for his house" (Exod 12:3), so that from the tenth day there may be sanctified to the Tenth the sacrificial offerings which are kept in the soul (cf. Exod 12:6), which is but two-thirds illuminated, until it becomes in its entirety a heavenly brightness, as the moon becomes full by its waxing in the second week,[c] and is able not only to keep but also to offer in sacrifice its sinless and spotless advances.[d]

4. FLAVIUS JOSEPHUS, *Jewish Antiquities* 2, 14, 6, 312–313

312. [Moses] accordingly had the Hebrews ready betimes for departure, and ranging them in fraternities[a] kept them assembled together; then when the fourteenth day was come the whole body, in readiness to start, sacrificed, purified the houses with the blood, using bunches of hyssop to sprinkle it, and after the repast burnt the remnants of the meat as persons on the eve of departure. 313. Hence comes it that to this day we keep this sacrifice in the same customary manner, calling the feast *Pascha*, which signifies "passing over,"[b] because on that day God passed over[c] our people when he smote[d] the Egyptians with plague.

5. A Palestinian Targum on Exodus 12:42: The Night of Watching

It is *a night kept* and appointed[a] *for the liberation* in the name *of the* LORD[b] at the moment when *the sons of Israel* went[c] liberated *out of the land of Egypt* (Exod 12:42). Now[d] four nights have been inscribed in the Book of Memorials.

First night: when the LORD[e] manifested himself to the world in order to create it,[f] *the world was confusion and chaos, and darkness was spread over the surface of the abyss* (Gen 1:2). And the Word of the LORD was the light and shone. And he called it First Night.

Second night: when the LORD[e] manifested himself to the one-hundred-year-old Abraham[g] and to the ninety-year-old Sarah his wife, to accomplish what the Scripture says: "Is one-hundred-year-old Abraham going to engender, and is ninety-year-old Sarah his wife going to give birth?" (Gen 17:17).[h] And Isaac was thirty-seven years old when he was offered on the altar.[i] The heavens were lowered and came down and Isaac saw their perfections and because of their perfections *his eyes were dimmed* (Gen 27:1). And he called it Second Night.

Third night: when the LORD[e] manifested himself to the Egyptians *in the middle of the night*: his hand *slew the first-born of the Egyptians* (Exod 12:29) and his right hand protected the first-born of Israel, to accomplish what the Scripture says: "Israel is my first-born son" (Exod 4:22). And he called it Third Night.

Fourth night: when the world will come to its end, to be dissolved.[j] The iron yokes will be broken (cf. Jer 28:2-14), and the perverse generations will be annihilated, and Moses will come up from the midst of the desert [and the king Messiah[k] from on high[l]].[m] One will proceed at the head of a flock,[n] and the other will proceed at the head of a flock,[n] and his Word[o] will proceed between the two, and I[p] and they will proceed together.

It is the night of *the Pascha for* the name of *the* LORD (Exod 12:11), a *night kept* and appointed[a] *for the liberation of all Israel throughout their generations* (Exod 12:42).[q]

6. *Haggadah for Pesach*: Rabban Gamliel's Aphorism and the Thanksgiving for the Redemption

Rabban Gamliel[a] used to say: Whoever has not spoken[b] these three words on Pesach has not done his duty. These are: *pesach*, *matzah*, and *marôr*.

Pesach,[c] which our fathers ate when the Temple was still standing: what is the explanation? The explanation is that the Holy One, blessed be he, *pasah* ["passed over," "protected"] the houses of our fathers in Egypt, as it is said: "You shall say, 'It is the Pesach-sacrifice to the LORD, because he *pasah* the houses of the Israelites in Egypt when he smote the Egyptians, but saved our houses.' The people then bowed low in homage" (Exod 12:27).

Matzah, this unleavened bread which we eat: what is the explanation? The explanation is that there was not enough time for the dough of our fathers to rise before the supreme king of kings, the Holy One, blessed be he, revealed himself to them and redeemed them. As it is said: "And they baked unleavened cakes of the dough that they had taken out of Egypt, for it was not leavened, since they had been driven out of Egypt and could not delay; nor had they prepared any provisions for themselves" (Exod 12:39).

Marôr, these bitter herbs which we eat: what is the explanation? The explanation is that the Egyptians embittered the life of our fathers in Egypt, as it is said: "Ruthlessly they made life bitter for them with the various labors that they made them perform, with harsh labor at mortar and bricks and with all sorts of tasks in the field" (Exod 1:14).

In every generation each person must regard himself as having come out of Egypt himself, as it is said: "And you shall explain to your son on that day, 'It is because of what the LORD did for me when I went free from Egypt'" (Exod 13:8). The Holy One, blessed be he, redeemed not only our fathers but us as well, together with them,[d] as it is said: "And us he freed from there, that he might bring us in, to give us the land that he had promised on oath to our fathers" (Deut 6:23).

(Lifting the cup:) Therefore we should thank, praise, glorify, magnify, exalt, honor, bless, extol, and give the victory to him who did all these marvels for our fathers and for us. He has brought us from bondage to freedom, from sadness to joy, from mourning to festivity, from darkness to great light, and from servitude to redemption.[e] And so let us sing before him a new song: Hallelujah.

NEW TESTAMENT WRITERS

7. MATTHEW, MARK, and LUKE: The Institution of the Eucharist

Matt 26:20-21, 26-29	Mark 14:17-18, 22-25	Lk 22:14-20
20. When it was evening, he sat at table with the twelve[a] disciples; 21. and as they were eating, he said, "Truly I say to you, one of you will betray me."	17. And when it was evening he came with the Twelve. 18. And as they were at table eating, Jesus said, "Truly, I say to you, one of you will betray me,	14. And when the hour came, he sat at table, and the apostles with him. 15. And he said to them, "I have earnestly desired to eat this passover[b] with

Matt 26:20-21, 26-29	Mark 14:17-18, 22-25	Lk 22:14-20
	one who is eating with me.''	you before I suffer; 16. for I tell you I shall not eat it[c] until it is fulfilled in the kingdom of God.'' 17. And he took a cup, and when he had given thanks he
26. Now as they were eating, Jesus took bread, and blessed, and broke it, and gave it to the disciples and said, ''Take, eat; this is my body.'' 27. And he took a cup,[f] and when he had given thanks he gave it to them, saying, ''Drink of it, all of you; 28. for this is my blood of the[g] covenant, which is poured out for many for the forgiveness of sins. 29. I tell you I shall not drink again[i] of this fruit of the vine until that day when I drink it new[k] with you in my Father's kingdom.''	22. And as they were eating, he took bread, and blessed, and broke it, and gave it to them, and said, ''Take; this is my body.'' 23. And he took a cup, and when he had given thanks he gave it to them, and they all drank of it. 24. And he said to them, ''This is my blood of the covenant,[h] which is poured out for many. 25. Truly, I say to you I shall not drink again[j] of the fruit of the vine until that day when I drink it new[k] in the kingdom of God.''	said, ''Take this and divide it among yourselves; 18. for I tell you that from now on I shall not drink of the fruit of the vine until the kingdom of God comes.'' 19. And he took bread, and when he had given thanks he broke it and gave it to them, saying,[d] ''This is my body[e] which is given for you. Do this in remembrance of me.'' 20. And likewise the cup after supper, saying, ''This cup which is poured out for you is the new covenant in my blood.''[e]

8. The Fourth Gospel, John 19:31-37: The Fulfillment of the Passover

31. Since it was the day of Preparation, in order to prevent the bodies from remaining on the cross on the Sabbath (for that Sabbath was a high day), the Jews asked Pilate that their legs might be broken, and that they might be taken away.   32. So the sol-

diers came and broke the legs of the first, and of the other who had been crucified with him; 33. but when they came to Jesus and saw that he was already dead, they did not break his legs. 34. But one of the soldiers pierced his side with a spear, and at once there came out blood and water. 35. He who saw it has borne witness—his testimony is true, and he knows that he tells the truth—that you also may believe. 36. For these things took place that the scripture might be fulfilled, "Not a bone of him shall be broken" (Exod 12:46).[a] 37. And again another scripture says, "They shall look on him whom they have pierced" (Zech 12:10).

9. PAUL, 1 Corinthians 5:7-8

7. Cleanse out the old leaven that you may be a new lump, as you really are unleavened. For our paschal lamb has been sacrificed,[a] (which is) Christ. 8. Let us, therefore, celebrate the festival,[b] not with the old leaven, (the leaven) of malice and evil, but with the unleavened bread of sincerity and truth.

SOURCES FOR THE HISTORY OF THE PASCHAL CONTROVERSY OF THE SECOND CENTURY

10. EUSEBIUS OF CAESAREA, *Ecclesiastical History* 5, 23-25

23, l. At this time, to be sure, a considerable controversy was stirred up, because the dioceses[a] of all Asia,[b] alleging a more ancient tradition, considered it necessary to reserve for the feast of the saving Pascha the fourteenth (day) of the moon, on which the Jews were commanded to sacrifice the sheep, so that the fast always had to be brought to an end on this date, no matter what day of the week it happened to be. It was not (however) the custom of the Churches throughout the rest of the (Roman) world to act in this fashion, preserving as they did in accordance with apostolic tradition the custom which is still in force that it is not proper to terminate the fast on any other day than that of our Savior's resurrection.[c]

2. Then synods and episcopal conferences were held on this subject, and all unanimously, in letters to the (faithful) everywhere, laid down the ecclesiastical decree that the mystery of the Lord's resurrection from the dead should never be celebrated on any other day than the Lord's Day, and that on that day alone should we observe the close of the paschal fasting.

3. There is a letter still circulating today from those who then assembled in Palestine under the presidency of Theophilus, bishop of the diocese of Caesarea, and Narcissus,[d] of that of Jerusalem; likewise from those at Rome, another (letter) bearing the name of Bishop Victor, about the same question; and one from the bishops of Pontus under the presidency of Palmas, since he was the eldest; and one from the dioceses of Gaul which were under Irenaeus' supervision.   4. Furthermore, (a letter) from those of Osrhoene and the cities of that region, and personal (letters) from Bacchylus, bishop of the Church of the Corinthians, and from very many more, who expressed one and the same opinion and judgment and voted the same way. Their one norm was that indicated above.[e]

24, 1. But the bishops of Asia insisted that they had to defend the custom transmitted to them long ago. Their leader was Polycrates, who wrote a letter to Victor and the Church of the Romans, setting out in the following terms the tradition which had come down to him:

> 2. For our part we keep the day scrupulously, without addition or subtraction. For Asia too holds the resting place of great luminaries,[f] such as will rise again on the day of the Lord's parousia, when he comes with glory from heaven and will search out[g] all his holy ones: Philip of the twelve apostles, who rests in Hierapolis, and his two daughters who had grown old in virginity, and the other daughter who lived her life in the Holy Spirit and rests in Ephesus.   3. There is also John, the one who leaned on the Lord's breast and who became a priest wearing the insignia of holiness,[h] both a martyr and a teacher;   4. he rests at Ephesus.[i] Then there is Polycarp in Smyrna, a bishop and martyr as well; and Thraseas, bishop and martyr, from Eumenia (but) buried in Smyrna.   5. Must I mention Sagaris,[j]

bishop and martyr, buried in Laodicea, and the blessed Papirius and the eunuch[k] Melito,[l] who lived all his life in the Holy Spirit and lies in Sardis awaiting the visitation[m] from heaven in which he will rise from the dead? 6. All of them observed the fourteenth as the day of the Pascha according to the gospel, not deviating in the least but following the rule of the faith. Finally, so do I, Polycrates, the least of all of you, in accordance with the tradition of my kinsmen, some of whom I have succeeded. Seven of them, in fact, were bishops, and I am the eighth. And my kinsmen always kept the day when the people[n] put away the leaven. 7. And so, brethren, after living sixty-five years in the Lord and conversing with brethren from the whole world and perusing all of Holy Writ, I am not terrified by these threats; for better men than I have said, "One must obey God rather than men" (Acts 5:29).

8. He followed this up by speaking of the bishops who were with him as he wrote and who thought as he did:

> I could mention the bishops with me, whom you directed me to call together and whom I have convoked. If I should write their names, it would be a long list. But, although they know me for a quite unimportant person, they approved my letter in the knowledge that I did not get my grey hairs for nothing but have always lived in Christ Jesus.

9. Whereupon Victor, head of the (Church) of the Romans, tried with one blow to cut off from the common unity the dioceses of all Asia together with the neighboring Churches, as though they were heterodox, and wrote letters proclaiming all the brethren there totally excommunicate. 10. But this did not please all the bishops. Their answer was to request him to be mindful of *the cause of peace* (Rom 14:19) and of union and love towards the neighbor; we still have the text of the stinging rebuke they gave to Victor.

11. Irenaeus too was of their company, writing in the name of the brethren over whom he presided in Gaul. He agreed that the mystery of the Lord's resurrection ought to be celebrated only on the Lord's Day, but on the other hand he politely urged Victor not to cut off entire Churches of God for observing an an-

cient traditional custom. After giving him much more advice, he added the following, which I quote exactly:

> 12. For the controversy is not only about the date or day,[o] but also about the very form of the fast. For some think it necessary to fast one day, others two, others even more days; and others measure their day as lasting forty hours, day and night.[p] 13. And such variation in the observance did not begin in our time but much earlier, in our forefathers' time. Incorrectly, as it would seem, they kept up an ignorant custom of their own that they had made for posterity. And nonetheless they were all at peace, and we are at peace with one another; and the difference in fasting confirms our agreement in the faith.

14. He continues with the following narrative, which I shall carefully reproduce:

> In their number were the presbyters before Soter, who headed the Church of which you are now the leader—namely, Anicetus and Pius, Hyginus and Telephorus, and Xystus.[q] They themselves did not observe, nor did they permit those with them to do so, and, in spite of the fact that they were not observant, they were at peace with those who came to them from the dioceses in which it was observed[r]—although observance was more offensive to the non-observant.[s] 15. And no one was ever repulsed on these grounds; rather the presbyters before you, though they did not observe, used to send the Eucharist[t] to the observants from the dioceses. 16. And when the blessed Polycarp arrived in Rome in the time of Anicetus,[u] while they had minor differences about certain other matters, they made peace immediately, not wishing to quarrel over this matter. For neither was Anicetus able to persuade Polycarp not to observe, since he had always done so with John the disciple of our Lord and with the rest of the apostles, with whom he had lived; nor did Polycarp persuade Anicetus to observe, for he said it was incumbent upon him to maintain the practice of the presbyters before him. 17. And still they remained in communion with each other, and in the church Anicetus ceded the Eucharist to Polycarp,[v] obviously out of respect, and they parted from one another in peace, while the whole Church, both observants and non-observants, were at peace.

18. And Irenaeus (a man well-named, for he was a peacemaker both in appellation and in character) urged and advocated such a course of action for the peace of the Churches. He discussed the various aspects of the problem in letters, not only to Victor but also to very many distinguished persons in charge of Churches.

25, 1. However, those in the region of Palestine—Narcissus and Theophilus, whom we have just mentioned, and Cassius, bishop of the Church at Tyre, Clarus of the one in Ptolemais, and those assembled with them—put into writing most of the elements of the tradition about the Pascha which had come to them directly from the apostles, and at the end of the document they subjoined this (which I quote exactly):

> Try to have copies of our letter distributed to every diocese, so that we may not be responsible for those who recklessly lead their own souls astray. We inform you that even in Alexandria they celebrate on the very same day as we do; for letters travel from us to them and from them to us, so that we keep the holy day in harmony and at the same time.

11. HIPPOLYTUS OF ROME, *Refutation of All the Heresies* 8, 18, 1-2

1. But certain others,[a] contentious by nature, deficient in knowledge, and rather pugnacious in behavior, maintain that the Pascha must be kept *on the fourteenth of the first month* (Exod 12:18) according to the prescription of the Law, on whatever day (of the week) it may fall. They fail to notice what is written in the Law, (namely that) he will be accursed who does not keep (it) just [as] it is laid down. They ignore the fact that this legislation was made for the Jews, who were going to do away with[b] the true Pascha, which would spread to the Gentiles and be understood in faith, though now not observed [according to the letter]. 2. While paying attention to this one commandment, they disregard what was said by the apostle: "I bear witness to everyone who is circumcised that he is under obligation to observe the whole Law" (Gal 5:3).[c] Otherwise they are in accord as to everything transmitted to the Church by the apostles.[d]

GREEK WRITERS

12. *The Gospel of the Ebionites,* Quotation

But they deprived themselves of the consistency of the truth[a] and changed the saying, (the meaning of) which is clear to everyone from the context.[b] They make the disciples say, "Where do you wish us to prepare for you to eat the Pascha?"[c] and make him reply, "Have I then set my heart on eating flesh meat—this Pascha—with you?"[d]

13. *The Gospel of the Hebrews*, Indirect Quotation

The eight days of the Pascha, on which Christ the Son of God rose, signify the eight days after the remission of the Pascha,[a] when the whole seed of Adam will be judged, as is told in the Gospel of the Hebrews. For this reason wise men are of the opinion that the day of judgment will come in the time of the Pascha,[b] inasmuch as Christ rose on that day so that the saints in turn might rise on it.

14. *The Epistle of the Apostles*, 15

[Jesus said,] "After I have gone to the Father, 15. you are to remember my death (cf. 1 Cor 11:24-26). Now when the Pascha comes,[a] then one of you will be thrown into prison *for my name's sake* (cf. John 15:21; Luke 21:12; Rev 2:3), and he [will be] in grief and anxiety that you celebrate Pascha while he is in prison and [away] from you; for he will grieve that he does not celebrate the Pascha [with] you. Thereupon I will send my power in the [form] of the angel Gabriel, and the gates of the prison will open, and he will come out and come to you (cf. Acts 12:3-11); he will spend a night of watching with [you] and stay with you until the cock crows. But when you have completed the memorial that is for me, and my Agape,[b] he will again be thrown into prison *for a testimony* (cf. Mark 13:9), until he comes out of that place and preaches what I have delivered to you."

But we said to him, "Lord, is it then necessary that we take the cup and drink?"[c] He said to us, "Yes, it is necessary, until the day when I shall come (cf. 1 Cor 11:26) with those who were killed for my sake."[d]

15. *The Epistle of the Apostles*, 17

But we said to him, "O Lord, after how many years yet will this happen?" (cf. Matt 24:3). He said to us, "When the hundredth and the twentieth[a] is completed, between the Pentecost and the feast of the Unleavened (Bread)[b] will the coming of the Father take place." But we said to him, "Now you are telling us, 'I will come,' and how do you say, 'he that sent me is the one who will come'?" Then he said to us, "*I am* wholly *in the Father and the Father* is *in me* . . . ."[c]

16. HERACLEON, Fragment 12

116. It would be more opportune to review in another setting the problems about the time of the Pascha, held around the spring equinox, and any other problem that demands explanation. 117. Anyway, Heracleon says: "This (was) the great feast; for it was the figure of the Savior's passion,[a] when the sheep was not only slain, but by being eaten, brought repose. By being sacrificed it signified the Savior's suffering in the world; by being eaten, (it signified) the repose in the wedding."[b]

17. PTOLEMY, *Letter to Flora* 5, 8-10. 13-15

8. Then there is the typical part (of the Law), laid down according to the image of the spiritual and transcendent—I mean, the legislation regarding sacrifices, circumcision, Sabbath, fasting, Pascha, unleavened bread, etc.   9. For all these things, being but images and symbols, have been changed at the revelation of the Truth. As to their being carried out in a material, perceptible way, they have been abolished, while their spiritual content has been exalted; the names have remained the same, while there has been

a change in what is really done.   10. And so the Savior commands us to offer sacrifices, not with dumb animals or incense, but with spiritual praises and by giving glory and thanks and by fellowship and good deeds towards the neighbor . . . .   13. And to fast—but he wishes us to fast not the bodily but the spiritual fast, in which one abstains from all evil.[a] For the perceptible fast is kept even by our people, since this can profit the soul somewhat when done with reason, whenever it is done not to imitate others and not out of habit and not on account of a day being fixed for it.   14. At the same time, (one may fast) for a remembrance of the true fasting, in order that those who cannot fast in that way at all may have a remembrance of it from the perceptible fasting.   15. Likewise the Pascha[b] and the unleavened bread: Paul the Apostle makes it clear that they are images when he says, "Christ has been sacrificed as our paschal lamb," and further, "that you may be unleavened bread, having no share in the leaven"—by leaven he means wickedness—"but that you may be a new dough" (cf. 1 Cor 5:7).

18. JUSTIN, *Dialogue with Trypho* 40, 1-3

1. The mystery of the lamb which God ordered you to sacrifice as the Passover was truly a type of Christ, with whose Blood the believers, in proportion to the strength of their faith, anoint their homes (cf. Exod 12:7), that is, themselves.[a] You are all aware that Adam, the result of God's creative act,[b] was the abode of his inspiration (cf. 1 Cor 3:16). In the following fashion I can show that God's precept concerning the paschal lamb was only temporary.   2. God does not allow the paschal lamb to be sacrificed *in any other place than where his name is invoked* (that is, in the Temple at Jerusalem; Deut 16:5-6),[c] for he knew that there would come a time, after Christ's Passion, when the place in Jerusalem (where you sacrificed the paschal lamb) would be taken from you by your enemies, and then all sacrifices would be stopped.   3. Moreover, that lamb which you were ordered to roast whole was a symbol of Christ's Passion on the cross.[d] Indeed, the lamb, while being roasted, resembles the figure of the cross, for one spit transfixes it horizontally from the lower parts

up to the head, and another pierces it across the back, and holds up its forelegs.

19. JUSTIN, *Dialogue with Trypho* 111, 3

And the blood of the Passover, which was smeared on the side posts and transoms of the doors, saved those fortunate ones in Egypt who escaped the death inflicted upon the first-born of the Egyptians. The Passover, indeed, was Christ,[a] who was later sacrificed, as Isaiah foretold when he said: "He was led as a sheep to the slaughter" (Isa 53:7). It is also written that on the day of the Passover you seized him, and that during the Passover you crucified him.[b] Now, just as the blood of the Passover saved those who were in Egypt, so also shall the blood of Christ rescue from death all those who have believed in him.

20. MELITO OF SARDIS, *On the Pascha*, 1-10: Introduction

1. The Scripture from the Hebrew Exodus has been read[a]
and the words of the mystery have been plainly stated,[b]
how the sheep is sacrificed,
how the people is saved,
and how Pharaoh is scourged through the mystery.[c]
2. Understand, therefore, beloved,
how it is new and old,
eternal and temporary,
perishable and imperishable,
mortal and immortal, this mystery of the Pascha:[d]
3. old as regards the Law,
but new as regards the Word;
temporary as regards the model,[e]
eternal because of the grace;
perishable because of the slaughter of the sheep,
imperishable because of the life of the Lord;
mortal because of the burial in earth,[f]
immortal because of the rising from the dead.
4. Old is the Law,
but new the Word;

temporary the model,
but eternal the grace;
perishable the sheep,
imperishable the Lord;
not broken[g] as the lamb,
but resurrected as God.
For, although *as a sheep he was led to slaughter*
    (Isa 53:7; Acts 8:32),
yet he was not a sheep;
although *as a lamb, speechless* (ibid.),
yet neither was he a lamb.
For the model indeed existed,
but then the reality appeared.
5. For instead of the lamb there was a Son;[h]
and instead of the sheep,[i] a Man;
and in the Man, Christ, who has comprised all things
    (cf. Col 1:17; Heb 1:3).
6. Hence the slaying of the sheep
and the distribution of the blood[j]
and the writing of the Law have led to and issued in Christ,
for whose sake everything happened (Heb 2:10) in the
    ancient Law,
and even more so in the new Gospel.[k]
7. For indeed the Law has become Word,
and the old, new
(*having gone out* together *from Zion and Jerusalem*);[l]
and the commandment, grace;
and the model, reality;
and the lamb, a Son;
and the sheep, a Man;
and the Man, God.
8. For the one who was born as Son,
and led to slaughter as a lamb,
and sacrificed as a sheep,
and buried as a man,
rose up from the dead as God, since he is by nature both God
    and man.[m]
9. For he is all things:
inasmuch as he judges, Law;

inasmuch as he teaches, Word;[n]
inasmuch as he saves, Grace;
inasmuch as he begets, Father;
inasmuch as he is begotten, Son;[o]
inasmuch as he suffers, Sheep;
inasmuch as he is buried, Man;
inasmuch as he is raised, God.
10. This is Jesus the Christ,
to whom be glory for ever and ever. Amen
   (2 Tim 4:18; 1 Pet 4:11).

21. MELITO OF SARDIS, *On the Pascha*, 46: The Mystery of
   the Pascha

46. Now that you have heard the explanation of the type and of
its corresponding reality,
listen also to what went into making up the mystery.
What is the Pascha?
Its name is taken from an accompanying circumstance:
paschein (to keep Pascha) comes from *pathein* (to suffer).[a]
Therefore learn who the sufferer is
and who he is who suffers along with the sufferer,
and why the Lord is present on the earth
in order to clothe himself with the sufferer
and carry him off to the heights of heaven.

22. MELITO OF SARDIS, *On the Pascha*, 65-69: Redemption
   through Christ

65. Many other things have been proclaimed by many prophets
about the mystery of the Pascha,
which is Christ.[a]
To him be the glory for ever. Amen (2 Tim 4:18).
66. It is he who, coming from heaven to the earth because of the
suffering one,
and clothing himself in that same one through a virgin's womb,
and coming forth a man,

accepted the sufferings[b] of the suffering one[c]
through the body which was able to suffer,
and dissolved the passions[b] of the flesh;
and by the Spirit which could not die
he killed death, the killer of men.
67. For, having been himself led as a lamb
and slain as a sheep,
he ransomed us from the world's service
as from the land of Egypt
and freed us from the devil's slavery
as from the hand of Pharaoh;
and he marked[d] our souls with his own Spirit,
and the members of our body with his own blood.
68. It is he that clothed death with shame
and put the devil into mourning
as Moses did Pharaoh.
It is he that struck down crime
and made injustice childless
as Moses did Egypt.
It is he that delivered us from slavery to liberty,
from darkness to light,
from death to life,
from tyranny to eternal royalty,[e]
and made us a new *priesthood*[f]
and an eternal *people personal* (to him).[g]
69. He is the Pascha of our salvation.[h]

23. MELITO OF SARDIS, *On the Pascha*, 71: Redemption
   through Christ

71. He is the lamb being slain;
he is the lamb that is speechless[a]
he is the one born from Mary the lovely ewe-lamb;[b]
he is the one taken from the flock[c]
and dragged to slaughter[d]
and sacrificed at evening
and buried in the night;[e]
who on the tree was not broken,[f]

in the earth was not dissolved,
arose from the dead,
and raised up mortals from the grave below.

24. MELITO OF SARDIS, *On the Pascha*, 100-103: The
Triumph of Christ

100. The Lord, when he had clothed himself with man
and suffered because of him that was suffering
and been bound because of him that was held fast
and been judged because of him that was condemned
and been buried because of him that was buried,
101. arose from the dead and uttered this cry:
"Who takes issue with me? Let him stand against me (Isa 50:8).
I released the condemned;
I brought the dead to life;
I raise up the buried.
Who (is there) that contradicts me?
102. I (am the one)," says the Christ,[a]
"I am the one that destroyed death
and triumphed[b] over the enemy
and trod down Hades
and bound *the strong one*[c]
and carried off mortals to the heights of heaven;
I (am the one)," says the Christ.[a]
103. "Come then, all you families of men
who are permeated[d] with sins
and get *forgiveness of sins* (cf. Acts 10:43; 26:18).
For I am[e] your forgiveness,
I (am) the Pascha of salvation,[f]
I (am) the lamb slain for you,
I (am) your ransom,[g]
I (am) your *life,*[h]
I (am) your *light* (cf. John 8:12),
I (am) your salvation,[i]
I (am) your *resurrection* (cf. John 11:25)
I (am) your king.[j]
I will raise you up by my right hand;[k]

I am leading you up to the heights of heaven;[l]
there[m] I will show you the Father from ages past.'"[n]

25. MELITO OF SARDIS, Another Work *On the Pascha*, Quotation

In his *On the Pascha*,[a] at the beginning, he [Melito] indicates the time when he composed it, in the following words: "Under Servillius Paulus, proconsul of Asia,[b] at the time when Sagaris was martyred, there was a great deal of discussion about the Pascha,[c] which fell according to season[d] in those days, and this was written."

26. APOLLINARIUS OF HIERAPOLIS, *On the Pascha*, Fragments

And Apollinarius, the most holy bishop of Hierapolis in Asia, who was close to apostolic times, tells us approximately the same thing[a] in his treatise on the Pascha, when he says:

> There are some, therefore, who, on account of ignorance, stir up disputes[b] about these things, but what they do is excusable, since ignorance does not receive accusation but requires instruction. They say, then, that the Lord ate the sheep with his disciples on the fourteenth and suffered on the great day of the Unleavened Bread, and they explain Matthew's words (Matt 26:17) according to their interpretation. Wherefore their opinion is contrary to the Law[c] and, according to them, the Gospels seem to disagree.[d]

And again in the same treatise he wrote:

> The fourteenth is the true Pascha of the Lord, the great sacrifice:[e] the Son of God in place of the lamb; the one bound who bound *the strong one* (cf. Matt 12:29); the one judged, "judge of living and dead" (Acts 10:42); handed over to sinners to be crucified; raised upon the horns of the unicorn;[f] whose sacred side was pierced; who poured out of his side the double purification, water and blood (cf. John 19:34), word and spirit; and

who was buried on the day of the Pascha with the stone placed over the tomb (cf. Matt 27:60).

27a. AN UNNAMED QUARTODECIMAN (PSEUDO-HIPPOLYTUS), *Homily on the Holy Pascha*, 1–3

1, 1. Already the sacred rays of the light of Christ are shining, the pure lights of the pure spirit[a] are beaming, and the heavenly treasures of glory and divinity are opening. The great dim night is swallowed up, and the impenetrable darkness is dissolved in him, and the sad shadow of death is overshadowed. Life is poured out upon all things, they all overflow with unlimited light, dawns of dawns occupy the universe, and he who was *before the morning star*[b] and the lights of heaven, immortal and immense, the great Christ shines upon everything, brighter than the sun. 2. And for this reason a shining day,[c] great, eternal, and imperishable is established among all of us who have believed in him: the mystic Pascha, celebrated as a foreshadowing by the Law, fulfilled as a reality by Christ;[d] the wondrous Pascha, prodigy of the excellence of God and work of his power; truly *a festival* and *everlasting memorial* (Exod 12:14); impassibility out of suffering, immortality out of mortality, life out of death, healing out of wounding, rising out of falling, ascent out of descent.[e] 3. Thus God works great things, thus he creates marvels out of impossibilities, so that it may be known that he alone can do whatever he wills.

2, 1. Let Egypt, then, declare the foreshadowings, and let the Law set forth the images of the reality beforehand, a messenger heralding the great visitation of a great king.[f] Thereupon let the Egyptian multitude of first-born die, but let the mystic blood save Israel. All these things are a shadow of the future: we have the substances to which the images refer and the realizations of the models and, in place of the shadow, the exact, corroborated truth. 2. This is why the Law went before, indicating in a model the shapes of the truth; the model indeed came to be, but the truth was discovered.[g] There a lamb from the flock, here a lamb from the heavens; there the sign of blood and feeble protection of the whole, here the whole chalice[h] filled with divine blood and spirit;

there the sheep from the flock, here the shepherd himself in place of the sheep.[i]

3, 1. How then do the works not proclaim the complete salvation of all beings, when the mere models of these works are salvific?   2. And so let the heavens of heavens—who, as the divine spirit cries out, *tell the glory of God* (Ps 19:2), and who are the first to receive the fatherly dawning of the divine spirit[j]—keep holiday; let the angels and archangels of the heavens keep holiday; and let all the celestial population and army keep holiday, seeing the commander-in-chief of the army on high come bodily into the world. Let the choirs of stars keep holiday, declaring the one who rises *before the morning star* (cf. Ps 109:3 LXX). Let the atmosphere keep holiday, measured in its immeasurable depths and breadths. Let the briny sea water keep holiday, honored by the sacred footprints (cf. Mark 7:48); let the earth keep holiday, bathed in the divine blood; let every human soul keep holiday, refreshed by the resurrection for the new rebirth.[k]   3. This is the Pascha: a festival in which everybody and everything has a share, a sending[l] of the Father's will upon the world, the God-filled dawning of Christ around the earth, everlasting feast of angels and archangels, the deathless life of the whole world, a mortal blow to death, the incorruptible nourishment[m] of mortals, and the heavenly soul of everything, sacred initiation rite[n] of heaven and earth, prophet of mysteries *ancient and new* (cf. Matt 13:52), seen visibly on earth but understood in the heavens.

27b. AN UNNAMED QUARTODECIMAN (PSEUDO-HIPPOLYTUS), *Homily on the Holy Pascha* 17, 1-3

1. Taking up our subject again from the beginning, let us say first then why this[a] month is "the beginning of months" and why the month of the Pascha "is the first of the months of the year" (Exod 12:2).   2. Now the esoteric doctrine of the Hebrews says that this is the season in which the divine craftsman and maker of all things[b] created the universe[c] . . . .   3. I do not refuse to believe this explanation, but I think, or rather am convinced, that the spiritual feast of the Pascha is the reason why the beginning and head and supreme authority of all time and

of the whole age is considered to be this month of the Pascha, in which this great mystery is accomplished and celebrated,[d] so that, as the Lord is the first-begotten and the first-born of all the intelligible and invisible[e] beings from the beginning (cf. Col 1:15), so this month, which celebrates the sacred rite, has become the first of the year and the beginning of every age.

27c. AN UNNAMED QUARTODECIMAN (PSEUDO-HIPPOLYTUS), *Homily on the Holy Pascha*, 49–50

49, 1. This is the Pascha which Jesus desired (Luke 22:15) to suffer[a] for us. By suffering he freed from suffering,[b] and by death he conquered death, and by means of the visible food he provided his deathless life. This is the saving desire of Jesus, this is his completely spiritual love: to show the models as models and to give in their place his sacred body to his disciples. "Take, eat, this is my body; take, drink, this is my blood, the new testament: it is poured out for many for the remission of sins" (Matt 26:26-28; cf. 1 Cor 11:25). 2. For this reason he did not so much desire to eat as to suffer,[c] in order to deliver us from the suffering[d] that came from eating. 50, 1. And for this reason, having planted one tree in the place of another (cf. Gen 3:6), and having piously nailed his own innocent hand [in place of] the criminal hand impiously stretched out of old (cf. Gen 2:6), he showed that all life truly hung from it.[e] You, O Israel, could not eat of it,[f] but we, with a spiritual, indestructible knowledge, eat and eating do not die (cf. Gen 2:17; John 6:50).

27d. AN UNNAMED QUARTODECIMAN (PSEUDO-HIPPOLYTUS), *Homily on the Holy Pascha* 62, 1–4

1. O (Pascha) of the mystical expenditure![a] O (Pascha) of the spiritual feast! O divine Pascha, who made your way from the heavens to earth and again went up from earth into the heavens! 2. O festivity in which everything has a share, cosmic solemnity! O joy and honor and sustenance and delight of the universe! Through you dark death was destroyed and life extended to all, and the gates of heaven were opened, God appeared as man and

man ascended as God.[b] Through you the gates of hell were shattered and the iron bars broken (cf. Ps 107:16), and the people below, hearing the gospel, rose [from] the dead, and a choir from earth is assigned to the ranks above.[c] 3. O divine Pascha, in no mean measure you brought God out of the heavens and now you have joined him (to us) spiritually. Through you the great hall for the wedding has been filled and all wear their bridal garments and no one is cast out for not having the wedding garment. 4. O Pascha, illumination of the new torchlight procession, splendor of the virginal feast of lights,[d] because of you the lamps of the souls are extinguished no more, but in a divine way the spiritual fire of grace is transmitted to everyone, fed by the body, spirit, and oil of the Anointed One.[e]

28. IRENAEUS, *Against the Heresies* 4, 10, 1

The passages in which Moses reveals the Son of God are innumerable. He was aware even of the day of his passion: he foretold it figuratively by calling it Pascha.[a] And on the very day which Moses had foretold so long before, the Lord suffered in fulfillment of the Pascha.[b] And he pointed out not only the day but also the place and the lateness of the times[c] and the sign of sunset, when he says: "You may not sacrifice the Pascha in any of your towns which the LORD your God gives you; but at the place which the LORD your God will choose, to make his name dwell in it, there you shall sacrifice the Pascha, in the evening at the setting of the sun" (Deut 16:5-6).

29. IRENAEUS, *The Demonstration of the Apostolic Preaching*, 25

And since they were greatly afflicted and oppressed by cruel servitude, and turned with sighs and tears to God, the God of the patriarchs, Abraham and Isaac and Jacob, led them forth from Egypt at the hand of Moses and Aaron, striking the Egyptians with ten plagues, in the tenth of which he sent a killer angel, destroying their firstborn, from mortals to brute. From this he saved the children of Israel, showing forth in a mystery[a] the passion of

Christ by the immolation of a spotless lamb and by its blood, given as a guarantee of immunity to be smeared on the houses of the Hebrews; and the name of this mystery is the Passover [*pathos*[b]], source of freedom.[c]

30. IRENAEUS, *On the Pascha*, Indirect Quotation

Not kneeling on the Lord's Day is a symbol of the resurrection through which by Christ's grace we have been freed from our sins and from the death they made us die. The aforesaid custom had its beginning from apostolic times,[a] says the blessed Irenaeus, the martyr and bishop of Lyons, in his book *On the Pascha*. In it he also mentions the Pentecost, during which we do not kneel, since it is the equivalent of the Lord's Day,[b] for the aforementioned reason.

31. ARCHAEUS (or IRENAEUS), Fragment

The Pascha should be celebrated on the Lord's Day; for it was then that the joy of the Church Catholic was accomplished and everyone was destined to eternal life. For on that day, the mystery of the resurrection, of unchangeable hope, and of inheriting the kingdom was established. At this time, the Lord triumphed over humanity's enemy, death, having revived his body, which will never die any more but with the spirit[a] continues on unchangeable. This is the body, enveloped in glory, which he offered to the Father, when the gates of heaven opened to him.[b]

32. *The Letter to Diognetus* 12, 9

And salvation is set forth, and apostles are given understanding,[a] and the Pascha of the Lord[b] advances, and the seasons[c] are assembled and arranged in order,[d] and the Word rejoices in teaching the saints, (the Word) through whom the Father is glorified, *to whom be glory for ever. Amen* (Gal 1:5; 2 Tim 4:18; Heb 13:21).

33. CLEMENT OF ALEXANDRIA, *Miscellanies* 2, 11, 51, 2

Wherefore the tithes,[a] both of the ephah and of the sacrifices, were presented to God; and with the tenth day began the paschal feast, the transition[b] from all trouble and from all objects of sense.

34. CLEMENT OF ALEXANDRIA, *On the Pascha*, Fragment 25

And in his book *On the Pascha,* he [Clement] acknowledges that he was constrained by his companions to transmit to posterity in writing traditions that he happened to hear from the early presbyters; there he mentions Melito and Irenaeus and some others, whose explanations he has also set down.

35. CLEMENT OF ALEXANDRIA, *On the Pascha*, Fragment 26

Clement of Alexandria mentions this treatise[a] [by Melito] in his own book on the Pascha, which he says he compiled because of Melito's work.[b]

36. CLEMENT OF ALEXANDRIA, *On the Pascha*, Fragment 28

But also Clement, the most holy priest of the Church of the Alexandrians, a man most ancient and not much removed from apostolic times, tells us approximately the same thing in his treatise on the Pascha, when he writes:

> In the celebrations of previous years, the Lord ate the paschal victim sacrificed by the Jews. But after he preached, being himself the Pascha, *the lamb of God* (John 1:29), *led like a sheep to the slaughter* (Isa 53:7), he immediately taught his disciples the mystery of the type, on the thirteenth, the day on which

they asked him, "Where do you wish us to prepare for you to eat the Pascha?" (Matt 26:17). On this day, you must know, occurred both the sanctification of the unleavened bread and the preparation of the feast. Wherefore John records that suitably on this day the disciples had their feet washed by the Lord as a preparation (cf. John 13:4-5). The passion of our Savior took place on the following day, himself being the paschal victim offered in pleasing sacrifice by the Jews.

Afterwards he writes:

> This is why on the fourteenth, the day on which he suffered, the high priests and scribes, having brought him to Pilate early in the morning, "did not enter the pretorium so that they might not be defiled but might eat the Pascha" (John 18:28) unhindered in the evening. All the Scriptures harmonize and the Gospels concord with this precise reckoning of the days.[a] The resurrection too testifies: he rose on the third day, which was the first of the weeks of the harvest and (the day) on which the priest was commanded by the Law to offer the sheaf (Lev 23:10-11).[b]

37. ORIGEN, *On the Pascha*, 1

Most, if not all, of the brethren think that the Pascha is named Pascha from the passion of the Savior.[a] However, the feast in question is not called precisely Pascha by the Hebrews, but *phas*[*h*]. The name of this feast is constituted by the three letters phi, alpha, and sigma, plus the rougher Hebrew aspirate.[b] Translated, it means "passage."[c] Since it is on this feast that the people goes forth from Egypt, it is logical to call it *phas*[*h*], that is, "passage." In the speech of Hellas the name itself cannot be pronounced as the Hebrews say it, because, not using[d] the rougher Hebrew aspirate, the Hellenes cannot say *phas*[*h*]. Consequently the name was Hellenized, and in the prophets we read *phasek,* which upon further Hellenization has become *pascha*.[e] And so, if any of our people in the company of Hebrews makes the rash statement that the Pascha is so named because of the passion of the Savior, they will ridicule him for being completely ignorant of the meaning of the appellation.

38. ORIGEN, *Commentary on John* 10, 18, 108-111

108. Nevertheless, this aforementioned prophecy[a] about the lamb (Exod 12:3-10) ought to be our nourishment only during the night of the darkness in life. For, of that food which is thus useful to us only in the present, we are not to leave anything over till the dawn of the day of what follows this life. 109. For, the night being past and the day after these things having arrived, we have the unleavened bread that is entirely free of the old earthly leaven. We eat this, and it will be useful to us until that is given which comes after the unleavened bread, namely the manna, the food of angels (cf. Ps 78:25) rather than of mortals.

And so let each of us sacrifice his sheep in the house of his family,[b] with the possible result that one breaks the law by not sacrificing the sheep while another keeps the entire commandment by sacrificing and boiling[c] and not breaking a bone of it.[d]

110. This, then, is the way in which we would summarize the meaning of Christ sacrificed as our Pascha (1 Cor 5:7), in harmony with what the gospel says about the lamb.

For it is not to be thought that the historical events are types of historical events nor that corporeal things typify corporeal things; rather the corporeal things are types of spiritual realities and the historical events represent ideal realities.[e]

111. Raising our minds to the third Pascha,[f] which will be celebrated among myriads of angels in the most perfect festivity (cf. Heb 12:22) and with the happiest exodus, is not necessary at this time, especially since we have spoken more fully and lengthily than the text required.

39. ORIGEN, *Homilies on Exodus* 5, 2

Let us see what camping place they came to from Ramesse. "They came," it says, "to Sochoth" (Exod 12:37) . . . . But they were not allowed to stay there either: they were pressed to depart, the camp was to be moved from Sochoth too, and they were to hasten to arrive at Othon.[a] In our language, they say, *Othon* means "signs for them."[b] And rightly, for this is the place where you will hear it said that God "went before them, by day in a pillar of cloud . . . and by night in a pillar of fire" (Exod 13:21).

You will not find this happening at Ramesse, or at Sochoth, which was specified as the second camping place on their journey; no, it is the third camp where the divine signs occur. Remember the previous passage where Moses told Pharaoh, "We will go a three-days' journey into the wilderness and sacrifice to the LORD our God" (Exod 5:3). This then was the triduum on which Moses was intent and which the Pharaoh forbade; for he said, "You shall not go very far" (Exod 8:28 [LXX 24]). Pharaoh would not allow the children of Israel to go as far as the place of signs, he would not allow them to go far enough to be able to enjoy the mysteries of the third day.[c]

Now listen to what the prophet says: "God will revive us after two days, and on the third day we shall rise and live in his sight" (Hos 6:2). For us the first day is the passion of the Savior; the second, on which he descended into hell; and the third, the day of resurrection.[d] And therefore it was on the third day that God went before them, in a column of cloud by day, in a column of fire by night. But if, in accord with what we said above, the apostle is rightly teaching us that these words contain the mysteries of baptism,[e] it must be that those who are baptized in Christ are baptized in his death, and are buried together with him and rise from the dead with him on the third day (cf. Rom 6:3-4). And according to the words of the apostle, he has also raised them together with himself and made them to sit together with him in the heavenly places.[f] When, therefore, you will have received the mystery of the third day, God will begin to lead you, and himself show the way of salvation.

40. ORIGEN, *Homilies on Exodus* 7, 4

Why does Scripture mention also the day on which the people murmured? "In the second month," it says, "on the fifteenth day of the month" (Exod 16:1). This was not written without a reason. Recall what was said about the laws of the Pascha, and you will find there that this is the time prescribed for celebrating the Pascha by those who were unclean in soul or taken up with the business of a journey (cf. Num 9:9-12). Therefore those who were not unclean in soul or were not traveling far kept the Pascha on the fourteenth day of the first month, while those who were journeying far and were unclean keep the second Pascha at this time, which is also the time when the manna comes down from heaven (cf. Exod 16:15). The manna does not descend on the day on which the first Pascha is kept but today, when the second Pascha is kept.

Therefore now, let us see the various levels of mystery in these prescriptions. The first Pascha is that of the first people, the second Pascha is ours. For we were unclean in soul, "worshipping wood and stone" (Ezek 20:32) and "in our ignorance of God serving things which were not divine in nature" (Gal 4:8). We were also travelers afar: the apostle says of us that we were "aliens and strangers with respect to the testaments" of God, "without hope and without a god in this world" (cf. Eph 2:12). Nevertheless, the manna is not given from heaven on the day on which the first Pascha is kept, but on that of the second. For "the bread which came down from heaven" (John 6:51; cf. Ps 78:24) did not come to those who kept the first solemnity but to us who have received the second. "For Christ is sacrificed as our Pascha" (1 Cor 5:7) and he is "the true bread which comes down from heaven" (John 6:32-33).

41. ORIGEN, *Homilies on Numbers* 23, 6

The fourth place[a] among the festivals of God is occupied by the solemnity of the Pascha, the feast on which the lamb is slain. Here you should see the true lamb, "the lamb of God," the lamb "who takes away the sin of the world" (John 1:29) and say, "Christ has been sacrificed as our paschal lamb" (1 Cor 5:7). Let the Jews eat the flesh of the lamb in a carnal way, but let us eat the flesh of the Word of God; for he himself said, "Unless you eat my flesh, you will not have life in you" (John 6:53). The words we speak at this moment are the flesh of the Word of God—as long as the nourishment we offer is not vegetables for the sick or milk for babies. If we express mature, robust, strong ideas, we are setting before you the flesh of the Word of God for your consumption. For where you hear a mystical discourse, dogmatic, solid, and full of Trinitarian faith, where the veil of the letter is removed and the mysteries of the spiritual law of the world to come are laid bare,[b] where the soul's hope is torn away from earth, hurled into heaven, and fixed on those things "which eye has not seen nor ear heard and which have not risen into the heart of man" (1 Cor 2:9), these are all the flesh of the Word of God. Whoever can feed on them with perfect understanding and a purified heart, that man truly offers the sacrifice of the paschal festival and keeps holiday with God and his angels.

42. ORIGEN, *Homilies on Jeremiah* 19, 13

Paschor struck Jeremiah the prophet *and threw him into the waterfall which was at the gate* of Benjamin, from *the upper story* (Jer 20:2 LXX). There was an upper story in the house of the LORD, and *he threw* the prophet *into the waterfall*. And we urge that we take Jeremiah now and make him go up to *the upper story in the house of the Lord*. The upper story is the sublime and elevated sense, as I will show from Scripture, when it testifies that the saints gave hospitality to the prophets *in the upper story* . . . . And the admirable apostles, . . . united for prayer . . . were *in the upper story* . . . , not below . . . .

But Jesus too, as he was about to celebrate with his disciples this feast, as a symbol of which we keep the Pascha,[a] and in reply to their question, "Where do you wish us to prepare the Pascha for you?" (Mark 14:12), said, "As you are on your way, a man will come to meet you carrying a jar of water: follow him. He will show you a large upper room furnished with cushions, cleaned and ready. There you shall prepare the Pascha" (cf. Mark 14:13, 15; Luke 22:10-12). Therefore, no one celebrating the Pascha as Jesus wishes is below the upper room. But if he feasts with Jesus, he is upstairs in the large upper room, in the clean room, in the upper room which has been arranged and readied.[b] And if you go up[c] with him to celebrate the Pascha (cf. Matt 20:18), he will give you the cup of the new testament (cf. Matt 26:27-28), he will also give you the bread of benediction, his body (cf. 1 Cor 10:16), and he will make you a present of his blood.[d]

43. ORIGEN, *Against Celsus* 8, 22

If anyone makes a rejoinder to this by talking of our observances on certain days, the Lord's Day which we keep, or the

Preparation,[a] or the Passover, or Pentecost,[b] we would reply to this that the perfect man, who is always engaged in the words, works, and thought of the divine Logos who is by nature his Lord, is always living in his days and is continually observing the Lord's Day. Moreover, since he is always making himself ready for the true life and abstaining from the pleasures of this life which deceive the multitude, and since he does not nourish "the mind of the flesh" (Rom 8:6-7), but "buffets" his "body and makes it" his "slave" (1 Cor 9:27), he is always observing the Preparation. Furthermore, if a man has understood that "Christ our Passover was sacrificed" (1 Cor 5:7), and that he ought to "keep the feast" (cf. 1 Cor 5:8) by eating the flesh of the Logos, there is not a moment when he is not keeping the Passover,[c] which means "offerings before making a crossing."[d] For he is always passing over in thought and in every word and every deed from the affairs of this life to God and hastening towards his city. In addition to this, if one is able to say truthfully, "We are risen with Christ," but also that "he raised us up with him and made us sit with him in the heavenly places in Christ" (Eph 2:5-6), one is always living in the days of the Pentecost—particularly when, like the apostles of Jesus, one goes up "to the upper room" (Acts 1:13) and gives time to supplication and "prayer" (cf. Acts 1:13-14), so as to become worthy of the "mighty rushing wind from heaven" (cf. Acts 2:2), which compels the evil in mortals and its consequences to disappear, and so that one becomes worthy also of some share in the fiery tongue given by God (cf. Acts 2:3).[e]

44. HIPPOLYTUS OF ROME, *The Apostolic Tradition*, 33

At the Pascha, no one may eat before the offering is made; for the one who does so is not accounted as having fasted. If anyone is pregnant or[a] sick and cannot fast for two days,[b] let that person fast (just) on the Sabbath on account of (his or her) necessity, being content with bread and water. But if a person was at sea or in some necessity[c] and did not know the day, when he will have found it out, let him make up the fast after the Pentecost. For it is not the Pascha which we keep,[d] since the type has passed away and hence is no longer observed in the second month. Having learned the truth, one needs to keep (only) the fast.

45. HIPPOLYTUS OF ROME, *Against All the Heresies*, Quotation

Hippolytus, later a martyr of piety, having become bishop of a place called Portus, near Rome, in his treatise *Against all the Heresies*, wrote word for word the following: "I see, therefore, that the matter is controverted. For he[a] says, 'Christ kept the Pascha on that precise day and[b] died; therefore I too must do exactly as the Lord did.' But he errs, not recognizing that at the time when Christ died, he did not eat the legal Pascha. For he himself was the Pascha which had been foretold and which was fulfilled on the day set for it."

46. HIPPOLYTUS OF ROME, *On the Pascha*, Quotation

And again the same person,[a] in the first book of his treatise *On the Holy Pascha*, said: "It is clear that he lied neither in the first case nor in the last,[b] because he who had previously declared, 'I eat[c] the Pascha no more,' took his dinner in suitable fashion before the Pascha. He did not eat the Pascha: he suffered it. For it was not the right time to eat it."[d]

47. HIPPOLYTUS OF ROME, *On Elkanah and Hannah*, Quotation

Wherefore three[a] seasons of the year prefigured the Savior himself, that he might fulfill the mysteries prophesied about him. In the Pascha, that he might show that he was going to be sacrificed as a sheep and revealed as the true Pascha[b]—as the Apostle says, "Christ was sacrificed" for us "as our Pascha" (1 Cor 5:7). In the Pentecost, that he might make an advance sign of the kingdom of heaven, going up into heaven first himself[c] and offering humanity as a gift to God.[d]

48. HIPPOLYTUS OF ROME, *Commentary on Daniel* 1, 16

1. "Once, while they were watching for an opportune day, she went in as before with only two maids, and wished to bathe in the garden, for it was very hot" (Dan 13:15 LXX). 2. What kind of day is opportune, if not that of the Pascha?[a] On that day the bath is made ready for those going to be burnt and Susanna[b] while she is being bathed is presented to God as a pure bride, as faith and love[c] prepare the oil and lotions. 3. What were the lotions if not the commandments of the Word? What is the oil if not the power of the Holy Spirit? With these after the bath the believers are anointed[d] as with perfumed ointment.

49. DIONYSIUS OF ALEXANDRIA, *Letter to Basilides*, 1

You sent to me, my most faithful and learned son, to inquire at what hour one ought to end the fast before Easter.[a] For you say that some of the brethren maintain one should do so at cockcrow: and some at evening. For the brethren in Rome, so they say, await the cockcrow:[b] but concerning those in the Pentapolis you said (they broke the fast) sooner. And you ask me to set an exact limit and a definite hour, which is both difficult and risky. For it will be acknowledged by all alike that one ought to start the feast and the gladness after the time of our Lord's resurrection, up till then humbling our souls with fastings (cf. Ps 35:13). But by what you have written to me, you have quite soundly and with a good insight into the divine Gospels established the fact that nothing definite appears in them about the hour at which he rose. For the evangelists described those that came to the tomb diversely—that is, at different times, and all said that they have found the Lord already risen . . . .[c]

As things stand thus, we pronounce this decision for those who inquire to a nicety at what hour or what half-hour, or quarter of an hour, they should begin their rejoicing at the resurrection of our Lord from the dead: those who are premature and relax before midnight, though near it, we censure as remiss and wanting in self-restraint; for they drop out of the race just before the end, as the wise man says: "that which is within a little in life is not little."[d] And those who put off and endure to the furthest

and persevere till the fourth watch,[e] when our Saviour appeared
to those who were sailing, "walking on the sea" (Matt 14:25,
Mark 6:48, John 6:19), we shall approve as generous and pains-
taking. And those midway who stop as they were moved or as
they were able, let us not treat altogether severely. For not all continue during the six days of the fast[f] either equally or similarly:
but some remain without food till cockcrow[g] on all the days,
some on two, or three, or four, and some on none of them. And
for those who strictly persist in these prolonged fasts and then
are distressed and almost faint, there is some pardon if they take
something sooner. But if some, so far from prolonging their fast
do not fast at all, but feed luxuriously during the earlier days of
the week, and then, when they come to the last two and prolong
their fast on them alone, viz. on Friday and Saturday, think they
are performing some great feat by continuing till dawn, I do not
hold that they have exercised an equal discipline with those who
have practised it for longer periods. I give you this counsel in accordance with my judgment in writing on these points.

50. ANATOLIUS OF LAODICEA, *Canons about the Pascha*, Quotation

14. It [the Paschal Table] has therefore in the first year the new
moon of the first month, which is the beginning of the whole
nineteen-year cycle, on the 26th of Phamenoth according to the
Egyptians[a] . . . .

15. [On this day] the sun is found . . . not only to have arrived at the first sign of the zodiac, but already to be passing
through the fourth day within it. This sign is commonly called
the first of the twelve divisions and the equinoctial (sign) and the
beginning of months and head of the cycle and the starting point
of the planetary course. But the preceding sign is the last of the
months and the twelfth sign and the last of the twelve divisions
and the end of the planetary circuit. Therefore we say that they
who place the first month in it, and determine the fourteenth of
the Pascha accordingly,[b] are guilty of no small or ordinary
mistake.

16. And this is not our own statement, but the fact was known
to the Jews, those of old time even before Christ, and it was care-

fully observed by them. One may learn it from what is said by Philo, Josephus and Musaeus,[c] and not only by them but also by those of still more ancient date, the two Agathobuli, surnamed the Masters of Aristobulus the Great. He was reckoned among the Seventy who translated the sacred and divine Hebrew Scriptures for Ptolemy Philadelphus and his father; and he dedicated books exegetical of the Law of Moses to the same kings.[d]

17. These writers, when they resolve the questions relative to the Exodus, say that all equally ought to sacrifice the Passover[e] after the vernal equinox, at the middle of the first month; and that this is found to occur when the sun is passing through the first sign of the solar, or, as some have named it, the zodiacal cycle. And Aristobulus adds that at the feast of the Passover[e] it is necessary that not only the sun should be passing through an equinoctial sign, but the moon also.

18. For as the equinoctial signs are two, the one vernal, the other autumnal, diametrically opposite each to other, and as the fourteenth of the month, at evening, is assigned as the day of the Passover,[e] the moon will have its place in the station that is diametrically opposed to the sun, as may be seen in full moons; the one, the sun, will be in the sign of the vernal equinox, while the other, the moon, will of necessity be in that of the autumnal.

51. TRICENTIUS, Quoted by PETER OF ALEXANDRIA in a Fragment of *On the Pascha*

[Peter quotes Tricentius as saying:]

And so it makes no difference to us whether the Jews erroneously sometimes celebrate their Pascha in the month Phamenoth, according to the course of the moon, or every third year in the month Pharmuthi, according to the intercalary month.[a] For we are interested only in keeping the remembrance of his passion,[b] and that at such time as the eyewitnesses from the beginning handed down, before the Egyptians believed.[c] For this is not the first time that by observing the course of the moon they are compelled to celebrate it twice[d] in the month of Phamenoth and once every three years in the month Pharmuthi; for from the beginning, and before the advent of Christ, they seem to have always done so. And therefore, reproving them, God said through the prophet, "And I said, 'They always err in their heart; thus I have sworn in my wrath that they shall not enter into my rest' " (Ps 94:10-11 LXX).

[Peter replies:]

. . . On this point the Jews never went wrong (because they were in everyday contact with those who were eyewitnesses and attendants), and certainly not from the beginning before the birth of Christ. For it was not because of the Paschal legislation that God says they always erred in their heart, as you wrote; but because of their evil and indecent deeds, when he saw them turning back to idolatries and fornications.[e]

52. CONSTANTINE THE GREAT, *Letter to the Churches*, 18

[1.] Then also, when there was a question about the most holy day of the Pascha, it was decided by common accord that it would be well for everyone everywhere to celebrate on the same day.[a] . . . 2. And firstly it seemed unsuitable that we should celebrate that holy festival following the custom of the Jews . . . . 4. . . . In this matter they do not see the truth, so that, erring as much as they can instead of (making) the appropriate correction, they celebrate the Pascha twice in the same year.[b] Why then should we follow them, when it is acknowledged that they are afflicted with frightful error? For we will never accept the celebration of the Pascha a second time in the same year . . . . 5. In addition, it must be kept in mind that it is wicked for discord to prevail in a matter of such gravity and on the feast of such religious importance. For our Savior left us (but) one day as the day of our liberation, that is, the day of his most holy passion.[c]

53. THE FIRST COUNCIL OF NICAEA, *Decree on Easter*, Report

And thus were enacted the decisions taken by all those attending the holy synod in the days of the pious and great Constantine, who not only gathered the aforenamed bishops in one place, making peace for our nation, but was also present at their meeting and participated in the examination of the affairs of the universal Church.[a] When, therefore, in the course of examining the matter of the need for the whole (Church) under heaven to keep the Pascha harmoniously, the three parts of the empire were found acting in harmony with the Romans and Alexandrians, and only one region, that of the Orient, disagreed,[b] it was decided that, putting aside all contention and contradiction, the brethren in the Orient too should do as the Romans and Alexandrians and all the rest do, so that all in harmony on the same day may send up their prayers on the holy day of the Pascha. And, while disagreeing with the others, those of the Orient subscribed.[c]

54. PSEUDO-CHRYSOSTOM, *Homilies on the Holy Pascha* 1, 1-4: The Excellence of our Pascha

1. The Jews celebrate an earthly Pascha, having refused the heavenly one; we, celebrating a heavenly (Pascha), have transcended[a] the earthly one. The one performed by them was a symbol of the salvation of the Jews' firstborn, when their firstborn were not destroyed together with those of the Egyptians, being protected by a symbol, the sacrificial blood of the paschal lamb, whereas the Pascha which we perform is the cause of the salvation of all humanity, beginning with the one first molded, who is saved and brought to life in all.

2. The partial and transitory, as images and figures of the perfect and eternal, prepared for and foreshadowed the reality which has now emerged. When the reality arrives, the figure is obsolete, just as when a king comes, no one who sees the living king would think of prostrating himself before his image.[b]

3. The inferiority of the figure when compared to the reality is self-evident, where the figure celebrates the short life of the firstborn of the Jews, while the reality (celebrates) the enduring life of all humanity. For it is no great thing to escape death for a short time, if one dies shortly thereafter; but it is a great thing to escape death altogether—which is what happens to us, for whom "Christ has been sacrificed as the paschal lamb" (1 Cor 5:7).

4. And the very name of the feast acquires its greatest reknown when interpreted in relation to the truth:[c] for *Pascha* means

"passing over,"[d] when the Destroyer who struck the firstborn passed over the houses of the Hebrews; but we (experience) the true passing over of the Destroyer when he passes over us once for all as we are being raised by Christ to eternal life.

55. PSEUDO-CHRYSOSTOM, *Homilies on the Holy Pascha* 1, 6-7: The Beginning of a New Life

6 . . . Seen directly in relation to the truth,[a] what is the meaning of defining the time in which we have the Pascha and the salvation of the firstborn as the beginning of the year? (It means) that for us too the sacrifice of the true paschal lamb is a beginning of eternal life—for the year is a symbol of eternity inasmuch as it keeps turning and coming around on itself, never coming to an end and stopping[b]—and that Christ, offered as a sacrifice for us, is the "father of the age to come" (Isa 9:5), who makes our whole previous life obsolete and gives us the beginning of another one "through the bath of" the "regeneration" (Titus 3:5) according to the "pattern of his own death and resurrection" (cf. Rom 6:5).[c]

7. Wherefore everyone who knows the Pascha sacrificed for him should consider as the beginning of his life the moment when Christ has been sacrificed for him. And he has been sacrificed for him when he recognizes the grace and becomes aware that he is alive because of that sacrifice.[d] And knowing this, he should strive to possess the principle of the new life and never turn back to the old, to the end of which he has already come. For he says: "we who have died to sin, how shall we still live in it?" (Rom 6:2).

56. EUSEBIUS OF CAESAREA, *On the Paschal Solemnity*

1. And now perhaps it will not be out of place to treat of the Pascha, which in olden times was given to the children of the Hebrews as a symbol. When, therefore, the Hebrews, foreshadowing future realities, first celebrated the feast of the *Phasek*, they took an animal from the flock (it was a lamb or a sheep), they sacrificed it themselves, and then the first thing was for each man to smear the blood on the lintel and doorposts of his house,

bloodying thresholds and beams so as to fend off the Destroyer. Then, eating the flesh of the sheep and, with belts around their waists, partaking of the food of unleavened bread joined to bitter herbs, they passed from place to place, from the land of the Egyptians to the desert. This is what they had been commanded, together with the killing and eating of the sheep. Hence the migration[a] from Egypt is the basis they have for calling it the Crossing-Feast.[b]

But "these things happened to them as a figure, and were written" on our account (cf. 1 Cor 10:11). Paul too interprets it this way, unveiling the truth of the ancient symbols when he says, "For Christ was sacrificed as our paschal lamb" (1 Cor 5:7). The Baptist tells us why he was sacrificed when he says, "Behold the lamb of God, who takes away the sin of the world" (John 1:29). Indeed, the body of the Savior was handed over to death as a sacrificial victim which would avert all evils and, after the manner of an expiation, it took away the sin of the whole world. In fact, Isaiah has clearly exclaimed, "He bears our sins and is afflicted in our regard" (Isa 53:4 LXX).

2. Fed, then, with the spiritual flesh[c] of this saving victim, who has saved the whole human race with his own blood—that is, with the teachings and words announcing the kingdom of heaven[d]—we are suitably regaled with divine delights. Furthermore, with faith in his blood (cf. Rom 3:25), which he has given us as a propitiation in exchange for our salvation, we mark the houses of the soul, our bodies,[e] and drive from ourselves every kind of treacherous demon. And as we celebrate the Crossing-Feast, we hasten to cross over to the divine things, like those who long ago passed over from Egypt into the desert . . . .

3. This time of festivity brought destruction to the demon-loving Egyptians but deliverance from evils to the Hebrews, who were keeping a feast for God. This was that very season which had been reserved[f] for the first creation of the universe, the season in which the earth sprouted, in which the lights (of heaven) came into existence, in which heaven and earth were produced and everything in them.[g] In this season the Savior of the whole world accomplished the mystery of his own feast, and the light brightened the world with the rays of true religion, and the season seemed to embrace the birthday of the world. In this season too

was performed the figurative rite of the ancient Pascha, also called the Crossing; it brought the symbol of the slaughter of the sheep and hinted at the image of feeding on unleavened bread.

All these things were brought to completion at the saving festival. For the sheep was he . . . ; he is also the sun of justice . . . ; all regions have brought forth welcome flowers of virtue . . . .

4. Such are the new teachings, formerly hidden in shadowy symbols but recently laid open to the light. And for our part, every year with the recurrent cycles[h] we rekindle the beginning of the feast. Before the feast we undertake the exercise of the Forty Days[i] to prepare ourselves, in imitation of the zeal of saints Moses and Elijah, but the feast itself we keep repeating forever without forgetting.[j] And so, setting out on our journey towards God, we gird our loins well with the girdle of temperance; we cautiously guard the steps of the soul so that we remain shod and ready to travel in response to the heavenly call. Using the staff of the divine word in the power of prayers for fending off enemies, with utmost eagerness we make the crossing that leads to heaven, hastening from what is here to what is in heaven and from mortal to immortal life. For when we have well and duly passed the Passage, another, greater feast awaits us there. The children of the Hebrews call it by the name of Pentecost, and it bears the likeness of the kingdom of heaven.[k]

Moses in fact says, "*When thou* art *putting the sickle to the crop*, thou shalt reckon *to thyself seven weeks* (Deut 16:9), and thou shalt present to God new loaves from the new harvest" (cf. Lev 23:16-17). With the prophetic figure of the harvest he revealed the call of the nations;[l] and with that of the new loaves, the souls offered to God through Christ and the Churches of the nations, for whose sake is celebrated the grand feast of God, the lover of humankind. Reaped by the spiritual sickles of the apostles and brought together under one as to a threshing floor the Churches[m] of all the earth, formed into a body by our concordant profession of faith, and salted with the teachings derived from the divine words, reborn through water and the fire of the Holy Spirit, we are presented to God through Christ as nourishing loaves, soft and tasty.

5. In this way, with the prophetic symbols from Moses becoming realities by means of more august completions, we ourselves

have learned to celebrate a festival still more splendid, as though we were already gathered to the Savior and shared his kingdom. Wherefore we are not allowed to toil during this festival; rather we are instructed to bear the likeness of the refreshment we hope for in heaven. Consequently, we neither bend the knee at prayers nor afflict ourselves with fasting.[n] For those deemed worthy of the resurrection according to God should never again fall to the ground, nor should those who have been freed from their passions suffer the same things as those still enslaved. This is why, after the Pascha, we celebrate the Pentecost for seven complete weeks, having soldiered through the previous forty-day period of asceticism in the six weeks before the Pascha. For the number six is effective and active; that is why God is said to have made the universe in six days. The labors of that observance are fittingly succeeded by the second feast, seven weeks long, with an increase of repose for us, symbolized by the number seven.[o] But the number of the Pentecost is not constituted by these seven weeks: going one day beyond, it seals them on the last day with the solemnity of Christ's assumption.[p] In these days of the holy Pentecost, therefore, we are right to represent our future refreshment by rejoicing our souls and resting the body as though we were already united to the Bridegroom and incapable of fasting (cf. Matt 9:15; Mark 2:19-20) . . . .

7. Moses' followers used to sacrifice the paschal sheep only once a year, on the fourteenth of the first month, toward evening; but we of the New Testament, performing our Pascha every Lord's day, are always satiating ourselves with the saving body and always partaking of the sheep's blood.[q] We always have the loins of our soul girt (cf. Exod 12:11; Luke 12:35; Eph 6:14) with purity and moderation; we always have our feet shod "in the readiness of the gospel" (Eph 6:15);[r] we always have our staves in hand and rest upon "the rod" which came forth "from the root of Jesse" (Isa 11:1); we are always departing from Egypt; we are always seeking after the lonely desert of human life;[s] we are always setting out on the journey towards God; we are always celebrating the Crossing-Feast. For the gospel word would have us do these things not once a year but always, even daily.[t] And that is why we keep the feast of our Pascha every week on the salvific Day of the Lord, peforming the mysteries of the true sheep through whom we have been purified . . . .

8. . . . But if anyone says,[u] as indeed it is written, *"On the first day of unleavened bread, the disciples approached* the Savior and said, *'Where do you wish that we prepare for you to eat the Pascha?'* And he sent them *to a certain man* to say, *'I keep the Pascha at your house'* " (Matt 26:17-18), then we reply that this is not a command but a narrative, telling what happened at the time of the Savior's Passion. It is one thing to explain what happened long ago and quite another to legislate and leave ordinances for posterity.[v]

9. Nor did the Savior observe the Pascha with the Jews at the time of his passion. He did not keep his own Pascha with his disciples at the time when the Jews were sacrificing the sheep; for they did this on the Parasceve, (the day) on which the Savior suffered. That is why "they did not enter the pretorium," but "Pilate went out to them" (John 18:28-29). Rather, he reclined (at table) with his disciples a whole day before, on Thursday, and while he was eating with them he said, "With desire I desired to eat this Pascha with you" (Luke 22:15). You see how it was not with the Jews that the Savior ate the Pascha.[w] Because this was something new and strange, against the custom and practice of the Jews, he had to insist saying, "With desire I desired to eat this Pascha with you before I suffer." For the primitive, or rather antiquated, customary foods which he used to eat with the Jews were not the objects of his desire; it was the new mystery of his new covenant, which he gave to his disciples, that he actually desired . . . .

10. But before he suffered he did eat the Pascha and celebrate the feast—with his disciples, not with the Jews. After he had feasted in the evening, the high priests, in alliance with the traitor, "laid hands on" him (Matt 26:50); for they were not eating the Pascha in the evening or they would have left him alone . . . . But on the very day of the passion[x] they ate the Pascha to their souls' destruction, having demanded the Savior's blood, not for but against themselves (cf. Matt 27:25). But our Savior kept the feast which he desired, reclining with his disciples, not then but on the previous day . . . .

11. Wherefore we too should eat the Pascha with Christ . . . filling ourselves with the unleavened bread of truth and sincerity . . . . And this not for one period out of the whole year, but every week. Friday should be a fast for us, a sign of grief, on

account of our former sins and to commemorate the saving passion.

57. ASTERIUS THE SOPHIST, Homily 11: *Sixth Homily on Psalm 5*, On Monday in the Octave of Easter 6, 4

O night brighter than day![a] More radiant than the sun! Whiter than snow! Flashing brighter than lightning! More visible than torches! More delicious than paradise! O night set free of darkness! Replete with light! Chasing sleep away! Teaching watchfulness with the angels! Terrifying to the demons! Desired of the year! Leading the Church to her Bridegroom! Mother of the newly enlightened! O night in which the Devil is despoiled in his sleep! O night in which the heir led the heiress into the inheritance— "Unto the end. For the heiress."[b]

58. ATHANASIUS OF ALEXANDRIA, *Festal Letter* 1 (for 329), 10

We shall begin the holy fast on the fifth of Pharmuthi[a] and immediately join to it those six holy and magnificent days which symbolize the creation of this world.[b] We shall terminate the fast on the tenth of the same month, on the Holy Sabbath of the week,[c] and the Holy Sunday will dawn on us on the eleventh of the month. From this day we count one by one seven more weeks and celebrate the holy day of Pentecost. This was formerly foreshadowed among the Jews under the name of the Feast of Weeks; it was the time for freeing (those in bondage) and forgiving debts,[d] in sum, it was a day of all kinds of freedom. Since that time is for us a symbol of the world to come, we shall celebrate the great Sunday,[e] enjoying here the first installment of that eternal life. But when we shall depart hence, then we shall celebrate the full feast with Christ.[f]

59. ATHANASIUS OF ALEXANDRIA, *Festal Letter* 5 (for 333), 4

In truth, the Pascha is abstinence from evil, the practice of virtue, and a transition from death to life. It is this which one learns from the ancient type: for then they labored to pass from Egypt to Jerusalem; now we pass from death to life; then, from Pharaoh to Moses; now, from the devil to the Savior. And just as then the type of the help given them was represented every year, so now also we commemorate our salvation. We fast, because we think of death, so that afterwards we can live. We watch, not as mourners, but as those who await their Lord's return from a banquet, so that we may take a cue from one another and proclaim the sign of victory over death as soon as possible.[b]

60. ATHANASIUS OF ALEXANDRIA, *Festal Letter* 6 (for 334), 13

But just as Israel, advancing toward Jerusalem, was purified and instructed in the desert, so that they would forget the customs of Egypt, so it is right that during the holy Lent, which we have taken upon ourselves, we should give our attention to our cleansing and purification, so that setting forth from here and mindful of fasting we can ascend to the upper room with the Lord and dine with him and share the joy in heaven. For otherwise, without keeping Lent, it would not be allowed us either to go up to Jerusalem or to eat the Pascha.

61. ATHANASIUS OF ALEXANDRIA, *Festal Letter* 14 (for 342), 6

Let us keep the holy feast [of Pascha] on the sixteenth of Pharmuthi, and then, adding day by day the holy Pentecost, which we regard as feast upon feast, we shall keep the festival[a] of the Spirit who is already near (us) through Christ Jesus.[b]

62. ATHANASIUS OF ALEXANDRIA, *Festal Letter* 42 (for 370), Excerpt

For we have been called, brethren, and are now called together, by Wisdom, and according to the evangelical parable, to that great and heavenly supper, and sufficient for every creature; I mean, to the Passover, to Christ, who is sacrificed; for "Christ our Passover is sacrificed" (1 Cor 5:7).

63. CYRIL OF JERUSALEM, *Catechesis* 14, 10

At what season does the Savior rise? Is it in summer or at another time? In the same Canticles, just before the words quoted above, he says: "The winter is past, the rains are over and gone. The flowers have appeared on the earth, the time of pruning has come" (Cant 2:11-12 LXX). Is not the land now full of flowers, and are not the vines being pruned? You see how he said also that the winter was past. For in this month Xanthicus, spring is already come. This is the time, the first month among the Hebrews, in which is celebrated the feast of the Pasch, formerly the figurative Pasch, but now the true. This is the season of the creation of the world; for God then said: "Let the earth bring forth vegetation, yielding seed according to its kind and according to its likeness" (Gen 1:11 LXX). Now, as you see, every herb is in seed. At that time God made the sun and the moon and gave them courses of equal day and night; just a few days ago we had the equinox. Then God said: "Let us make man in our image and likeness" (Gen 1:26); he received the image but he obscured the likeness by his disobedience. Humanity's loss of grace and its restoration[a] took place in the same season. When the man who had been created disobeyed and was cast out of Paradise, then the one who had believed[b] obeyed and was brought in. And so salvation took place at the same time that the Fall had taken place: when "the flowers have appeared" and the pruning "has come" (Cant 2:12 LXX).

64. EPIPHANIUS OF CONSTANTIA, *Panarion* 70, 9, 2-3

2. For they [the Audians] wish to celebrate the Pascha with the Jews, that is, in their love of dissension they keep the Pascha during the period when the Jews are keeping their (feast of) Unleavened Bread, and give as their reason the fact that this was the usage of the Church.[a] They also lay a slanderous charge against the people of the Church in regard to this matter, asserting:

3. "From the time of Constantine, because of special considera-
tion for the emperor, you have abandoned the observance of the
fathers concerning the feast of the Pascha," and: "You have
changed the day to one decreed by the emperor."

65. EPIPHANIUS OF CONSTANTIA, *Panarion* 70, 10, 1-6

1. To this purpose the same Audians adduce the *Diataxis of
the Apostles*, which many consider suspect, but it is not worth-
less, for it embraces the whole of canon law while containing nothing contrary to the faith, whether to the Creed or to the
ecclesiastical administration of both canon and faith.

2. But the phrase with which the aforementioned support their
opinion about the Pascha they misinterpret and ignorantly take
in a wrong sense. For in the same *Diataxis* this is what the apostles
decree: "You shall not calculate, but celebrate the feast whenever your brethren from the Circumcision do. Keep it together
with them."[a] And they did not say, "brethren in the Circumcision," but "from the Circumcision," so as to designate those who
had passed from the Circumcision to the Church to be thereafter
the leaders, whom the others should obey, so that one would not
be doing one thing and another (doing it) at another time.[b]

3. They agreed upon this whole plan for the sake of unity, to
prevent schisms and divisions. But these (schismatics), not having understood the apostles' intention and the sense of the
pronouncement in the *Diataxis*, concluded: "How then is it not
necessary to celebrate the Pascha with the Jews?"

4. Now altogether fifteen men from the Circumcision became
bishops,[c] and since the bishops from the Circumcision were established in Jerusalem, it was necessary at that time that the whole
world follow them and celebrate with them, so that there should
be a single confession, with all singing in unison, as it were, and
celebrating one feast.

5. Wherefore their concern, bringing the mind of men together
into the unity of the Church. It having been impossible for such
a long time to celebrate [the feast together with the Jews],[d] with
God's approbation, under Constantine [a correction] was made
for the sake of concord.

6. It was for the sake of concord that the apostles made that decree, as they attest when they say, "Even if they err, do not be concerned." The answer (to the Audians) becomes clear from the very things said there. For they [the apostles] tell (us) to hold the vigil during (the week of) the Unleavened Bread,[e] but, given the Church's way of computing (the date of Easter), this cannot always be done.

66. EPIPHANIUS OF CONSTANTIA, *Exposition of the Faith* 22, 10-14

10. All the peoples pass the six days of the Pascha in xerophagy, that is, consuming only[a] salt, and water towards evening.   11. But the fervent take on themselves a two- or three- or four-day (fast), and some (go without food) the whole week[b] until cockcrow of Sunday morning. They hold vigils on all six days. Furthermore they assemble for services[c] from the ninth hour till vespers on these six days and for the whole forty-day period.
12. In some places[d] they only keep vigil after Thursday until dawn of Friday, and [after Saturday until dawn] of Sunday.
13. And in some places the Worship of the Dispensation is held on Thursday at the ninth hour[e] and so breaks the fast, though they remain in the same xerophagy.   14. In other places the Worship of the Dispensation is not held before Sunday begins to dawn, when it breaks the fast around the sound of cockcrowing on the Day of Resurrection and great festive day of the Pascha, as has been prescribed.[f]

67. AERIUS, *Quotation and Report*

4. Then he [Aerius] says: "What is the Pascha which you celebrate? You still cling "to Jewish fables" (cf. Titus 1:14). "There is no need," he says, "to celebrate the Pascha, *for Christ has been sacrificed as our paschal lamb*" (1 Cor 5:7) . . . .
6. "Neither should fasting be enjoined," says he; "for these are Jewish (observances) and *under the yoke of servitude* (cf. Gal 5:1; 1 Tim 6:1). *For the Law was not laid down for the just but for patricides and matricides* and the rest (1 Tim 1:9). If then I decide to fast, I fast on whatever day I shall choose by myself."

7. That is why they glory in fasting[a] on Sunday and eating on Wednesday and Friday. But often they also fast on Wednesday, not by law but, as they say, by their own choice.[b]   8. In the days of the Pascha, when we are sleeping on the floor, being chaste, afflicting ourselves, eating dry food,[c] praying, watching, and fasting, and performing all the soul-saving practices of the sacred sufferings,[d] they are up at dawn, laying in stocks of meat and wine, stuffing their veins, and indulging in bursts of laughter as they mock those who are performing the sacred rites of the week of the Pascha.

68. BASIL OF CAESAREA, Homily 13: *Exhortation to Holy Baptism,* 1

Different times are suitable for different things. There is a proper time for sleep and a proper time for staying awake, "a time for war and a time for peace" (cf. Qoh 3:8), but the time for baptism is the whole of human life . . . . Every time, therefore, is opportune for being saved through baptism—night, day, hour, minute, no matter how brief. But it is surely reasonable that what corresponds more closely is more opportune—and what would correspond more closely to baptism than the day of the Pascha?[a] The day is a memorial of the resurrection, and baptism is a power for resurrection. Therefore we shall receive the grace of the resurrection on the Day of the Resurrection.[b]

69. GREGORY OF NAZIANZUS, Oration 1: *First Oration on the Pascha*, 3-4

3. Yesterday the lamb was slain and the doorposts were anointed, and Egypt bewailed her firstborn, and the Destroyer passed us over, and the Seal was dreadful and awesome, and we were walled in[a] with the "precious blood" (1 Pet 1:19). Today we have clean escaped from Egypt and from our harsh master, the Pharaoh, and from the oppressive overseers, and we have been freed from the mortar and the brick, and there is no one to keep us from celebrating a feast to the Lord our God—the feast of departure—and from feasting, not "with the old leaven of wicked-

ness and depravity but with the unleavened bread of sincerity and truth" (1 Cor 5:8), bringing with us none of the godless Egyptian dough.[b]

4. Yesterday I was crucified with Christ, today I am glorified with him; yesterday I died with him, today I am brought to life with him; yesterday I was buried with him, today I am raised up with him.[c]

70. GREGORY OF NAZIANZUS, Oration 45: *Second Oration on the Pascha*, 10

The Pascha of which I speak, the great and holy (feast), is called by the Hebrews in their tongue *Phaska*.[a] The word means "crossing"—historically, because of the escape and migration out of Egypt into Canaan; spiritually, on account of the progress and ascent from the things below to those above and to the land of the Promise.[b] And we find that a thing which often occurs in Scripture, the change of certain names from a dubious to a clearer meaning, or from a coarser to a more refined signification, has taken place here too. For some people, thinking this to be the name of the saving passion, and then Hellenizing the word by changing *phi* to *pi* and *kappa* to *chi*, named the day *Pascha*.[c] Custom took up the word and confirmed it since people approved of it as being a more pious way of speaking.

71. GREGORY OF NAZIANZUS, Oration 45: *Second Oration on the Pascha*, 23

The Pascha in which we are going to participate is still a figurative one, and if it is less veiled than it was in the past (for the Pascha of the Law, I make bold to say, was the more obscure figure of another figure), in a little while it will be purer and more perfect, when the Logos drinks it "new with" us "in the kingdom of the Father" (Matt 26:29), revealing and teaching what he indicated now in a limited way.[a] For what is now being learned is always new.[b]

72. GREGORY OF NYSSA, *On the Three-Day Interval between Our Lord's Death and Resurrection*

Behold the blessed Sabbath[a] of the first creation of the world,[b] and in that Sabbath recognize this Sabbath, the day of the Repose,[c] which God has blessed above the other days. For on this day the only-begotten God truly rested from all his works, keeping Sabbath in the flesh by means of his death;[d] and, returning to what he was before through his resurrection, he raised up with himself all that lay prostrate,[e] having become Life and Resurrection (cf. John 11:25) and East and Dawn and Day "for those in darkness and the shadow of death" (Luke 1:79).[f]

73. AMPHILOCHIUS OF ICONIUM, Oration 5: *For Holy Saturday*, 1

Today we celebrate the feast of our Savior's burial. He, with the dead below, is loosing the bonds of death and filling Hades with light and awakening the sleepers, while we, upon earth, have the resurrection in mind and rejoice.[a] We have no fear of decay, as though it might prevail over incorruption . . . .

Yesterday the crucified one darkened the sun, and night fell in the middle of the day; today Death is undone because he swallowed up a dead man who was not his. Yesterday the creation was in mourning, seeing the frenzy of the Jews, and it put on darkness as a mourning garment; today "the people who sat in darkness have seen a great light" (Matt 4:16; Isa 9:2).[b]

74. JOHN CHRYSOSTOM, *Orations Against the Jews* 3, 4

The Pascha and Lent are not the same thing: the Pascha is one thing, Lent is another. For Lent comes once a year, but the Pascha three times a week, sometimes even four,[a] or as often as we wish.[b] For the Pascha is not fasting but the offering of the sacrifice which takes place in every synaxis. And that this is so, listen to Paul, who says, *"Our Pascha was sacrificed* for us, *namely, Christ"* (1 Cor 5:7), and "As often as you eat this bread and drink this cup, you proclaim the death of the Lord" (1 Cor 11:26).

Hence, as often as you approach with a clean conscience, you celebrate Pascha—not whenever you fast, but whenever you partake of that sacrifice. For "as often as you eat this bread and drink this cup, you proclaim the death of the Lord." The Pascha is the proclamation of the death of the Lord.[c] For the offering made today and the one carried out yesterday and the one (made) every day is one and the same sacrifice happening that day of the week. This (offering) is not holier than that, and that is not less worthy than this; rather they are one and the same, equally awesome[d] and salvific.

75. PSEUDO-CHRYSOSTOM, *Homilies on the Holy Pascha* 7, 3-4: A Complex Mystery

3. For often we have heard people ask: How is it that the Savior's birthday is celebrated on a fixed day (it comes, as everyone knows, on the eighth day before the Kalends of January, according to the Roman calendar); the Epiphany likewise (it is celebrated on a fixed day, the thirteenth of the fourth month, according to the Asian calendar); and similarly, in celebrating the memory of martyrs, we put the commemoration on a fixed day; but for the Pascha this is not the case?[a] Because the sacred rite[b] is not a matter of a single day or of the simple coincidence of days, but of many occurrences [which] we intentionally put together into one occasion for the purpose of explaining the mystery.[c]

4. . . . Since, therefore, we observe the beginning of time and the equinox, and after this also the fourteenth of the moon, and with this the triduum (that is, Friday-Saturday-Sunday), and the Pascha cannot be celebrated when one of these elements is missing, for this reason we cannot adopt one fixed day for the mystery of the Pascha, but by putting all these occurrences together[d] we reveal the inner meaning of the saving passion.

76. PSEUDO-CHRYSOSTOM, *Homilies on the Holy Pascha* 7, 35-36: The New Beginning

35. But the equinox is observed on (the day of) the passion[a] on account of its recapitulation[b] of the first time; likewise Good

Friday,[c] since the first man was molded on this day, and it was expedient that he be put back on his feet[d] on the same day on which he was molded and fell. The Sabbath has been taken over for repose by the Scripture which says, "And . . . God . . . rested from all his works on the seventh day . . . and he sanctified it" (Gen 2:2-3). Therefore, in the same fashion, the Lord, having once worked the recapitulation by suffering on Friday,[c] and having finished the works by which fallen man is reformed,[d] rests on the seventh day[e] and remains "in the heart of the earth" (Matt 12:40) having, moreover, bestowed on those in Hades the freedom deriving from his passion[f]. . . .

36. Thus, having observed the equinox and Friday and Saturday according to the original sequence of the passion, "on the first day of the week" (Mark 16:2; Luke 24:1) he reveals the light of the resurrection, again in (proper) temporal order. For this was again the first day of all time, which he established of old as the beginning of visible light and in line with that now as the beginning of the spiritual light of the resurrection.[g]

77. PSEUDO-CHRYSOSTOM, *Homilies on the Holy Pascha* 7, 39: The New Paschal Sacrifice

39. . . . Wherefore, since the Only-Begotten was sacrificed once for all and satisfied (the requirements of) the Dispensation, the lamb[a] is no longer sacrificed, but the Savior, come to the threshold of his passion,[b] gives bread and a cup as a representation of the most excellent sacrifice, with ineffable invocations making his own body from the one, his blood from the other, and commanding (us) to perform the Pascha[c] with these symbols.[d]

78. DIDYMUS OF ALEXANDRIA, *Commentary on* Zechariah 5, 88

That is why, when the spiritual spring arrives and the month of the first fruits is at hand, we keep the Crossing-Feast,[a] called in the Hebrew tongue *Pascha*. On this day Christ has been sacrificed, in order that, consuming his spiritual flesh and his sacred blood, "we should feast with the unleavened bread of sincerity and truth" (1 Cor 5:7).[b] After this solemnity we shall also celebrate the Feast of Weeks, called Pentecost, on which we shall reap as perfect sheaves and fullest ears that which flowered in the spring.

79. *Apostolic Constitutions* 5, 20, 1–2. 4. 14.

1. After eight days you are again to have a sumptuous feast, the eighth day itself[a]—on which he convinced me, the unbelieving Thomas, of his resurrection, having shown me the marks of the nails and the lance-wound in his side.[b] 2. And again, from the first Sunday[c] count forty days, and on Thursday celebrate the feast of the Assumption[d] of the Lord. . . . 4. After ten days of the Assumption, when the fiftieth day from the first Sunday arrives, you are to have a great feast; for on it, at the third hour, the Lord Jesus sent us the gift of the Holy Spirit[e]. . . . 14. After having celebrated the Pentecost, feast for one week,[f] and after that fast for a week; for it is right to rejoice at the gift of God and to fast after the relaxation.

80. SEVERIAN OF GABALA, Fragment

Now, the Law was given on the day of the Pentecost. . . . Therefore, it was right that the grace of the Spirit be given on the same day as the old Law was given.

81. THEOPHILUS OF ALEXANDRIA, *Festal Letter for 401* 20, 4

If the divine mercy permits, we shall be thought worthy to celebrate the Lord's Pascha with the angels. Lent will begin on the eighth day of the Egyptian month Famenoth, and with God's help we shall fast more strictly in the Great Week of the venerable Pascha, beginning on the thirteenth day of the month Farmuthi, so that, according to gospel traditions, we end the fast in the depth of night on the eighteenth day of the said month Farmuthi[a] and on the next day, which is the symbol of the Lord's resurrection, let us celebrate the true Pascha. Then let us add to these seven more[b] weeks, which compose the festivity of Pentecost, and present ourselves worthy of the Communion of the Body and Blood of Christ.[c] For thus we shall deserve to receive the kingdom of heaven in Christ Jesus.

82. THEODORET OF CYRRHUS, *Cure for the Greek Illnesses* . 9, 24

. . . On the very day of the saving passion, on which we solemnize the memory both of the passion and of the resurrection of the Lord,[a] they destroyed all the Churches in the Roman empire.[b]

83. EUTYCHIUS OF CONSTANTINOPLE, *Sermon on the Pascha and the Eucharist*, 2

"I have earnestly desired to eat this Pascha with you before I suffer" (Luke 22:15). Therefore, before he suffered he ate the Pascha—the mystical Pascha, of course.[a] For it would not be called "Pascha" without the passion. And so he sacrificed himself in mystic fashion[b] when, after supper, he took the bread in his own hands, gave thanks, pointed to it and broke it, having mingled himself with the antitype.[c]

84. *The Paschal Chronicle*

There are not lacking some who dare to move not only tongue but hands against the feasts celebrated in all the holy Churches of God throughout the whole earth under the sun and to bring this accusation against the holy Church of God, that she designates the august feast of the resurrection from the dead of Christ our God as the Pascha.[a] They seem to have been ignorant of the meaning of this word. For what is signified by the Greek words *diabasis* (crossing over), *ekbasis* (going out), and *hyperbasis* (passing above) is expressed in Hebrew by the word *phasoch*, that is, *pascha*.

Necessarily, therefore, the Church of God gives the name *Pascha* not only to the passion of the Lord but also to his resurrection.[b] For, on account of the Lord's passion and resurrection, the nature of mortals has received from him who holds "the power of death"[c] the crossing over, going out from, and passing above[d] death itself and Hades and corruption. If Christ's death has bestowed this gift upon us, how much more will his resurrection, when he rose from the dead as *the first-fruits of them that sleep* (1 Cor 15:20), destined never again to return to corruption. For "death no longer has dominion" (Rom 6:9), according to the teaching of the divine apostles.

SYRIAN WRITERS

85. *Diataxis of the Apostles*, Fragment

For the apostles themselves say: When they are feasting, you should be fasting and mourning for them,[a] because they crucified the Christ on the day of the festival, and when they mourn by eating unleavened bread[b] with bitter herbs,[c] you should feast.

86. *Didascalia Apostolorum*, 21

[5, 17, 1] It behooves you then, our brethren, in the days of the Pascha to make inquiry with diligence and to keep your fast with all care. And do you make a beginning when your brethren who are of the People[a] keep the Pascha.[b] For when our Lord and Teacher ate the Pascha with us, he was betrayed by Judas after that hour; and immediately we began to be sorrowful, because he was taken from us. . . .

[8] . . . In the night when the fourth day of the week drew on, (Judas) betrayed our Lord to them. But they made payment to Judas on the tenth of the month, on the second day of the week; wherefore they were accounted by God as though on the second day of the week they had seized him, because on the second of the week they had taken counsel to seize him and put him to death;

and they accomplished their malice on the Friday: as Moses had said concerning the Pascha, thus: "It shall be kept by you from the tenth until the fourteenth: and then all Israel shall sacrifice the Pascha."

[5, 18] Therefore you shall fast in the days of the Pascha from the tenth, which is the second day of the week;[c] and you shall sustain yourselves with bread and salt and water only, at the ninth hour, until the fifth day of the week. But on the Friday and on the Sabbath fast wholly, and taste nothing.[d] [V 19, 1] You shall come together and watch and keep vigil all the night[e] with prayers and intercessions, and with reading of the Prophets, and with the gospel and with psalms, with fear and trembling and with earnest supplication, until the third hour in the night after the Sabbath;[f] and then break your fasts.

[2] For thus did we also fast, when our Lord suffered, for a testimony of the three days; and we were keeping vigil and praying and interceding for the destruction of the People, because that they erred and confessed not our Saviour. [3] So do you also pray that the Lord may not remember their guilt against them unto the end for the guile that they used against our Lord, but may grant them a place of repentance and conversion, and forgiveness of their wickedness. . . .

[6] Especially incumbent on you therefore is the fast of the Friday and of the Sabbath; and likewise the vigil and watching of the Sabbath, and the reading of the Scriptures, and psalms, and prayer and intercession for them that have sinned, and the expectation and hope of the resurrection of our Lord Jesus, until the third hour in the night after the Sabbath.[f] [7] And then offer your oblations; and thereafter eat and make good cheer, and rejoice and be glad, because that the earnest of our resurrection, Christ, is risen. . . .[g]

[5, 20, 10] . . . Wherever, then, the fourteenth of the Pascha falls, so keep it; for neither the month nor the day squares with the same season every year, but is variable. When therefore that People keeps the Passover, do you fast; and be careful to perform your vigil within their (feast of) unleavened bread. [11] But on the first day of the week make good cheer at all times; for he is guilty of sin, whosoever afflicts his soul on the first of the week. [12] And hence it is not lawful, apart from the Pascha, for any one to fast during those three hours of the night between the Sabbath and the first of the week, because that night belongs to the first of the week; but in the Pascha alone you are to fast these three hours of that night,[f] being assembled together, you who are Christians, in the Lord.

87. APHRAATES, *Demonstration* 12: *On the Pascha*, 6-8, 12-13

6. Our Savior ate the Pascha with his disciples in the hallowed night[a] of the fourteenth,[b] and he performed the sign of the Pascha in truth[c] for his disciples. For, after Judas departed from them,[d] "he took bread and blessed and gave it to his disciples and said" to them, "This is my body; take, eat of it, all (of you)." Likewise over the wine he blessed and said to them, " 'This is my blood, the new covenant, which is shed for many for the remission of sins. Do likewise in memory of me' when you gather" (cf. Matt 26:26,28; Luke 22:19-20). Our Lord said these things before he was arrested.

And our Lord rose from where he had performed the Pascha and given his body to be eaten and his blood to be drunk, and went with his disciples to the place where he was arrested. Now one whose body is eaten and whose blood is drunk[e] is counted among the dead. With his own hands our Lord gave his body to be eaten, and before being crucified he gave his blood to be drunk. And he was taken in the night of the fourteenth, and his trial lasted until the sixth hour, and at the time of the sixth hour they sentenced him and lifted him up in crucifixion. When they were judging him, he said nothing and answered not a word to his judges: he was of course able to speak and answer, but it is impossible for one who is counted among the dead to speak.

And from the sixth to the ninth hour there was a darkness, and he gave over his spirit to his Father at the ninth hour. And he was among the dead in the night in which the fifteenth dawned, the night of the Sabbath, and for the whole day, as well as for three hours on the Parasceve.[f] And in the night in which the first of the week dawned, at the time when he had given his body and blood to his disciples, he rose from the dead.[g]

7. Now show us, O wise one, what are the three days and three nights which our Savior spent among the dead. For we see that

there were the three hours on the Parasceve and the night in which the Sabbath dawned, and its whole day; and in the night of the first of the week he rose. Reckon for me the three days and three nights. Where are they? Behold it is only one whole day and night.

And yet in truth it is as our Savior said: "*Just as Jonah, son of Mattai, was in the belly of the fish for three days and three nights, so shall the Son of Man be in the heart of the earth. . . ."* (Matt 12:40; cf. Jonah 1:7). There are indeed three days and three nights, beginning from the time when he gave his body for food and his blood for drink.[h] For "it was nighttime" when Judas departed from them (cf. John 13:30) and the eleven disciples ate the body and drank the blood of the Savior: behold, therefore, one night, the one in which the Parasceve dawned. And he stood trial until the sixth hour: behold, therefore, one day and one night. And the three hours of darkness, from the sixth to the ninth hour, and the three hours after the darkness: behold two days and two nights. And so the entire night in which the Sabbath dawned and the whole day of the Sabbath completed for our Lord three days and three nights among the dead. And in the night of the first of the week he rose from among the dead.

8. Indeed the Pascha of the Jews is the fourteenth day, its night and its day; but our great day of the passion is the day of the Parasceve, the fifteenth day,[i] its night and its day. After the Pascha Israel eats unleavened bread for seven days, until the twenty-first of the month (cf. Exod 12:18); we too observe the Unleavened Bread—as a feast of our Savior. They eat the unleavened in bitterness;[j] but our Savior rejected this cup of bitterness and took away all the bitterness of the nations when "he tasted and would not drink" (Matt 27:34). The Jews call to mind their sins from year to year; but we remember the crucifixion and insults of our Savior. On the Pascha they escaped the slavery of Pharaoh; on the day of the crucifixion we were delivered from the service of Satan.[k]

12. Be instructed and in turn instruct the brethren belonging to thy Church who have difficulties about the time of the Pascha. For those of sound mind these things are not hard to grasp. If, now, the day of the Pascha of the passion of our Savior[l] falls on the first of the week, according to the law[m] we should celebrate it on the second day, so as to observe the whole week in his pas-

sion and in his Unleavened Bread, because after the Pascha come the seven days of unleavened bread, until the twenty-first. But if the passion occurs on another day, a weekday, this need not cause us any difficulty; but our solemn day is the day of the Parasceve.[n]

And if we count the days of the month, the Day of Crucifixion, on which our Savior suffered and was among the dead for the night and the day, was the fifteenth, from the sixth hour of the Parasceve to the dawn of the first of the week. And on the first of the week, on the sixteenth, he rose. For at dawn of the fourteenth day he ate the Pascha with his disciples according to the Law of Israel, and on this day of the Parasceve, the fourteenth day, he was judged until the sixth hour and was crucified for three hours, and he descended to the dead in the night in which the fifteenth dawned. On the day of the Sabbath, which was the fifteenth, he was among the dead; and the night in which the first of the week dawned, which was the sixteenth day, he rose and appeared to Mary Magdalen and to two of his disciples where they were walking on the road.

Hence the one who has difficulties about these days will understand that at dawn of the fourteenth our Lord celebrated the Pascha and ate and drank with his disciples, but from the time when the cock crowed he ate and drank no more, because they took him captive and began to judge him. And, as I have shown thee above, the fifteenth day, night and day, he was among the dead.

13. But for us the requirements are: that we observe the feast from date to date[o] at the proper time, fast with purity, pray unwaveringly, praise with enthusiasm, and sing the hymns properly, give the sign[p] with baptism properly administered, bless the holy (gifts)[q] at the proper times, and perform all the customary rites. . . .

For if we were contentious about these things and only cared about the fourteenth day, but not about the custom (of keeping the feast) from year to year,[o] we might choose to observe the fourteenth day of every month and to mourn on the Parasceve of every week.[r] But it behooves us (rather) to take each day of the week to "do what is right" before "the Lord" our God (cf. Deut 6:18; 21:9). . . .

88. EPHRAEM THE SYRIAN, *Hymns on the Crucifixion* 3, 1-2

1. On the fourteenth was slain the paschal lamb—
toward evening, as it is written.
It was written beforehand (a testimony for him)
that he would prophesy even his time.
The time of the true lamb's slaying
shows us how fulfilled (he was):
on the fifteenth he was slain—on the day
on which both sun and moon were full.[a]

2. Blessed art thou also, final evening!
For in thee the evening of Egypt was fulfilled.[b]
In thy time our Lord ate the little Pascha
and became himself the great Pascha.
Pascha was mingled with Pascha,
feast joined to feast;
a temporary Pascha, and another that abides;
type and fulfillment.[c]

89. CYRILLONAS, *First Homily on the Pascha*

[Verse 1] The true paschal lamb speaks joyfully to those who
will eat him, and the First-Born announced the Pascha in the
dining room to his disciples. Our Savior invited himself to his immolation and bloodshedding. His lifegiving bread was nutritious
and well prepared, and his sheaf of ears came home full. The
matter of his body was permeated [10] with the yeast of his divinity. His mercy welled up and his love overflowed, so that he
might become food for his own. He took the "heap of wheat"
(Cant 7:2) away from Zion and gave it to the Church in holiness.
He had prepared a new banquet, and now he invited his companions to it and called them to come. A feast he prepared for
his Bride, to allay her hunger. Our Lord slew his own body, [20]
and (only) then did mortals slay it. He pressed it out into the cup
of salvation and (only) then did the People also press it out on
the cross. As priest he offered himself ahead of time, so that
strangers might not exercise the priestly office. . . .

[96]ᵃ He found the upper room readied and put in order; for it had been waiting for him and was therefore ready (cf. Mark 14:15-16). [100] Moses went down and prepared a Pascha for the earthly ones in the depths, that is, in Egypt, the grave of the Hebrews. Our Lord, however, went up to the bright and airy height and there prepared his Pascha, [110] in order to lift us up into his kingdom. The lamb was sacrificed in Egypt, and our Lord in the upper room; the lamb in the depths and the First-Born on the height.

Our Lord led his group (in) and reclined in the dining room. He went up and was the first to recline, and his disciples (reclined) after him (cf. Luke 22:14). There they lay with him at table and watched him, [120] how he ate and was changed. The Lamb ate the lamb, the Pascha consumed the Pascha. He brought his Father's institution to an end and began his own; he concluded the Law and inaugurated the new covenant of reconciliation.

Who ever saw such a marvellous banquet, to which mortals sit down [130] with their Creator? . . . Take note, O listeners! Fishermen and tax collectors [150] recline at table with him, while angels and archangels stand trembling before him! . . .

[478]ᵇ Happy are you, O my disciples, who with your mouths [480] have eaten me! But so that you will not forget this evening, which should be more precious than the day, so that you will not forget this hour in which you tasted divinity, I give you this further command, [490] O my dear ones, intimates of my secrets: This memorial shall not cease among you until the end of the world! Thus, my brothers, shall you do in every time, [500] and remember me (cf. Luke 22:19). You have eaten my body, forget me not. You have drunk my blood, do not neglect me. In my Church let this be my noble memorial and throughout the world let this become the Pascha! This day [510] of all days shall be for you holy, blessed, and glorious. On it shall all sufferers be comforted, all the troubled comforted, all the tortured saved! On it shall [520] all prisoners be freed. On it shall the visible water of baptism be consecrated. On it shall baptism be administered, and the perfect people be born. On it shall the Old Man, grown gray in sin, be rejuvenated (cf. Eph 4:22-23), [530] my children multiplied on earth, and mortals drawn up to heaven. See, all "is consummated" (John 19:30), the mysteries are sealed equally with

the prophecies. Leave the dining room now joyfully, and go out into the world like merchants. Preach me in all lands, and give me as food to mortals.

90. PSEUDO-EPHRAEM, *Sermons for Holy Week* 2, 605–629

605. "Longingly I have longed to eat[a]
    with you before I suffer;
For from now on I shall not eat"
    the Pascha with you at the feast.
This is for me the last Pascha
    that I will celebrate among the Jews.
Let it not sadden you that I say:
    I shall not eat the Pascha again.
For you it is profitable and useful
    that I give you a new Pascha to eat.
615. I give you leavened bread to eat.
    Renounce this unleavened bread![b]
I give you my cup, Life, to drink.
    Flee this (feast) of the bitter herbs!
In this old Pascha
    you experience the new Pascha.
You receive new hope,
    extending into eternity.
A pure, clean Pascha
    you eat here and over there.[c]
625. A leavened, perfect bread,
    kneaded and baked by the Holy Spirit;[d]
I can give you a wine to drink
    that is a mixture of fire and spirit:[e]
Body and Blood of God,
    made a victim for everyone.

LATIN WRITERS

91. TERTULLIAN, *On the Prayer* 18, 3-7

3. What prayer is complete without the bond of a holy kiss?
4. With whom does the kiss of peace interfere in his service of
the Lord? 5. What kind of sacrifice is it from which one departs
without giving the kiss of peace? 6. Whatever the reason may
be, it will not outweigh the observance of the precept whereby
we are bidden to conceal our fasting (Matt 6:16-18). For, when
we refrain from the kiss, it is recognized that we are fasting. But
even if there is some reason for it, still, that you may not be guilty
of transgressing this precept, you may, if you wish, dispense with
the kiss of peace at home, since there you are among those from
whom it is not entirely possible to conceal your fasting. But, wherever else you can conceal your acts of mortification,[a] you ought
to remember this precept; in this way you will satisfactorily comply
with religious discipline in public, and with ordinary usage at
home. 7. Thus, too, on Good Friday,[b] when the fasting is a
general and, as it were, a public religious obligation, we rightly
omit the kiss of peace, having no anxiety about concealing that
which we are doing along with everyone else.

92. TERTULLIAN, *On the Prayer* 23, 1-2

1. With regard to kneeling,[a] too, prayer allows a difference in
custom because of certain people, a very few, who stay off their
knees on the Sabbath—an opposing point of view, which is just
now strongly defending itself in the Churches. 2. The Lord will
give his grace so that either they will yield, or else maintain their
own opinion without giving scandal to others. As for ourselves,
according to our tradition, only on the day of the Lord's resurrection should we refrain from this custom; and not only from
this, but from every sign that bespeaks solicitude and every
ceremony arising therefrom. This includes deferring business, lest
we give any opportunity to the Devil. The same holds for the season of Pentecost,[b] which is marked by the same joyous
celebration.

93. TERTULLIAN, *On Baptism* 19, 1-3

1. The Pascha[a] affords a more (than usually) solemn day for baptism,[b] since the passion[c] of the Lord, in which we are baptized (cf. Rom 6:3), was accomplished (then).[d] And there is nothing wrong with seeing a symbolic foreshadowing of it in the fact that, when the Lord was about to keep his last Pascha, he said to the disciples he sent to prepare (it), "You will meet a man carrying water" (cf. Mark 14:13; Luke 22:10). With the sign of water he showed them the place for celebrating the Pascha.

2. After this, the Pentecost is an extremely happy period[e] for conferring baptisms, because the Lord's resurrection was celebrated[f] among the disciples and the grace of the Holy Spirit was inaugurated and the hope in the Lord's coming indicated, because it was then, when he had been taken back into heaven, that angels told the apostles that he would come exactly as he had gone up to heaven—meaning, of course, during the Pentecost.[e] Moreover, when Jeremiah says, "And I will gather them from the farthest parts of the earth on the festal day of the Pascha" (Jer 38:8 LXX),[h] he also means to say, "the day of Pentecost," which is properly the festal day.

3. For that matter, every day is the Lord's (Day); every hour and every time is suitable for baptism.[i] If there is a question of solemnity, it has nothing to do with the grace.

94. TERTULLIAN, *To His Wife* 2, 4, 2

Who would permit his wife to go about the streets, entering other people's dwellings, especially the poorer sort, in order to visit the brethren? Who will cheerfully tolerate her leaving his side for nighttime meetings when required? And finally, who will allow her to be away the whole night for the rites[a] of the Pascha,[b] without worrying about her?

95. TERTULLIAN, *Against Marcion* 4, 40, 1

Accordingly, he also knows when the person must suffer, whose passion is foreshadowed in the Law. For out of so many Jewish feasts he chose the day of the Pascha. For, in reference to this mystery,[a] Moses had proclaimed, "It is the Pascha of the Lord" (Exod 12:11). This is also why he manifested his longing: "With desire I have desired to eat the Pascha with you before I suffer" (Luke 22:15). A fine "destroyer of the Law"—who desired even to keep the Pascha![b] Could it be that he was so fond of Jewish lamb's meat? Was it not rather that he, who was going to be led like a sheep to the sacrifice, and who, like a sheep before the shearer, was not going to open his mouth (cf. Isa 53:7), desired to fulfill the figure of its saving blood?[c]

96. TERTULLIAN, *On Fasting* 2, 2

They think that the gospel prescribes for fasting the days during which the Bridegroom is taken away,[a] and that these are the only legitimate days of Christian fasting, now that the prescriptions of the Old Law and the Prophets have been done away with.

97. TERTULLIAN, *On Fasting* 14, 2-3

2. But if there is a new creation in Christ, then (our) fasts and feasts[a] must also be new. Otherwise, if the apostle has abolished absolutely all consecration of times and days and months and years, why do we celebrate the Pascha every year in the first month? Why do we spend the next fifty days in so much exultation? Why do we set aside Wednesday and Friday for stations[b] and Friday for fasting? 3. Anyhow, you sometimes continue your fasting on Saturday, (a day) on which we should never fast—except at Easter, for a reason explained elsewhere.

98. PSEUDO-TERTULLIAN, *Against the Jews* 10, 18

Moses too prophesied that you would do this at the beginning of the first month of the new (crops)[a] when the whole people of the sons of Israel would sacrifice the lamb "at eventide" (Exod 12:6). He predicted that you would eat the ritual food of this day,[b] the Pascha of Unleavened Bread, with bitterness (cf. Exod

12:8), and added, "It is the Pascha of the Lord" (Exod 12:11), in other words, the passion of Christ. And this too was fulfilled when you killed Christ on the first day of the Unleavened Bread[c] and, that the prophecies might be fulfilled, the day hastened to make an eventide, that is, to bring on the darkness, which fell at noon (Matt 27:45; Mark 15:33; Luke 23:44).

99. PSEUDO-TERTULLIAN, *Against All the Heresies* 8, 1

And besides all of these, we have Blastos[a] too, who secretly wants to introduce Judaism.[b] For he says that the Pascha should not be kept in any other way than according to the Law of Moses, on the fourteenth of the month.[c] But who does not know that the grace of the gospel is rendered nil if you reduce Christ to Law? (cf. John 1:17).

100. PSEUDO-CYPRIAN, *Computus for the Pascha*, 2

Therefore God commanded the whole assembly of the sons of Israel through Moses in the new month, which is "the beginning of months, the first of the months of the year" (Exod 12:2), to wear certain clothes when they ate the Pascha on the fourteenth of the moon, doubtless with the purpose of manifesting his divinity to us who believe in Christ and of demonstrating, already from the beginning of the world, the murderous act of those who in Egypt at eventide (Exod 12:6), that is, in the last age of the world,[a] came out "with swords and clubs" (Matt 26:47, 55; Mark 14:43, 48), girt and shod (cf. Exod 12:11), against the immaculate lamb (cf. Exod 12:5) of God "on the first day of the Unleavened Bread" (Matt 26:17; Mark 14:12)[b] at eventide (cf. Matt 26:20; Mark 14:17), and did to him everything that had been foretold by the Prophets. And therefore we, who celebrate the Pascha, no longer symbolically, as they did, but in truth, to commemorate the passion of the son of God,[c] ought to search out carefully, with all the forces of our faith, nothing other than the new month—which one it is, and when it begins and ends. And then we shall find that the Pascha cannot be observed by the Jews themselves before or after the fourteenth of the moon.

101. COUNCIL OF ELVIRA, Canon 43

It has been decided to correct a bad custom according to the authority of the Scriptures, so that we all celebrate the day of Pentecost;[a] and that anyone who does not should be marked as having brought in a new heresy.

102. LACTANTIUS, *Divine Institutes* 4, 26, 40

Finally, the very people who keep the Pascha call the sacrifice of the sheep after the word *paschein*[a] because it is a figure of the passion, which God in his foreknowledge gave through Moses to his people to celebrate.

103. LACTANTIUS, *Divine Institutes* 7, 19, 3

This is the night which we celebrate by watching until morning on account of the coming of our king and God. There are two meanings for this night: in it he received life when he had suffered, and afterwards he is to receive the kingship over the world.[a]

104. FIRST COUNCIL OF ARLES, Canon 1

Marinus and the group of bishops united in the town of Arles,[a] to the most holy lord, brother Silvester:[b] so that all may know what they should observe in the future, we are informing Your Charity of what we have decided after deliberating together.

[Canon 1] First of all, on keeping the Pascha of the Lord: that we should keep it on the same day and at the same season everywhere in the whole world, and that you should send letters to all according to custom.[c]

105. ZENO OF VERONA, *Treatise on the Pascha* 1, 57

In its regular way,[a] crowned with graces of all kinds, through the [changes[b]] of the seasons, with stately step arrives the day of salvation. Successor as well as predecessor of itself, always young in its great age, the parent of the year as well as its child, it both precedes and follows infinite centuries and ages. From the end it gives birth to its own beginning, while never leaving its cradle. Undoubtedly it bears the image of the mystery of the Lord; for at sunset it celebrates the passion and at sunrise the resurrection. Through it the gift of future bliss is promised us, and it will confer the same upon our candidates for baptism—those whom the happy evening now invites to plunge into the milky depth of the sacred ocean,[c] and from it to arise rejuvenated[d] with the new day, and with us to attain to the glory of immortality.[e]

106. AMBROSE OF MILAN, *On Cain and Abel* 1, 8, 31

The *Pascha of the Lord*[a] is the passage from the passions to the practices of virtue.[b] That is why it is called the "Pascha of the Lord": because in that symbol of the lamb, the reality of the Lord's passion was foretold[c] then and its grace is celebrated now.

107. AMBROSE OF MILAN, Letter 1, to Justus, 9-10

9. . . . the Pascha is the lamb. . . .

10. . . . And so the Lord has commanded all to bring an equal measure of devotion and faith to the Pascha of the Lord, that is to the Passage. For it is Pascha when the soul puts off unreasoning passion and puts on the good compassion,[a] so as to suffer with Christ and take his passage upon herself, so that he may "dwell in" her and "walk in" her and become her God (cf. 2 Cor 6:16).

108. AMBROSE OF MILAN, *Exposition of the Gospel according to Luke* 10, 34

In spring we have the Pascha, when I am saved;[a] in summer we have the Pentecost, when we celebrate the glory of resurrection after the manner of the age to come.[b]

109. AMBROSE OF MILAN, *On the Sacraments* 1, 4, 12

To come immediately to the subject of baptism [among all the sacraments of the Old Testament]: what excels the passage of the Jewish people through the sea?[a] And yet the Jews who made that passage died in the desert, every one. But he who passes through this font, that is, from earthly to heavenly things—for it is a passing (therefore Pascha, which means "his passing"), a passing from sin to life, from guilt to grace, from defilement to sanctification—he who passes through this font does not die but rises.[b]

110. The Paschal Proclamation: *Exsultet*

1. Now let the angelic heavenly choirs exult; let joy pervade the unknown beings who surround God's throne;[a] and let the trumpet of salvation sound the triumph of this mighty King. Let earth, too, be joyful, in the radiance of this great splendor. Enlightened by the glory of her eternal King, let her feel that from the whole round world the darkness has been lifted. Let mother Church likewise rejoice, arrayed in the brilliance of this dazzling light; let these walls echo with the multitude's full-throated song.

2. Dear brethren who are present at this wondrous lighting of the holy flame,[b] I pray you join with me and invoke the loving-kindness of almighty God, that he who, not for any merit of mine, has deigned to number me among his ministers,[c] may shed his own bright light upon me and enable[d] me to glorify this candle with fitting praise,[e] through our Lord Jesus Christ, his Son, who lives and reigns with him in the unity of the Holy Spirit, God; for ever and ever.

(The people answer: Amen.)
The Lord be with you.
(Answer: And with you.[f])
Let us lift up our hearts.
(Answer: We lift them up to the Lord.)
Let us give thanks to the Lord our God.
(Answer: It is right and proper.)

3. It is indeed right and proper with all the ardor of our heart and mind and with the service of our voice to acclaim God, the invisible almighty Father, and his only-begotten Son, our Lord Jesus Christ, who repaid Adam's debt for us to his eternal Father, and with his dear blood erased the bond contracted through that ancient sin.

4. This is the Paschal feast wherein is slain the true Lamb[g] whose blood hallows the doorposts of the faithful (cf. Exod 12:7). This is the night when, long ago, thou didst cause our forefathers, the sons of Israel, in their passage out of Egypt, to pass dry-shod over the Red Sea. This is the night which swept away the blackness of sin by the light of the fiery pillar (cf. Exod 13:22). This is the night which at this hour[h] throughout the world restores to grace and yokes to holiness those who believe in Christ, detaching them from worldly vice and all the murk of sin.[i] On this night Christ burst the bonds of death and rose victorious from the grave.

5. [. . .[j]] What good would life have been to us without redemption? How wonderful the pity and care thou has shown us; how far beyond all reckoning thy loving-kindness! To ransom thy slave, thou gavest up thy Son! O truly necessary sin of Adam, that Christ's death blotted out; and happy fault, that merited so great a Redeemer![k] Blessed indeed is this, the sole night counted worthy to mark the season and the hour in which Christ rose again from the grave.[l] It is this night of which the Scripture says: "And the night shall be bright as day" (Ps 138:12 OL). "Such is my joy that night itself is light!" (Ps 138:11 OL). So holy, this night, it banishes all crimes, washes guilt away, restores lost innocence, brings mourners joy; it drives forth hate, fosters harmony, and humbles the pride of earthly rule.

6. On this gracious night, then, holy Father, accept the evening sacrifice of this flame, which Holy Church, by the hands of her ministers, renders to thee in the solemn offering of wax the bees have made. Who now can doubt the message that this candle brings?[m] A brilliant fire burns here to the glory of God, which though it be divided into parts, yet suffers no loss of light, being fed from the ever-melting wax that the parent bee brought forth to form the substance of this precious torch.[n]

Blessed indeed is the night, which despoiled the Egyptians and enriched the Hebrews! The night on which heaven is wedded to earth, the Godhead to humanity![o]

9. We, therefore, pray thee, Lord, that this candle hallowed in honor of thy name, may continue bravely burning to dispel the darkness of this night. Welcome it as a sweet fragrance, mingling with the lights of heaven. May the morning-star find its flame alight, that Morning-Star[p] which knows no setting,[q] which came back from the grave and shed its clear light upon humankind.

10. We pray thee, Lord, to grant us a season of peace at this time of Easter gladness. Be pleased to preserve us thy servants, and all the clergy and faithful people, [together with our Father, the most blessed N.[r]]. . . .

111. AMBROSIASTER, *Old and New Testament Questions* 96, 1

Does *Pascha* mean *passage*, as the Greeks maintain?

The apostle cannot be mistaken, and he says, "Christ has been sacrificed as our Pascha" (1 Cor 5:7). Of course, this is not his own statement, but the Law's, for Moses says, "And there will come a time when your children will say to you: What is this worship? and you shall say: This Pascha of the Lord is a sacrifice"[a] (Exod 12:26-27). Do we need any further testimony? The Law says it, the apostle confirms it; all that remains is for the one who contradicts them[b] to be dismissed as obstinate. For it is plain that the passage came after the Pascha. They put the blood of the lamb that had been sacrificed on the doorposts and lintel, so that the angel who passed in the night should not strike the house on which there was the sign of blood. Salvation came, therefore, from the blood, not from the passage, because it was the blood that kept the passage from being harmful.

112. AMBROSIASTER, *Commentary on the Thirteen Epistles of Paul*, on 1 Corinthians 5:7

Christ, our Pascha, has been sacrificed. According to the Law, he [Paul] teaches that the newness of the Pascha consists in the reason for it. And Christ was killed for this reason: that a new preaching from him might establish a new mode of life, in which we who accept the reason for the Pascha would not follow the old way. And so Pascha is sacrifice,[a] not passage, as some think. For the Pascha comes first, and then the passage; because the foreshadowing of the Savior's example comes first, and then the sign of salvation.[b] Nor is the sign prior to the Cross. For when the lamb had been slain at evening, the children of Israel in Egypt kept the Pascha and marked their doorposts with its blood, so that the angel who passed during the night did not touch the places which had been smeared with the lamb's blood (cf. Exod 12:22-23).

113. JEROME, *Commentary on the Gospel of Matthew* 4, on Matt 25:6

At midnight came the cry: Here comes the Bridegroom, go out to meet him! Yes, it will be very late at night, when everyone is fast asleep, without a care in the world, that Christ will make his coming heard through the shouts of angels and the trumpets of powers which go before him. Perhaps it will help the reader to know that Jewish tradition[a] tells us that the Messiah will come at midnight, as happened in Egypt, when they celebrated the Pascha, and the Exterminator came, and the Lord passed over the dwellings, and the doorposts of our foreheads[b] were consecrated with the lamb's blood. This is why I think we also have an apostolic tradition[c] that on the day of the paschal vigil the people should not be dismissed before midnight while they await the coming of Christ, and that after that time has passed and they presume they are safe (they may be dismissed) with everyone keeping the festal day.

114. JEROME, *Commentary on the Gospel of Matthew* 4, on Matt 26:2

The Pascha, which is called *phase* in Hebrew, does not get its name from *passio,* as many people think,[a] but from *passage,* either because the Exterminator, seeing the blood on the Israelites' doors, passed by[b] without striking them, or because the Lord himself walked above, giving help to his people.[c] Read the book of Exodus, which we will comment on more fully,[d] if we live long enough. But our *phase* or passage is celebrated if we let go of Egypt and the things of earth and hasten toward those of heaven.[e]

115. JEROME, *On the Sunday of Pascha*

This is the day the Lord has made: let us rejoice and be glad in it (Ps 118:24 = 117:2 Vg).[a] Just as Mary, the virgin mother of the Lord, holds the first place among all women, so among the other days of the year, the present day is the mother of all.[b] I say something new, but which is based on the words of Scripture: the present day is one of the seven and is outside the seven. This is the day called the octave:[c] hence some psalms are inscribed with the title, "For the octave."[d] This is the day on which the synagogue comes to an end and the Church is born. Its number is eight: eight souls were saved in Noah's ark. And that, says Peter, is the way the Church saves you (cf. 1 Pet 3:21).

116a. EGERIA, *Travels in the Holy Land*, 35–39

35, 1. Thursday[a] is like the other days from cockcrow till morning in the Anastasis,[b] at nine o'clock, and at midday. But it is the custom to assemble earlier than on ordinary days in the afternoon at the Martyrium,[c] in fact at two o'clock, since the dismissal has to take place sooner. The assembled people have the service; on that day the Offering is made in the Martyrium, and the dismissal takes place at about four in the afternoon. Before the dismissal the archdeacon makes this announcement: "Let us meet tonight at seven o'clock in the church on the Eleona. There is a great effort ahead of us tonight!"

2. After dismissal at the Martyrium they go Behind the Cross, where they have one hymn and a prayer; the bishop makes the Offering there, and everyone receives Communion.[d] On this one day the Offering is made Behind the Cross, but on no other day in the whole year. After the dismissal there, they go to the Anastasis, where they have a prayer, the usual blessings of catechumens and faithful, and the dismissal.

Then everybody hurries home for a meal, so that, as soon as they have finished it, they can go to the church on Eleona[e] which contains the cave which on this very day the Lord visited with the apostles.

3. There they continue to sing hymns and antiphons suitable to the place and the day, with readings and prayers between, until about eleven o'clock at night. They read the passages from the gospel about what the Lord said to his disciples when he sat in the very cave which is in the church.[f]

4. At about midnight they leave and go up with hymns to the Imbomon,[g] the place from which the Lord ascended into heaven. And there they again have readings and hymns and antiphons suitable to the day, and the prayers which the bishop says are all appropriate to the day and to the place.

36, 1. When the cocks begin to crow, everyone leaves the Imbomon, and comes down with singing to the place where the Lord prayed, as the Gospels describe in the passage which begins, "And he was parted from them about a stone's cast, and prayed" (Luke 22:41). The bishop and all the people go into a graceful church[h] which has been built there, and have a prayer appropriate to the place and the day, and one suitable hymn. Then the Gospel passage is read where he said to his disciples, "Watch, lest ye enter into temptation,"[i] and when the whole passage has been read, there is another prayer.

2. From there all of them, including the smallest children, now go down with singing and conduct the bishop to Gethsemane. There are a great many people and they have been crowded together, tired by their vigil, and weakened by their daily fasting— and they have had a very big hill to come down—so they go very slowly on their way to Gethsemane. So that they can all see, they are provided with hundreds of church candles.

3. When everyone arrives at Gethsemane, they have an appropriate prayer, a hymn, and then a reading from the gospel about the Lord's arrest. By the time it has been read everyone is groaning and lamenting and weeping so loud that people even across the city can probably hear it all.

Next they go with singing to the city, and walking they reach the gate at the time when people can first recognize each other. . . .

37, 1. Before the sun is up, the dismissal takes place At the Cross, and those with the energy then go to Sion[j] to prayer at the column at which the Lord was scourged, before going on home for a short rest. But it is not long before eveyone is assembled for the next service. The bishop's chair is placed on Golgotha Behind the Cross (the cross there now), and he takes his seat. A table is placed before him with a cloth on it, the deacons stand round, and there is brought to him a gold and silver box containing the holy Wood of the Cross.[k] It is opened, and the Wood of the Cross and the Title are taken out and placed on the table.

2. As long as the holy Wood is on the table, the bishop sits with his hands resting on either end of it and holds it down, and the deacons round him keep watch over it. They guard it like this because what happens now is that all the people, catechumens as well as faithful, come up one by one to the table. They stoop down over it, kiss the Wood, and move on. But on one occasion (I don't know when) one of them bit off a piece of the holy Wood and stole it away, and for this reason the deacons stand round and keep watch in case anyone dares to do the same again.

3. Thus all the people go past one by one. They stoop down, touch the holy Wood first with their forehead and then with their eyes, and then kiss it, but no one puts out his hand to touch it. . . .

4. At midday they go Before the Cross—whether it is rain or fine, for the place is out of doors—into the very spacious and beautiful courtyard between the Cross and the Anastasis, and there is not room even to open a door, the place is so crammed with people.

5. They place the bishop's chair Before the Cross, and the whole time between midday and three o'clock is taken up with readings. They are all about the things Jesus suffered: first the psalms on this subject, then the apostles (the Epistles or Acts) which concern it, then passages from the Gospels. Thus they read the prophecies about what the Lord would suffer, and the Gospels about what he did suffer.

6. . . . And between all the readings are prayers, all of them appropriate to the day.

7. . . . Then, when three o'clock comes, they have the reading from St John's Gospel about Jesus giving up the ghost,[l] and,

when that has been read, there is a prayer, and the dismissal. . . .

38, 1. The following day is the Saturday, and they have normal services at nine o'clock and midday. But at three they stop keeping Saturday[m] because they are preparing for the paschal vigil in the Great Church, the Martyrium. They keep their paschal vigil[n] like us, but there is one addition. As soon as the "infants"[o] have been baptized and clothed, and left the font, they are led with the bishop straight to the Anastasis.[p]

2. The bishop goes inside the screen and after one hymn says a prayer for them.[q] Then he returns with them to the church, where all the people are keeping the vigil in the usual way.

They do all the things to which we are accustomed, and, when the Offering has been made, they have the dismissal. After their dismissal in the Great Church they at once go with singing to the Anastasis, where the resurrection gospel is read, and once more the bishop makes the Offering. They waste no time during these services, so as not to detain the people too long; in fact they are dismissed from their vigil at the same time as we.

39, 1.[r] But in the late afternoon the paschal days are celebrated just as they are with us, and Masses are held in proper order for the eight days of the Pascha, just as is done elsewhere for the Pascha up to the eighth day.[s]

116b. EGERIA, *Travels in the Holy Land,* 42-43

42. The Fortieth Day after Easter[a] is a Thursday. On the previous day, Wednesday, everyone goes in the afternoon for the vigil service to Bethlehem, where it is held in the church containing the cave where the Lord was born. On the next day, the Thursday which is the Fortieth Day, they have the usual service, with the presbyters and the bishop preaching sermons suitable to the place and the day;[b] and in the evening everyone returns to Jerusalem.

43, 1. The Fiftieth Day is a Sunday, and a great effort for the people. At cockcrow they have the usual service, a vigil at the Anastasis with the bishop reading the regular Sunday gospel about the Lord's resurrection, and what follows in the Anastasis is what they do during the rest of the year.

2. . . . Straight after the dismissal in the Martyrium all the people, every single one, take the bishop with singing to Sion, where they arrive in time for nine o'clock (cf. Acts 2:15).

3. When they arrive, they have a reading of the passage from the Acts of the Apostles about the descent of the Spirit, and how all the languages spoken were understood, after which the service[c] proceeds as usual. . . .

4. So all the people go home for a rest, and as soon as they have had their meal, they go up Eleona, the Mount of Olives, each at his own pace, until there is not a Christian left in the city.

5. Once they have climbed Eleona, the Mount of Olives, they go to the Imbomon (the place from which the Lord ascended into heaven), where the bishop takes his seat, and also the presbyters and all the people. They have readings, and between them hymns and antiphons suitable to this day and to the place. Also the prayers which come between are concerned with subjects appropriate to the day and the place. They have the gospel reading about the Lord's ascension, and then the reading from the Acts of the Apostles about the Lord ascending into heaven after the resurrection.

6. When this is over, the catechumens are blessed, then the faithful. It is already three o'clock, and they go down with singing from there. . . .

117. GREGORY OF ELVIRA, *Treatises* [*of Origen*] *on the Books of Holy Scripture* 9, 9. 16. 20. 22

9. . . . Scripture says: "It is the Pascha of the Lord" (Exod 12:11). It did not say "of the people," for *pascha* is derived from *passio*, "suffering," and thus Scripture calls it "the Pascha of the Lord," for it was not the people, but the Lord, who was sacrificed at the Pascha in the form of the lamb. Then too, the blessed Apostle Paul says: "Christ, our Pascha, has been sacrificed" (1 Cor 5:7).[a] . . . 16. For Egypt stood for this world, Pharaoh stood for the devil, and the people of Israel was the type of ourselves. Just as that people was liberated from Egypt by the sacrifice of a lamb and the mystery of the Pascha, so we, who believe in him, are liberated from the captivity of this world

and of Pharaoh—that is, from the tyranny of the devil.[b] Pharaoh, who pursued the children of Israel, was overwhelmed and perished in the very water in which the people of Israel were liberated. So too now: Pharaoh, that is the devil, perishes in the shipwreck that the Savior causes; he perishes in the same water of baptism in which we are liberated.[c] 20. But we said that Pascha received its name from the Lord's passion. This showed that whoever believes in the Lord's passion and deserves to receive the Pascha of his sacred Body[d] has already cast out the leaven of wickedness and depravity from his soul. The blessed apostle says: "Cast out the old leaven, so that you may be new dough, in the unleavened bread of sincerity and truth" (1 Cor 5:7). . . . 22. This, I say, is the venerable and saving mystery of the Pascha,[e] by which Christ "the sun of justice" (Mal 4:2) killed the law of death and, by rising, revealed to us a new day, brighter than the sun. By this mystery pitiless hell has trembled and, when Christ rose, heaven was opened.

118. GAUDENTIUS OF BRESCIA, Tractate 1: *On Exodus* 3. 10. 13

3. So the Son of God, "through" whom "all things were made" (John 1:3), by his own resurrection raises up the fallen world on the same day, and at the same time, as he himself had earlier created it out of nothing. "All things" were to be restored "in Christ, all things in heaven and on earth" (Eph 1:10), "because," as the apostle says, "all things are from him and through him and in him; to him be glory forever" (Rom 11:36). . . . 10. For he had made man on the sixth day, and on the same day he suffered for him (cf. Gen 1:27, 31; John 19:31). And he rose on the Lord's Day, which the Scriptures call "the first day of the week" (Matt 28:1), the day on which the world had its beginning. On the first day he "created heaven and earth" (Gen 1:1, 5), and afterwards he made man, forming him from the earth (cf. Gen 2:7). On the first day, too, he restored the whole of humankind, on whose account he had made the world. I have made these few remarks to explain the Pascha.[a] . . . 13. The blessed and perfect Exodus is fulfilled in us, when the true Moses is taken up from the water

of the Jordan (cf. Mark 1:10). He is our Lord Jesus, God by nature, not by appellation. With the rod of his cross[b] he leads us through the water of baptism out of the captivity of Pharaoh, the devil, and the entire Egypt of his darkness. He calls us from the darkness of worldly acts into the works of light (cf. 1 Pet 2:9).[c]

119. GAUDENTIUS OF BRESCIA, Tractate 2: *On Exodus* 2, 25–26

25. Scripture says: "It is the Pascha of the Lord" (Exod 12:11)—that is, the "passing over" of the Lord. Do not think of it as earthly. He who passed over into it and made it his body and blood[a] brought about something heavenly. 26. For what we explained earlier, in general terms, about eating the flesh of the lamb should be observed in particular in partaking of the same mysteries of the Lord's passion. Do not think, as the Jews did, that it is brute flesh and brute blood. Do not spurn it, saying: "How can that man give us his flesh to eat?" (John 6:52). Do not boil that mystery in the pot of a fleshly heart, always naturally full of liquids.[b] Do not consider it common and earthly. Rather believe that, by the fire of the divine Spirit,[c] what is proclaimed is accomplished. What you receive is the body of that heavenly bread, and the blood of that sacred vine. For when he offered the consecrated bread and wine to his disciples he said: "This is my body, this is my blood" (Matt 26:26, 28).

120. CHROMATIUS OF AQUILEIA, Sermon 16: *On the Great Night*, 1

Every vigil celebrated in honor of the Lord is welcome and pleasing to God, but this vigil is so more than all other vigils. In fact this night has a distinctive name, "the vigil of the Lord." For we have read in the Scriptures: "This is the vigil of the Lord, to be kept by all the children of Israel" (Exod 12:42). This night is properly called "the vigil of the Lord," because he was awakened to life lest we should sleep in death. For our sake he took upon himself the sleep of death, through the mystery of his passion. But that sleep of the Lord has become the vigil of the whole world, because Christ's death staved off from us the sleep of eternal death. He himself says this when he speaks through the prophet: "Thereafter I slept and I kept watch,[a] and my sleep was made sweet to me" (Ps 3:5; Jer 31:26 [38:26 LXX]). That sleep of Christ was obviously made sweet, because from the bitterness of death he recalled us to the sweetness of life.

Hence this night is called "the vigil of the Lord," because even in the very sleep of his passion he kept watch. He shows this when he says through Solomon: "I sleep, and my heart keeps watch" (Cant 5:2). This clearly shows the mystery of divinity and flesh in his own person. For he slept in his flesh and kept watch in his divinity, since divinity could not sleep.[b] For we read this, said of the divinity of Christ: "Behold, he who guards Israel shall neither sleep nor fall asleep" (Ps 121:4). He says: "I sleep and my heart keeps watch" (Cant 5:2) because in the sleep of his passion, he slept in his flesh, but his divinity was scouring the underworld, so that he could carry off humankind, who was imprisoned in hell. For our Lord and Savior willed to scour every place, to have mercy on all. From heaven he came down to earth, to visit the world. From the earth, again, he went down to the underworld to bring light to those who were bound in hell, according to the word of the prophet, who said: "A light has dawned for you who sit in darkness and the shadow of death" (Isa 9:2). So this night is rightly called "the vigil of the Lord." In it he brought light not only to this world but also to those who were in the underworld.[c]

121. CHROMATIUS OF AQUILEIA, Sermon 17A: *On the Pascha*, 1

The passion of Christ is a true Pascha; it even received the name of "pascha" from "passion." The apostle's word clearly shows this when he says: "For Christ our Pascha has been sacrificed" (1 Cor 5:7). . . . "With desire have I desired to eat this Pascha with you" (Luke 22:15). Hence we eat the Pascha with Christ because he feeds[a] those whom he saves. For he is the source of the Pascha, he is the source of the mystery; he fulfilled the feast of this Pascha so as to renew us with the food of his passion and restore us with the cup of salvation.[b]

122. MAXIMUS OF TURIN, Sermon 54: *On the Holy Pascha*, 1

Hence when Christ rose again, his entire body rose with him by necessity. For while he passed from the underworld to the world above, he caused us to pass from death to life. For the Hebrew word *pascha* means "passing over" or "progress" in Latin, since through this mystery a passage from the worse to the better takes place. Thus the good passing over is the passage from sins to justice, from vices to virtue, from old age to infancy.[a] But I mean not an infancy of age, but of simplicity. For good acts, too, have their ages of life. Formerly we were among the dying, by the old age of our sins. When Christ rose we were renewed in the innocence of children.

123. PAULINUS OF NOLA, Poem 27: *On the Feast of St. Felix*

There is also the feast of the Pasch. Of course, the Church proclaims the Pasch in all lands on each successive day, witnessing to the Lord's death on the cross, and to the life gained by all from the cross.[a] Yet the whole world with equal devotion everywhere venerates this lofty mystery of great love towards humankind in a particular month each year,[b] when it celebrates the eternal King risen with body restored. After this solemn feast (we calculate seven weeks before this holiday comes round for mortals) comes the day on which the Holy Spirit was of old sent down from the heights of heaven in parted tongues of fiery light.[c]

124. AUGUSTINE OF HIPPO, Letter 55 to Januarius 1, 2

You ask what the reason is that the anniversary celebration of the Lord's passion does not return on the same day of the year, as does the day on which he is said to have been born.[a] Then you add: If this happens because of the Sabbath and the moon, what does this celebration have to do with the observation of the Sabbath and the moon? Here you must know, first of all, that the Lord's birthday is not celebrated in a sacrament[b] but his birth is simply remembered, and for this it was only necessary to mark with festive devotion each year the day on which the event took place. But there is a sacrament in any celebration when the commemoration of the event is done in such a way as to make us understand that it signifies something that is to be taken in a holy manner. This is in fact how we keep the Pascha. Not only do we call to mind again what happened, that is, that Christ died and rose again, but we also do not leave out the other things about him which confirm the signification of the sacraments.[c] For, since he "died for our sins and rose for our justification," as the apostle says (Rom 4:25),[d] a certain passage from death to life has been consecrated in the passion and resurrection of the Lord.[e]

125. AUGUSTINE OF HIPPO, Letter 55 to Januarius 14, 24

Pay attention, therefore, to the sacred three days of the Crucified, Buried, and Resurrected One.[a] Of these three the Cross is the one whose meaning we realize in the present life, while the Burial and the Resurrection signify something we believe and hope for.

126. AUGUSTINE OF HIPPO, *Exposition of Psalm 120* (Sermon Preached on the Feast of St. Crispina, Martyr), 6

Careful scholars[a] have discovered that *Pascha* is a Hebrew word, and they do not translate it with "suffering" but with "passage." For by suffering the Lord made the passage from death to life[b] and opened a way for us who believe in his resurrection by which we too might pass from death to life.[c]

127. AUGUSTINE OF HIPPO, *Tractate 55 on the Gospel of John*, 1 (on John 13:1-5)

Pascha ("Passover") is not, as some think,[a] a Greek noun, but a Hebrew: and yet there occurs in this noun a very suitable kind of accordance in the two languages. For inasmuch as the Greek word *paschein* means "to suffer," therefore *pascha* has been supposed to mean "suffering," as if the noun derived its name from his passion: but in its own language, that is, in Hebrew, *pascha* means "passover"; because[b] the Pascha was then celebrated for the first time by God's people, when, in their flight from Egypt, they "passed over" the Red Sea. And now that prophetic emblem is fulfilled in truth, when Christ is "led as a sheep to the slaughter" (Isa 53:7), that by his blood sprinkled on our doorposts, that is, by the sign of his cross marked on our foreheads,[c] we may be delivered from the perdition awaiting this world, as Israel from the bondage and destruction of the Egyptians (cf. Exod 12:23); and a most salutary transit we make when we pass over from the devil to Christ, and from this unstable world to his well-established kingdom. And therefore surely do we pass over to the ever-abiding God, that we may not pass away with this passing world. The apostle, in extolling God for such grace bestowed upon us, says: "Who has delivered us from the power of darkness, and has translated us into the kingdom of the Son of his love" (Col 1:13). This name, then, of *pascha*, which, as I have said, is in Latin called *transitus* ("pass-over"), is interpreted, as it were, for us by the blessed evangelist, when he says, "Before the feast of Pascha, when Jesus knew that his hour was come that he should pass out of this world to the Father" (John 13:1).[d] Here you see we have both *pascha* and "pass-over." Whence, and whither does he pass? Namely, "out of this world to the Father." The hope was thus given to the members in their Head, that they doubtless would yet follow him who was "passing" before. And what, then, of unbelievers, who stand altogether apart from this Head and his members? Do not they also pass away, seeing that they abide not here always? They also do plainly pass away: but it is one thing to pass from the world, and another to pass away with it; one thing to pass tò the Father, another to pass to the enemy. For the Egyptians also passed over [the sea]; but they did not pass through the sea to the kingdom, but in the sea to destruction.

128. AUGUSTINE OF HIPPO, Sermon 220: *On the Vigil of Pascha*

We know, brethren, and we hold with faith most firm, that "Christ died once for" us (1 Pet 3:18), the Just One for sinners, the Lord for his servants. . . . As the apostle says, "He was handed over for our sins, and he rose for our justification" (Rom 4:25). You know perfectly well that this event took place once; yet the feast takes place as if the event occurred often. As the seasons come round the feast recurs, although the truth[a] cries out in so many voices from the Scriptures that the event took place only once. But the truth and the feast do not contradict each other, as if the feast were a lie and the event true. For the truth points out what in deeds took place only once. The feast renews the event, which devout hearts should celebrate often. The truth reveals the events that took place, just as they happened, whereas the feast reveals the events not by making them happen but by rejoicing in them. The feast keeps the past from passing away; "Christ our Pascha has been sacrificed" (1 Cor 5:7) indeed. Surely he was slain once, "who now does not die; death will no longer have dominion over him" (Rom 6:9). Thus, according to the voice of the truth, we say that Pascha took place once, and will take place no longer; but according to the voice of the feast, we say that Pascha will come each year. . . . The magnificent feast of this night pertains to the latter. By keeping vigil, as it were, we effect the Lord's resurrection through the "remnants of our thought" (Ps 76:10 Vg); by thinking about it, we confess more truly that it took place once. The truth that was proclaimed has made us learned; neglect of the feast should not make us impious. The feast has made this night brilliant throughout the whole world. This feast shows forth the ranks of the Christian peoples; it confounds the darkness of the Jews; it overturns the idols of the pagans.[b]

129. AUGUSTINE OF HIPPO, Sermon Wilmart 4, 3

And so, in this vigil of ours, we do not await the Lord as if he were still about to rise; rather, our yearly feast renews the memory of his resurrection. But still, when we celebrate this feast we recall past events in such a way that, by this same vigil, we create a sign of something we do by living in faith.[a] For this whole time, in which this world passes as if in one night, the Church keeps vigil, gazing with the eyes of faith upon the holy Scriptures as if they were lamps in the night, until the Lord comes.

130. AUGUSTINE OF HIPPO, Sermon Wilmart 9, 2

So, dearly beloved, may untiring meditation on all these truths
be for us a daily celebration of the Pascha. For we should not
consider these days of the feast so special that we neglect the
memorial of the Lord's passion and resurrection at other times.
We have his Body and Blood as our daily banquet.[a] But this
feast commemorates it more clearly, rouses us to greater fervor,
and renews us in greater joy, because in the yearly cycle of seasons it recalls, as it were, to our very eyes the memory of what
Christ did.

131. AUGUSTINE OF HIPPO, Sermon Morin-Guelferbytanus 4, 2

Dearest brethren, we keep vigil on this night, on which we recall that our Lord was buried. We ought to keep vigil during that
time in which, for our sakes, he slept. Long before, he announced
his passion through his prophet: "I slept," he says, "and I rose
up, because the Lord received me" (Ps 3:5). He called the Father
"Lord." Hence on the night on which he slept, we keep vigil,
so that through the death he suffered we might have life.[a] During his short sleep we celebrate a vigil, so that he will keep watch
for us and, when we are raised, we can abide untired for the eternal vigil.[b] On this night he also rose; our hope keeps watch for
his resurrection.

132. AUGUSTINE OF HIPPO, Sermon Morin-Guelferbytanus 5, 1–2

1. The day that our Lord Jesus Christ made sorrowful by dying
he also made glorious by rising. We call both times into solemn
memory. As we ponder his death, let us keep vigil; and as we embrace his resurrection, let us rejoice. This is our yearly feast,[a]
and our Pascha—not represented by the slaughtering of an animal, as for God's people of old, but fulfilled for the new people
by the Savior's sacrifice. For "Christ our Pascha has been
sacrificed" (1 Cor 5:7), and "the old has passed away, and, be-

hold, the new has come to be" (2 Cor 5:17). For we do not grieve, except for the weight of our sins; nor do we rejoice, except for our justification by his grace. For "he was handed over for our sins, and he rose for our justification" (Rom 4:25). We grieve for sin, rejoice in justification, and so are gladdened. What is sad, happened on our account and for us; and what is joyous was sent as a sign for the same reason. We do not pass over these events in ungrateful forgetfulness, but celebrate them in thankful memory. So let us keep vigil, dearly beloved, because Christ's burial was prolonged up to this night, so that in this very night the resurrection of the flesh might take place. Once, on the cross, that flesh was mocked; now, in heaven and on earth, it is adored. Understood aright, this night is part of the day that follows, which we call the Lord's Day.[b] . . . 2. . . . . Why do Christians keep vigil today, on the yearly feast? We keep vigil most especially now; no other feast has the significance that this one has.[c] In our longing for it we ask about it and say, "When do we keep vigil?" "In so-and-so-many days we keep vigil."[d] In comparison with this one, other vigils should not even have the name.

133. AUGUSTINE OF HIPPO, Sermon Mai 158, 4

Why do the Jews celebrate Pentecost? This is a great mystery, brethren, and quite wondrous. Consider this: on the day of Pentecost they received the Law written by the finger of God, and on the day of Pentecost the Holy Spirit came.[a]

134. PSEUDO (?)-AUGUSTINE, Sermon Denis 7, 1

Everyone knows that we are celebrating the days of Pascha. On these days we sing "alleluia."[a] We should pay careful attention to this feast, brethren, so that we can preserve in our souls what we celebrate externally. For we say we are celebrating "Pascha." "Pascha" is a Hebrew word that means "passing over." But in Greek, *paschein* means "to suffer." In Latin *pascha* means "to feed"; we have the expression, "I will feed" [*pascam*]—that is, serve dinner to—"my friends." Who celebrate Pascha, except those who "pass over" from the death of their sins to the life of the just? As the apostle says: "We have passed from death to life, because we love the brethren" (1 John 3, 14). Who celebrates Pascha, if not he who believes in the one who "suffered" on earth, so that he might reign with him in heaven? Who celebrates Pascha, if not he who "feeds" Christ in the poor? For of the poor he himself says: "Whoever does this for one of my least ones, does it for me" (Matt 25:40). Christ is seated in heaven, and on earth he is needy. He intercedes with the Father for us, and here he begs bread from us. Hence, my revered brethren, if we wish to celebrate Pascha to our advantage, we should "pass over," "suffer," and "feed." We should pass from sins to justice, suffer for Christ, and feed Christ in the poor.[b]

135. LEO THE GREAT, Sermon 49: *On the Fast of Lent*, 1

Dearly beloved, in every day and season some sign of the divine goodness is shown to us, and no part of the year is bereft of the sacred mysteries. Assistance with our salvation is found everywhere, so we can more eagerly beg for God's mercy, which always summons us. But whatever works together for the salvation of human souls in the various deeds and gifts of grace is now presented to us more evidently and more abundantly. We do not commemorate single events; rather, we celebrate all of them together.[a] For the paschal feast is approaching. The greatest and most sacred fast has come. The observance of this fast is enjoined without exception on all the faithful.

136. APONIUS, *Explanation of the Song of Songs* 4, 25-26 (on Cant 2:11-12)

After the harsh winter of idolatry and the doctrine of philosophy, Christ our Lord, in the season of spring, decorated the face of the world with the flower of the martyrs and of all the holy deeds[a] (cf. Cant 2:11-12). This he did through his passion, because he is "our Pascha"[b] (1 Cor 5:7), the passing over from death to life.[c] At this season, in the beginning, every creature was created, as we know, and man himself was formed from the mud of the earth. . . . At this same season, Christ our Redeemer, by the example of his death, calls the Church from the deep valley of tears to the mountain of paradise.[d]

137. PSEUDO-AUGUSTINE, Sermon Caillau-St. Yves 1, 30

Beloved brethren, some think that *pascha* is a Greek word—that is, that it comes from "passion" or "suffering." That is not true. *Pascha*, or *phase*—and Scripture does not mention this *pascha* itself by another name—each of these short words means in Latin *transitus*, "passing over." It is called "passing over" because on this night, in the past, the Lord passed through Egypt when he struck down all the first-born of the Egyptians. The same Lord records this deed when he says: "And I shall pass through the land of Egypt, and I shall strike every first-born in the land of Egypt" (Exod 12:12).[a] But we celebrate this Pascha—that is, rather, this passing over—more profoundly; for on this night our Lord and Savior, after his passion, passed over from death to life, and from the underworld to the world above, when he rises.[b]

138. PSEUDO-AUGUSTINE, Sermon Caillau-St. Yves 1, 31

Listen to a mystery, and an account of the word *pascha*. In Hebrew *pascha* means "passing over." But as a Greek word it means "passion."[a] The Jews keep Pascha only as "passing over," the day on which their ancestors were freed from Egypt and passed over the sea, which hardened under their feet in dry waves. But we celebrate both the "passing over" and the "passion" of Christ the Lord.[b] For just as the passing over of a people, made on foot, was the redemption of captives, so the passion of Christ is the redemption of sinners.

139. PSEUDO-AMBROSE, Sermon 12: *On the Pascha*, 4

Brethren, since you are now celebrating the holy Pascha, you should know what Pascha is. *Pascha* means "passing over." This feast has been given that name because on it the children of Israel passed over out of Egypt, and on it the Son of God passed over "out of this world to the Father" (John 13:1).[a] What profit is there for you in celebrating Pascha if you do not imitate what you celebrate? What profit is there, if you do not pass over from Egypt—that is, from the darkness of sins to the light of virtues, and from love of this world to longing for the heavenly fatherland?[b]

140. RUPERT OF DEUTZ, *On the Divine Offices* 6, 26

Now, before we give an ordered account of the office, we ought to explain for how many, and for which, reasons the feast of Pascha is considered so illustrious and so important. For many see in this feast only this: that "on the first day of the week" (Matt 28:1) the Lord rose. This is why it is called the "day of the Lord's resurrection."[a] It is obviously a great cause for a feast and for joy in our hearts. Because he rose, we believe there is a resurrection of the dead; and we rightly rejoice in the hope that we are also going to be raised. But in the contemplation of this feast our eyes should never pass over the joy we feel in recalling the redemption of our souls. As we already said, this joy was postponed from Good Friday until this day. On Good Friday our Savior effected that redemption through his cross and the shedding of his blood.[b]

141. SICARD OF CREMONA, *Mitrale* 6, 15

Pascha is understood historically, allegorically, tropologically, and anagogically.[a] The historical sense is: Pascha is celebrated when the exterminating angel passes through Egypt and kills the first-born. . . . At that time the people of Israel also passed out of Egypt—that is, they went out, and on the third day they passed through the Red Sea. The allegorical sense: Through baptism the Church passes from infidelity to faith. The tropological sense: Through confession and contrition the soul should pass from vice to virtue. The anagogical sense: Christ passed from mortality to immortality, from death to life, from the prison of hell to the joys of paradise, so that he could have us pass from the misery of this world to eternal joys.[b]

Notes to the Texts

1a. Exodus 12:1-28: The Passover in Egypt and the Feast of Unleavened Bread

> Critical Hebrew text: *Biblia hebraica Stuttgartensia* eds. Karl Elliger and Wilhelm Rudolph (Stuttgart: Deutsche Bibelstiftung, 1967–1977) 104–105.

> Critical Greek text: *Septuaginta, id est Vetus Testamentum Graece iuxta LXX interpretes* ed. Alfred Rahlfs (Stuttgart: Württembergische Bibelanstalt, 1935), 1:104–105.

> English version used here: *Tanakh, A New Translation of the Holy Scriptures According to the Traditional Hebrew Text* (Philadelphia: Jewish Publication Society, 1985) 100–102.

Every verse of Exodus 12 had a typological or allegorical interpretation in Christian exegesis: see Huber, 139–147. The following notes, however, elucidate only the literal meaning and the history of the meanings assigned to various phrases.

a. Most modern scholars believe that the Pesach laws of Exodus 12, while deriving from the comparatively recent Priestly Source (P), reflect the most archaic stage of the festival, in which Israel was still a nomad people and a sheep or goat would be sacrificed in each household. In contrast, the laws of Deuteronomy 16:1-8 (text 1b) reflect the Pesach as the Israelites celebrated it in the land of Canaan, where they kept larger cattle. It was probably King Hezechiah (see 2 Chr 30) who transformed the Pesach from a family feast into a pilgrim feast at the central sanctuary. See Haag, *DBS* 6 (1960) 1130–1135.

b. The Greek version adds: "You are not to break any of its bones." The phrase comes from v. 46 below.

c. *Pesah*: origin and etymology of the term are uncertain. Here it refers to the lamb or kid slaughtered for the feast, as in Exodus 12:21, "kill the pesach," and Deuteronomy 16:2, 5, 6, "sacrifice the pesach." So also 2 Chronicles 30:18, "eat the pesach," and Matt 26:17; Mark 14:12; Luke 22:8, 11; John 18:28, "eat the *pascha*." Elsewhere the term denotes the festival connected with the lamb, e.g., Lev 23:5; Num 28:16; Deut 16:1; 2 Chr 35:1; Ezra 6:19, "keep (or do) Pesach."

d. *Pesah hû' le-YHWH* = it is a *pesah to* or *in honor of* YHWH. The LXX *pascha estin kyriôi* can also be understood in this sense. The pesach then will originally have been the object of a sacrificial action of men. But *pesah / pascha* was also taken to mean the feast, and then, by a very natural extension, the action of God which the feast commemorated and which is described in the next two verses: "I will pass over (or protect) you." Codex Alexandrinus (fifth cent. A.D.) and Theodoret testify to this possible understanding with the reading *kyriou:* "It is the Pascha *of* the Lord." This is the reading of the Old Latin and the Vulgate: *Pascha est enim Domini.* It was also that of Aquila and Symmachus. Taking *pesah,* then, as the action of God, Aquila could translate it *hyperbasis,* and Symmachus could render it *hypermachêsis.* The former would read the phrase as "It is the passage of the LORD"; the latter, "It is the LORD's defending (Israel)." Jerome and the Vulgate incorporate Aquila's translation of the word into the phrase: *est enim Phase, id est transitus, Domini,* "for it is the *phase(ch),* that is the passage, of the Lord." This again is open to two interpretations: the Lord's passage (over the houses), or: the people's passage (out of Egypt) under the Lord's guidance. The latter interpretation may underlie Philo's explanation of the Pascha as the "Crossing Feast" (text 2); the former accords with Josephus' understanding (see text 4, note c). "The Lord" was taken by fourth-century Latin Christians to refer to Christ, and "the passage of the Lord" to refer to Christ's passion (text 117) or his passage from death to life (texts 122, 124, 126, etc.; see also text 14, note c). For Aquila and Symmachus, see Field, 1:100; for the Old Latin, Sabatier, 1:157; for the Vulgate, Weber, 1:92. (Trans.)

e. The Hebrew word is *pasahtî* in v. 13, *pasah* in vv. 23 and 27. Since the root *psh* is also heard in the name of the feast, *pesah,* the text connects the two words. Elsewhere in the Bible, *psh* means "limp" or "hop"; many scholars think that the same verb is used here in a derived sense: "hop over," "skip," "pass over," "not strike," and hence "spare." However, T. Francis Glasson (*JThS* n.s. 10 [1959] 79–84) rejects the meaning "pass over" for *psh* in Exodus 12:13, 23, 27, asserting that in these three places it means "hover over" and "protect," as it does in Isaiah 31:5. In support of his translation, he can adduce the Septuagint, the targums, Symmachus, the Old Latin, the Midrash *Exodus Rabbah,* and the Mekhilta. Jerome showed that he knew this way of rendering the word when he offered *ipse Dominus praebens auxilium populo suo desuper ambulavit* as an alternative interpretation of Exodus 12:13 (see text 114). See also Botte, *OrSyr* 8 (1963) 213 ff.

f. The fifteenth, the day after the Pesach-offering and the first day of Unleavened Bread. This latter was originally a harvest feast which Israel adopted on settling in Canaan. It became linked to Pesach after the reform of Josiah in 617 B.C. (2 Chr 35:17). As a result Pesach became a seven-day festival like the Feast of Weeks (Pentecost) and the Feast of Tabernacles. (Trans.)

g. Moses' way of speaking seems to indicate that the Pesach was already known to the Hebrews. Probably the tenth plague of Egypt and the Exodus simply happened to coincide with the festival—as it is said in Exodus 12:17 that the Exodus occurred on the first day of Unleavened Bread, implying the pre-existence of the feast. Nevertheless, the earliest traditions of Israel connect the rites of the feast with the Exodus (e.g., eating the lamb in haste, Ex 12:11), and the explanations (Haggadah) of the Pesach ritual which evolved constitute a beautiful catechesis of salvation. Cf. *Bible de Jérusalem*, nouvelle éd., 95 = *New Jerusalem Bible*, 95. (Trans.)

h. *Zebah-pesah hû' le-YHWH.* LXX and Theodotion: *thusia to pascha touto kyriôi* = "this Pascha is a sacrifice to the Lord," which the Old Latin translates literally: *Immolatio pascha hoc domino.* Aquila, on the other hand, has: *thusia hyperbaseôs estin . . .* = "it is a sacrifice of passage . . .," and Jerome follows Aquila: "Victima transitus domini est, quando transivit super domos filiorum Israel." See Field, 1:101; Sabatier, 1:158; Weber, 1:92. (Trans.)

1b. Deuteronomy 16:1-10: The Passover in the Promised Land and the Feast of Weeks

Critical Hebrew text: *Biblia Hebraica Stuttgartensia*, 315.

Critical Greek text: Rahlfs, 1:316–317.

English version used here: *Tanakh*, 300.

a. A harvest festival adopted by the Israelites in Canaan. The date was variable until priestly legislation attached the feast to the relatively fixed date of Pesach with the prescription: "From the day on which you bring the sheaf of elevation offering—the day after the Sabbath—you shall count off seven weeks. They must be complete: you must count until the day after the seventh week—fifty days; then you shall bring an offering of new grain to the LORD" (Lev 23:15-16). The Pharisees understood "the Sabbath" as the first day of Unleavened Bread and began counting with the sixteenth of Nisan, finishing with the sixth of Siwan. A group of Sadducees, however, understood "the Sabbath" as the seventh day of the week and began counting on the Sunday after Pesach, so that their fiftieth day was always a Sunday. Still others began counting on the day after the last day of Unleavened Bread (the Falashas) or on the Sunday which followed the week of Unleavened Bread (Qumran). See Delcor, *DBS* VII (1966) 861-864.

2. PHILO OF ALEXANDRIA, *On the Special Laws* 2, 145-147

> Critical Greek text: *Philonis Alexandrini opera quae super-sunt*, vol. 5, ed. Leopoldus Cohn (Berlin: G. Reimer, 1906) 120-121.
>
> English version used here: *Philo*, vol. 7, with an English translation by F. H. Colson (LCL; London: Heinemann, 1937, repr. Cambridge [Mass.]: Harvard, 1950) 395-397.

Philo lived from about 20 B.C. to about A.D. 50.

a. *Ta diabatêria*. In classical Greek, these are offerings made before or after crossing a boundary, river, or the like. In translating *pascha* with *diabatêria* or *diabasis*—as he does in *On the Preliminary Studies* 106; *Allegorical Interpretation* (*Legum allegoria*) III 94, 154, 165; *On the Sacrifices of Abel and Cain* 63; *On the Migration of Abraham* 25; and *Who is the Heir?* (*Quis rerum divinarum heres*) 255—Philo initiates a new interpretation of the Pascha, one which will then become dominant among the Christians. It is possible that it underlies as early a text as John 13:1, in which the Pascha is identified with Christ's passing from this world to the Father.

b. The same theme is found in Philo's *Moses* 2, 224. In dependence on Exodus 19:6, he also called Israel a priestly people, in *On Abraham* 98.

c. For Philo, the historical meaning of the Pascha lies in its com-memorating the crossing of the Red Sea (Exod 14) rather than the slaugh-ter of a lamb and even the protection of Israel from the destruction of the first-born (Exod 12). Reading the Bible in Greek, he probably did not see the connection between *pascha* in Exodus 12:11 and *pasahtî* in v. 13 or *pasah* in v. 27, since these are translated *skepasô* and *eskepasen* respectively. He based his allegory, then, on an idea and an event (the Exodus) rather than on the Hebrew Bible's play on words.

d. Allegory is the soul of Scripture, as the literal sense is its body: *On the Contemplative Life* 78. In Philo, the allegory of the Pascha occupies the place that the Pascal liturgy held in Palestinian Judaism and that the typology of the Pascha came to hold in primitive Christianity: see Cantalamessa, *La Pasqua della nostra salvezza*, 52-66.

e. With this interpretation, the theological Pascha (God passes and saves) gives way to the moral or anthropological Pascha (humanity passes from vices to virtue). Elsewhere (in *Questions and Answers on Exodus* 1, 4), Philo distinguishes three types of passage: historical or spatial (out of Egypt), moral (out of evil), and contemplative or eschatological (out of the world)—all three anthropological.

3. PHILO OF ALEXANDRIA, *On the Preliminary Studies*, 106

Critical Greek text: *Philonis Alexandrini opera quae supersunt*, vol. 3, ed. Paulus Wendland (Berlin: G. Reimer, 1898), 93.

English version used here, and wherever no other translator is named, by James M. Quigley, S.J.

a. *Pathos*. The association between *pascha* and *pathos* will find significant development in Christian catechesis. Philo makes it explicit in *Who is the Heir?* 192: "It is Pascha whenever the soul endeavors to unlearn the irrational passion (*alogon pathos*) and voluntarily submits (*paschei*) to reasonable and good emotion (*eulogos eupatheia*)." Compare text 107.

b. Philo has devoted sections 94–105 to an allegorization of the tithes prescribed by the Law, showing how the tenth part of anything is a symbol of the divine. See also *On the Preliminary Studies* 94.

c. The moon is but two-thirds full on the tenth of a lunar month; its becoming full by the fourteenth symbolizes the progressive illumination of the soul. See also *On the Special Laws* 2, 149 and *Questions and Answers on Exodus* 1, 2, 9.

d. The spiritual progress of the soul is seen allegorically in the paschal lamb, using the etymology of "sheep" (*probaton*, from *probainô* = "walk forward," "progress") in *Allegorical Interpretation* 3, 165, *On the Sacrifices of Abel and Cain* 112, and *Questions and Answers on Exodus* 1, 7–8.

4. FLAVIUS JOSEPHUS, *Jewish Antiquities* 2, 14, 6, 312–313

Critical Greek text: *Flavii Josephi opera*, vol. 1, ed. Benedictus Niese (Berlin: Weidmann, 1887, reprinted 1955), 148–149.

English version used here: Josephus, vol. 4, *Jewish Antiquities, Books I–IV*, trans. Henry St. John Thackeray (LCL; London: Heinemann, 1930; repr. Cambridge: Harvard) 301.

Josephus (ca. A.D. 37–ca. 101) wrote the *Antiquities* in Greek in 93 or 94.

a. *Phatria* = *phratria*, a subdivision of a tribe in ancient Greece. Josephus uses the word to designate a group both large enough and small enough to eat the Passover together. In *The Jewish War* 6, 423, he says it consisted of from ten to twenty persons.

b. *Hyperbasia.*

c. *Hyperbas.* Josephus interprets *pasah* as "passed above" (see text 1a, note e) and remains faithful to the theological interpretation, in which the acting subject (one who passes) is God and not, as in Philo, human. Aquila follows this tradition (see text 1a, note c), as do a few Christian authors (see texts 54 and 114 with notes b and c to the latter).

d. *Ho theos autôn hyperbas . . . enapeskêpse*: literally, "their God, having passed above, smote. . . ." "Having passed above" has no object, and thus Thackeray's "God passed over our people" is an interpretation rather than an exact translation. It is based on the supposition that Josephus understood *psh* = *hyperbainein* to mean "skip over" rather than "hover over." This supposition as to the meaning of *pasah* is embedded in English-speaking culture ever since Tyndale's Bible translated *pesah* as "passover" (see text 1a, note e above). The noncommittal English term *Pasch*, which Wyclif (1382) spelled *Phask* at Exodus 12:43 and *pask* at Mark 14:14, is used in the Rheims New Testament (1582) and the Douay Bible (1609), but has passed out of common usage (see the *Oxford English Dictionary* [Oxford: Clarendon, 1933] 7:517 on these terms). (Trans.)

5. A Palestinian Targum on Exodus 12:42: The Night of Watching

> Critical edition, with Spanish, French, and English translations: Alejandro Díez Macho, *Neophyti 1, Targum Palestinense, MS de la Biblioteca Vaticana*, Vol. 2, *Exodo* (Textos y Estudios 8; Madrid: Consejo Superior de Investigaciones Cientificas, 1970) 77–79.

> Codex Neophyti is referred to below as N. The Fragmentary Targums V (Ms Vaticanum Ebr. 440), P (Paris, Bibliothèque Nationale, MS Hébr. 110), and C (Cambridge University Library MS T-S NS 182.69) have been edited by Michael L. Klein, *The Fragment-Targums of the Pentateuch according to Their Extant Sources* (*AnBib* 76; Rome: Biblical Institute Press, 1980) and *Genizah Manuscripts of Palestinian Targum to the Pentateuch* (Cincinnati: Hebrew Union College Press, 1986).

> Most of the following notes were contributed by the translator, with the author's approval.

The concept of the Pascha presented in this text is governed by two ideas: that of memorial (cf. Exod 12:14) and that of salvation. For a detailed commentary, see Le Déaut, *La nuit pascale*, where the passage is called "The Poem of the Four Nights."

a. *Lyly ntyr wmswmn* = "night reserved and fixed in time." This is the Aramaic interpretation of the first words of Exodus 12:42, *lêl simmurîm* = "night of observances," "night of watching." This targum, like that of Onqelos (Sperber, *The Bible in Aramaic*, 1:109) understands the phrase to mean "a night reserved," but the Old Latin version, which Jerome left unchanged, takes its cue from Exod 13:10 and translates it as "a night to be observed": *nox est ista observabilis* (Old Latin), *nox ista est observabilis* (Vulgate)—see Bonifatius Fischer, *Beiträge*, 426, and Weber, 93. The Septuagint preferred "a night of watching" or, more precisely, "a nighttime watch": *nyktos prophylakê*. Aquila, with *nyx paratêrêseôs*, and Symmachus, with *nyx paratetêrêmenê*, show that they are aware of all three interpretations: reserving, observing, and watching. (See Le Déaut, *La nuit pascale,* 272-273.) *Lê simmurîm* was commonly used in the first century B.C. to denote the night of Pesach under its eschatological aspect (Huber, 211; Le Déaut, *La nuit pascale* 272-73). Translated into Syriac from the targum, it is still the name of the paschal night among Christians in upper Mesopotamia in the fourth century A.D.: see text 87 with note a.

b. *Lsmh dyyy* = "for the name of Yahweh."

c. The whole sentence in C reads: "*Lyl smwrym*: it is a night preserved and trustworthy for deliverance, before the Lord; [it is] the time when the Israelites were brought forth."

d. In the margin of N: "Because."

e. V has: *Mymr' dyy'* = "the Word of Yahweh" (Klein, *The Fragment-Targums*, 1:167).

f. For the connection between Pesach and creation in Judaism, see Le Déaut, *La nuit pascale*, 218-237. Philo explains the words, "This month . . . shall be the first month of the year for you" (Exod 12:2) as based on the world's having been created in the month of the Pascha (*On the Special Laws* 2, 150-152). See also text 27b.

g. P and V add: "between the pieces." The Second Night is the night in which Abraham saw a smoking fire-pot and a flaming torch passing between the divided halves of his sacrifices and received God's covenant with its promise of descendants who should possess the Land (Gen 15:1-21). Rabbinic tradition puts this event on 15 Nisan, the night of Pesach (Füglister, 208-209). For the connection between Pesach and the covenant of Sinai, see Le Déaut, *La nuit pascale*, 76-87.

h. The biblical text is in the form of a question. The targum, according to Klein, *The Fragment-Targums*, 2:126, converts it into a statement: "Behold, it is possible for Abraham at one hundred years to beget, and it is possible for Sarah at ninety years to give birth."

i. The addition of a reference to the vision of Isaac, which occurred, according to the rabbis, as he lay bound on the altar, means that the Pascha encompasses the theme of sacrifice as well as that of covenant (Füglister, 208–214; Le Déaut, *La nuit pascale*, 100–115 and 133–208). The association of Pesach with the sacrifice (*'aqêdâh* = binding) of Isaac was prepared for by the tradition which identified the mountain "in the land of Moriah" (Gen 22:2) with the Temple mount ("Moriah" in 2 Chr 3:1).

j. *Lmtprq'* = "to be destroyed," or "to be set free."

k. Various witnesses attest to the Jewish tradition which expected the coming of the Messiah during the night of Pesach (see Strack-Billerbeck, 1:967, and Le Déaut, *La nuit pascale*, 279–298). The New Testament, with its warnings about the nocturnal coming of the Son of Man, does not focus on the paschal night (unless Luke 17:20, "the kingdom of God does not come with watching," *meta paratêreseôs,* is a rejection of such a paschal expectation), but it was surely a strong element of the Quartodeciman Pascha and is mentioned by Lactantius, Jerome, *The Testament of our Lord Jesus Christ*, and Isidore of Seville (Huber, 218–223). See text 13, note b.

l. *Mn gw rwm'* (originally *mrwm'*), which can also be translated "from Rome," in allusion to the belief that the Messiah would come from Rome, as mentioned in the Mishnah, *Sanhedrin* 98a (Le Déaut, *La nuit pascale*, 359–369).

m. The bracketed phrase, absent from N, is surely part of the traditional text; for the first revisor of the codex noted an omission at this point (Le Déaut, *La nuit pascale*, 271–272), and the phrase is found in P and V (Klein, *The Fragment-Targums*, 1:80, 167) and in the *Meturgeman* of Elias Levita (Ginsburger, *Das Fragmententhargum*, 105).

n. The reading "atop a cloud" is rejected by Le Déaut, *Targum du Pentateuque*, 2:98–99, note 49.

o. P and V: *wmymr' dyy'* = "and the Word of Yahweh" (Klein, *The Fragment-Targums*, 1:80 and 167).

p. P omits but V and C retain: and I. Klein, *The Fragment-Targums*, 1:126, note 19, explains "I" as referring to the Lord himself.

q. In C this sentence reads: "That is the night of Passover before the Lord, which the Master of All Worlds named the fourth night, at the end of the world. It is reserved and prepared for all the Israelites, throughout all their generations" (Klein, *Genizah Manuscripts*, 1:220–221).

6. *Haggadah for Pesach*: **Rabban Gamliel's Aphorism and the Thanksgiving for the Redemption**

> Hebrew text: E. D. (Daniel) Goldschmidt, *The Passover Haggadah: Its Sources and History* (Jerusalem: Bialik Institute, 1960).

a. Either Rabbi Gamaliel I, the teacher of St. Paul (Acts 5:34; 22:3), or Gamaliel II, grandson of the former, who lived at Jabneh around 100 A.D. The text, at least in part, is surely older than the middle of the second century A.D., because the antitheses at the end are echoed by Melito of Sardis (text 22, with note d). Our earliest witness to the text is the Mishnah, *Pesahim* 10, 5 (about A.D. 200); this whole passage is there, but four paragraphs are shorter than in later redactions. They read:

> *Pesah*, because the divinity passed over (or protected) the houses of our fathers in Egypt.
>
> *Massâh*, because our fathers were redeemed from Egypt.
>
> *Marôr*, because the Egyptians embittered the lives of our fathers in Egypt.
>
> In every generation each person must regard himself as having come out of Egypt "It is because of what the LORD did for me when I came out of Egypt" (Exod 13:8).

b. That is, explained in the course of his *'aggadâh* (narrative).

c. The lamb. Unlike the unleavened bread and the bitter herb, it is no longer consumed in the Seder of the Ashkenazim, but may be represented on the table by a roasted shank-bone. Lamb is eaten at the Pesach meal, however, by North African and Sephardic Jews, but only the Samaritans ritually sacrifice the lambs. However, animal sacrifices seem to have been performed by some Jews in various places after A.D. 70 and even after 135 (see *Encyclopedia Judaica* [Jerusalem: Keter, 1971–1972] 13, 164–168 and 172). (Trans.)

d. This unusual and distinctive notion of time, which regards the saving events of the past as contemporaneous with the present in the act of worship, is discussed by Gerhard von Rad in his *Old Testament Theology*, 2:99–112. It is the basis of the *hodie* of the Christian liturgy (ibid., 109).

e. The same antitheses are found in the Mishnah, *Exodus Rabbah* 12, 2, which shows many affinities also with the Targum on Exodus (text 5). See Le Déaut, *La nuit pascale*, 235.

7. MATTHEW, MARK, and LUKE: The Institution of the Eucharist

Critical text: Kurt Aland and others, eds., *The Greek New Testament*, 3d ed. (New York: American Bible Society, 1975). See also Kurt Aland, *Synopsis quattuor euangeliorum*, 13th ed. (Stuttgart: Deutsche Bibelgesellschaft, 1985) 436–437.

English translation used here: RSV, from *The New Oxford Annotated Bible*, (New York: Oxford University Press, 1973) 1207–1208, 1234, and 1279.

Mark's account was written between 65 and 70, probably at Rome; Matthew's, probably after 70 and probably at Antioch in Syria; Luke's, after 70 and before 85, traditionally in southern Greece.

a. (Matt 26:20) Many manuscripts have: "with the twelve disciples"; a few have: "with his disciples."

b. (Luke 22:15) The Synoptics describe Jesus' Last Supper as a Passover meal (Matt 26:17-20; Mark 14:12-18; Luke 22:7-15); the Eucharist, therefore, should be seen as the new Passover meal (Jeremias, *Eucharistic Words* [1966] 15–88), especially if one takes account of the idea of memorial expressed in Luke 22:19 = 1 Cor 11:24 (cf. Exod 12:14). Jaubert (*The Date*, 57) proposes that Jesus ate his Passover on the evening of Tuesday, the day on which the fourteenth always fell according to the solar calendar of *Jubilees* and Qumran, and that he was executed on Friday, the fourteenth according to the official, lunar calendar. The arguments pro and con are given by Carmignac, *RdQ* 5 (1964) 59–79. For a different solution, see text 56, § 9.

c. (Luke 22:16) Many manuscripts read: "never eat it again." Luke implies that Jesus did not eat his own body or drink his own blood, but he does not state that Jesus abstained from eating the Passover.

d. (Luke 22:19) Codex Alexandrinus adds: "Take."

e. (Luke 22:19-20) Many manuscripts omit vv. 19b–20. Some scholars regard these words as an interpolation into the gospel text from the liturgical tradition reflected in 1 Cor 11:24-25.

f. (Matt 26:27) Many manuscripts read: "the cup."

g. (Matt 26:28) Many manuscripts add: "new."

h. (Mark 14:24) Many manuscripts read: "my blood—that of the covenant." Others read: "my blood—that of the new covenant."

i. (Matt 26:29) *Ap' arti* = "henceforth," "from now on."

j. (Mark 14:25) *Ouketi ou mê piô* = "never again will I drink."

8. The Fourth Gospel, John 19:31-37: The Fulfillment of the Passover

Critical Greek text: Aland, *The Greek New Testament*, 408.

English version used here: RSV, from *The New Oxford Annotated Bible*, 1315.

a. John puts the death of Christ on the cross in the afternoon of the fourteenth of Nisan (cf. John 18:28) so that Jesus is seen as the new paschal lamb (cf. John 1:29, 36; Rev. 5:6, 9, 12; 12:11), taking the place of the victim prescribed by the Law. Nevertheless, it is not the theological interpretation that created the chronological datum, but vice versa: thus Strobel, *ZNW* 51 (1960) 69-101, and Cadman, *Studia Patristica 5* (1962) 8-16, contrary to Huber, 111, who follows Joachim Jeremias, *TDNT* 5, 900, § 2, and others. John is simply interpreting a datum traditional in the Asiatic communities: Schürmann, *ThQ* 131 (1951) 414-425; Ziener, *BZ* n.s. 2 (1958) 263-274.

9. PAUL, 1 Corinthians 5:7-8

Critical Greek text: Aland, *The Greek New Testament*, 588.

English version used here: RSV, from *The New Oxford Annotated Bible*, 1384.

a. *To pascha hêmôn etythê*, an allusion to *thysate to pascha* (Exod 12:21). Here, as often in both Old and New Testaments (e.g., Mark 14:12; see Jeremias, *TDNT* 5, 897), *pascha* refers to the paschal lamb. The typology of the paschal lamb standing for Christ is found not only in the Johannine writings (see text 8 with note a) but also in 1 Pet 1:19.

b. *Heortazômen*. If the word has here a real and not simply metaphorical meaning, we have in this text the first historical testimony to the existence of a Christian feast of Passover, distinct from the Jewish one. Much less certain is the Christian character of the Pentecost mentioned in Acts 20:16 and 1 Cor 16:8. For the connection between the Jewish and Christian Pentecosts, see Kretschmar, *ZKG* 66 (1954-1955) 213 and 229-232. See also Boeckh, *JLH 5* (1960) 9 ff.

10. EUSEBIUS OF CAESAREA, *Ecclesiastical History* 5, 23-25

Critical Greek text: *Eusebius Werke* 2, 1, by Eduard Schwartz (GCS 9/1; Leipzig: Hinrichs, 1903) 488-498.

The first edition of the *History*, in seven books, was put out before 303, and a revised edition, in ten books, shortly after 324.

a. *Paroikiai* = "sojourning communities"—a term applied to ecclesiastical dioceses, provinces, or parishes. In this selection, it will always be translated "dioceses." (Trans.)

b. Since Pontus and Osrhoene (ch. 23, § 3) and Phoenicia (Tyre and Ptolemais, ch. 25, § 1) kept the Pascha on Sunday, "all Asia" (ch. 23, § 1; ch. 24, § 9) should not refer to Greater Asia (the present Turkey, Syria, and Lebanon) but to Asia Minor (Diocletian's diocese of Asia, comprising Proconsular Asia, Caria, Lydia, the Hellespont and Cyzicus, the islands of Lesbos, Chios, Rhodes, and Cyprus, and the two provinces of Phrygia) or to some even more restricted area in the southwestern part of the peninsula around Ephesus.

c. The apostolic origin of the celebration of the Pascha on Sunday is defended by Van Goudoever (*Biblical Calendars*, 124–129; 164–175) and Rordorf (*ThZ* 18 [1962] 167–189). Huber (45 ff.) follows Holl in setting the origin of the practice in Jerusalem around A.D. 135.

d. Narcissus (bishop from 180–192) is said to have changed water into oil for the lamps "during the great vigil of Pascha" (Eusebius, *Eccl. Hist.* 6, 9, 2–3).

e. This universal accord at the end of the second century makes it hard to believe that the Sunday observance of Pascha was not introduced before 135. See Strand, *JBL* 84 (1965) 251–258. The fifth-century historians Socrates (*Eccl. Hist.* 5, 22; ed. Hussey-Bright [Oxford 1893] 239) and Sozomen (*Eccl. Hist.* 7, 19, 1; ed. Bidez, 330) tell us that the practice goes back to Peter and Paul, just as the Quartodeciman usage goes back to John.

f. Victor had probably claimed the authority of Peter and Paul, who are buried at Rome.

g. Jerome's Latin version agrees with some Greek codices in reading: "will raise up."

h. *To petalon*, the engraved metal plate attached to the Jewish high priest's headdress (Exod 28:36-38).

i. Polycrates is quoted previously in the *Ecclesiastical History* (3, 31, 3) as testifying to the burial of John at Ephesus. His title of martyr derives from the tradition that he was tortured under Domitian (ibid. 20, 1 ff.)

j. Sagaris was martyred between 164 and 166: see text 25.

k. Here, as in Clement of Alexandria, *Miscellanies* 3, 105, 1, and *Pedagogue* 3, 4, "eunuch" means one who voluntarily remained unmarried rather than one who was mutilated.

l. The mention of Melito in this context leaves no doubt about his being a Quartodeciman. See what I wrote in *RSLR* 6 (1970) 259–267 against the contrary view of Huber, 31 ff.

m. *Episkopê*, as interpreted by Mohrmann, *VigChr* 16 (1962) 157, and contrary to Nautin, *Lettres*, 67, who translates it as "episcopate"; for other instances of the term in the sense of "divine visitation" see *PGL*, 532.

n. The Jews.

o. The day on which the Pascha was to be celebrated (Richard), or the day on which the fast was to be concluded (Nautin and Campenhausen). See note s below.

p. Approximately the time from Christ's crucifixion to his resurrection, namely, from noon on Friday to dawn (about 4 a.m.) on Sunday.

q. With this list, Irenaeus does not deny the observance of the Pascha at Rome before the time of Xystus; he is only giving a series of examples. See Rordorf, *ThZ* 18 (1962) 169.

r. This is the crucial passage for understanding the status of the Pascha before Victor. The object of the verb "observe" (or "not observe") may be either the fourteenth of Nisan, or the feast of the Pascha, or the paschal fast. See the Introduction, Part IV.

s. An obscure phrase. Keeping in mind the three possible interpretations of "observe," we can say that what the Romans before Victor found objectionable was either (a) the observance of 14 Nisan at Rome by those who came from Asia (as Mohrmann and others hold), or (b) the introduction of the yearly feast of the Pascha under Soter, though by this time the disagreement would only be about the date on which it should be celebrated (Holl, Richard), or (c) the introduction of a fast before the Pascha, an observance allegedly unknown at Rome before Soter, though common elsewhere (Zahn, Campenhausen).

t. On this custom of the Roman church, see La Piana, HThR 18 (1925) 215–218.

u. Polycarp's visit to Rome under Anicetus is mentioned by Irenaeus, *Against the Heresies* 3, 3, 4. According to Eusebius, *Eccl. Hist.* 4, 14, 1, Polycarp went to Rome to confer with Anicetus "because of some controversy about the day for the Pascha." This seems to exclude Campenhausen's opinion (Introduction, Part IV) that the visit was about the paschal fast—unless, as Campenhausen suggests (*VigChr* 28 [1974] 136 ff.), Eusebius has modified the report.

v. Anicetus, who as local bishop normally presided at the liturgy, allowed his guest to preside in his place, or, as B. Lohse thinks (*Passafest*, 60), to distribute the Eucharist to the various Christian communities in Rome.

11. HIPPOLYTUS OF ROME, *Refutation of All the Heresies* 8, 18, 1-2

Critical edition: Paul Wendland, *Hippolytus Werke*, 3 (Leipzig: Hinrichs, 1916), 237-238.

a. According to Schwartz, *ZNW* 7 (1906) = *Gesammelte Schriften* 5 (1963) 18, Hippolytus is alluding to Blastos (see text 99); but it is more probable that he is referring to the Quartodecimans in general.

b. *Anairein* means either "exalt" or "kill"; hence the sentence may also be translated: "They pay no attention to the fact that it was enacted for the Jews who were to kill the true Pascha. Which [Law] has spread to the Gentiles and is understood by faith . . ." (*Philosophumena or the Refutation of all Heresies*, formerly attributed to Origen but now to Hippolytus, trans. Francis Legge [London: S.P.C.K., 1921] 2:113).

c. The meaning is: if the Quartodecimans want to hold to the Mosaic Law in celebrating the Pascha, then they ought to observe the whole Law, including the prohibition of celebrating the Pascha outside Jerusalem (Deut 16:5-6). In Justin (text 18), the prohibition is said to be a prophecy that all sacrifices would be abolished after the destruction of Jerusalem. Aphraates uses the prohibition to impugn the legitimacy of Jewish festivals and of the Pascha in particular (*Demonstratio* 12, 3-4).

d. This is Epiphanius' source for his report on the Quartodecimans, *Panarion* 50, 4, 4-8. His odd accusation that the Quartodecimans celebrate the Pascha "only once a year" is to be understood against his fourth-century background, in which the weekly Pascha, i.e. the Sunday celebration (see text 56, § 7), has taken on such importance. For further reports on the Quartodecimans, see Huber, 84-88.

12. *The Gospel of the Ebionites*, Quotation

Source: Epiphanius, *Panarion*, 30, 22, 4.

Critical edition: *Epiphanius*, vol. 1, ed. Karl Holl (GCS 25; Leipzig: Hinrichs, 1915), 363.

This *Gospel* was probably written in Greek between A.D. 120 and 140, possibly in the region east of the Jordan.

a. *Tēn tēs alētheias akolouthian* = "the logical sequence of ideas in the Gospels."

b. Montague Rhodes James (*The Apocryphal New Testament*, corrected ed. [Oxford: Clarendon, 1953], 10) translates: "as is plain to all from the combination of phrases." James Ogg (Hennecke, *New Testament Apocrypha* 1:158) translates: "But they abandon the proper sequence of the words and pervert the saying, as is plain to all from the readings attached." By "readings" Ogg probably means the other citations of the gospels in Epiphanius's document.

c. Matt 26:17; cf. Mark 14:12 and Luke 22:8-9.

d. The Ebionites take Jesus' statement, "I have set my heart on eating this Pascha with you" (Luke 22:15), as a question: "Have I set my heart on eating this Pascha with you?" and make this interpretation explicit by adding the ironical *mê* ("Is it not so?"). They also add the word *kreas* (flesh meat) to make clear that "this Pascha" means the lamb. Thus this *Gospel* portrays Jesus as refusing to eat meat. Ebionites were vegetarians (Epiphanius, *Panarion* 30, 15, 3; trans. Williams, 131); they celebrated the Pascha with unleavened bread and water, no more than once a year (ibid. 30, 16, 1). Marcion too, according to Epiphanius (ibid. 42, 11, 15, *Elenchus* 61; trans. Williams, 309–310), would not admit that the Savior ate the lamb; he interpreted "Pascha" in Luke 22:15 with reference to the Eucharist ("the mystery he was about to accomplish").

13. *The Gospel of the Hebrews*, **Indirect Quotation**

> Source: Codex Vaticanus Reginensis Latinus 49 (tenth century, Britain).

> Edition: André Wilmart in *Analecta Reginensia (StT* 59; Vatican City: Biblioteca Apostolica Vaticana, 1933) 58.

This *Gospel* was written for Greek-speaking Jewish Christians, possibly in Egypt, in the first half of the second century A.D. Jerome found it in use by Jewish Christians at Beroea in Syria.

a. *Post remi(ssionem) pascae* = "after breaking the fast of the Pascha." (Trans.)

b. The notion that the Judgment will come at Eastertime is not found in the surviving fragments of this *apocryphon* (for which see Hennecke, *New Testament Apocrypha* 1:163-165). If this citation in the codex Vat. Reg. Lat. 49 is authentic and this passage actually stood in the *Gospel of the Hebrews*, it may be the basis of Jerome's report about the tradition of expecting the parousia in the paschal night (text 113; cf. Lactantius, text 103; see also text 5 with notes j and k, and text 15 with note b).

14. *The Epistle of the Apostles*, **15**

> The Greek or Syriac original is lost. The Ethiopian version (ch. 1–62) with a French translation was published by Louis Guerrier as *Le Testament en Galilée de Notre Seigneur Jésus-*

Christ in PO 9/3 (1913). Ch. 15 is on 198–199. A German translation of the incomplete Coptic version (ch. 7–31, 38–48) and Isaak Wajnberg's German translation of the Ethiopian, together with fragments of a Latin version (ch. 12–17), was published by Carl Schmidt as *Gespräche Jesu mit seinen Jüngern nach der Auferstehung* (TU 43; Leipzig: Hinrichs, 1919; reprinted Hildesheim: Georg Olms, 1967). Ch. 15 is on 52–59.

A revision of the German translations of the Coptic and Ethiopian versions in Schmidt's edition was published as *Epistula Apostolorum nach dem äthiopischen und koptischen Texte* by Hugo Duensing (Kleine Texte für Vorlesungen und Übungen, 152; Bonn: Marcus & Weber, 1925).

Some scholars date this work to the first half, others to the second half of the second century A.D.; some place its composition in Egypt, others in Syria (see Manfred Hornschuh, *Studien zur Epistula Apostolorum* [Patristische Texte und Studien 5; Berlin: de Gruyter, 1965]). It was written to refute the Gnostic idea that Christ's body was unreal and to assure Christians that the parousia would occur soon.

a. Ethiopian version: "Thereupon I returned to my Father. 15. As to you, celebrate the remembrance of my death (cf. 1 Cor 11:24-26), that is, the Pascha." This equation of Pascha with the remembrance of Christ's death led some (notably Schmidt, *Gespräche*, 579) to suppose that the document originated in a Quartodeciman milieu, in which the Pascha commemorated exclusively the passion; but in the second century, non-Quartodecimans too thought of Pascha as *pathos* or *passio* (see Cantalamessa, *La Pasqua della nostra salvezza*, 158–171). In any case, it is only the Ethiopic version (made perhaps thirty years later than the Coptic and probably from an intermediary Arabic version) that puts the Pascha into apposition with the remembrance of Christ's death, so that this idea may well be absent from the original. (Trans.)

b. Here we have already the constitutive elements of the paschal celebration: vigil until cockcrow (cf. text 49, note 2) and the celebration of the Eucharist (as we see from "remembrance of me" and "Agape").

c. "Drink the cup" means "undergo the passion" (Matt 20:22-23; 26:39; Mark 10:38-39; 14:36; Luke 22:42). "Take the cup and drink" may also have a Eucharistic connotation (cf. Matt 26:27; Luke 22:17). The Ethiopian version is: "Lord, did you not complete the drinking of the Pascha? Are we obliged to do it again?" "Drink the Pascha" is an original phrase, which takes for granted the equivalence of "Pascha" and "passion." (Trans.)

d. Ethiopian version: "And he said to us, 'Yes, until I shall come from the Father with my wounds.'"

15. *The Epistle of the Apostles,* **17**

Edition with French translation of the Ethiopian version in Guerrier, PO 9/3 (1913) 199. German translations of the Coptic and Ethiopic versions in Carl Schmidt, *Gespräche,* 57–59. Revised German translation: Duensing, 14–15.

a. "Year" has evidently been omitted (not "part" as Schmidt and Duensing have it; see Gry, *RB* 49 (1940) 89. The Ethiopian version has: "when the hundred-and-fiftieth year is completed." (Trans.)

b. The Ethiopian version has: "between the Pentecost and the Pascha." Since Jesus is represented as predicting not only the year but also the day of his parousia, it would be absurd to understand this as referring to the ten-and-a-half-month period after the Pentecost and before the Pascha or Unleavened Bread. The author must mean the period before the Pentecost (or before the day of Pentecost) and after the Pascha. Hence Louis Gry (*RB* 49 [1940] 89–91) attributed a series of scribal errors to the translators or copyists of the document and reconstructed the underlying Greek text to read "on the feast of the Pascha." Then, recalling that some rabbis predicted the judgment of humankind for Pesach, A.D. 119, he suggested that our Christian author wished to predict the parousia for the same date, which he would have calculated as marking the completion of one hundred twenty years after the incarnation. Soon after, when the parousia did not occur, the date would have been changed by a copyist or by the Arabic or Ethiopian translator to one hundred fifty years. If, however, we retain the actual wording of the Coptic and Ethiopic versions and understand it as referring to the brief interval before the Pentecost and after the Pascha or first day of Unleavened Bread, we have a prediction of the parousia occurring after the fifteenth of Nisan and before the beginning of the counting of the *'omer* on the sixteenth (with the Pharisees) or on the following Sunday (with the Sadducees). This would be during the night leading to the sixteenth (the night of the resurrection) or during the handful of days which occurred in most years between the fifteenth and the following Sunday. In Churches which kept the Pascha on Friday and Saturday following the fourteenth, this would be during the night leading to Sunday, the time which soon became the paschal vigil for the greater part of the Church. (Lactantius, in text 103, expected the parousia during the paschal vigil, and Jerome, in text 113, records it as a belief based on an apostolic tradition.) One good manuscript of the Ethiopian version reads, "in the days of the Pentecost and of the Pascha," showing that the copyist was not sure that a particular day was meant, but was sure of the season. (Tertullian testifies to the expectation of the parousia during the Pentecost; see text 93 with note b.) (Trans.)

c. Cf. John 10:38; 14:10-20; 17:21-23. Gry, *RB* 49 (1940) 92, note 3, thought that "the coming of the Father" might be an adaptation of a Jewish phrase. Cf. *heôs parousias tou theou tês dikaiosynês* in the *Testament of Judah* 22, 2; *Testamenta XII Patriarcharum*, ed. Marinus de Jonge (Leiden: Brill, 1964) 34.

16. HERACLEON, Fragment 12

> Source: Origen, *Commentary on John* 10, 116-117.
>
> Critical text: *Origenes Werke* 4, *Der Johanneskommentar*, ed. Erwin Preuschen (GCS 10; Leipzig: Hinrichs, 1903) 190-191.
>
> All the fragments of Heracleon were collected by Werner Foerster in *Gnosis*, trans. R. McL. Wilson (Oxford: Clarendon, 1972), 1:162-183.

A disciple of Valentinus in the second half of the second century, Heracleon explained everything in John's Gospel as a symbol of some Gnostic doctrine. This quotation comes after Origen has explained "the Pascha of the Jews" (John 2:13).

a. The Gnostics of the second century also thought of *pascha* as *pathos*; indeed, the Barbelo-Gnostics took *pathos* in the sense of sexual passion and gave Pascha an obscene meaning (Epiphanius, *Panarion* 26, 4, 5-7; trans. Williams, 86).

b. In Valentinian Gnosticism, the wedding is the union of the aeons Christ and Sophia in the Pleroma; the "spiritual" race of mortals will enjoy it when, having laid aside body and soul, their spiritual elements become the brides of their angels. Heracleon makes eating the paschal lamb (and perhaps also the Christian Eucharist) a symbol of this esoteric idea. (Trans.). Heracleon mentions the "wedding" again in fragment 38 (Origen, *Commentary on John* 13, 349, ed. Preuschen, 281). Cf. Theodotus, *Excerpts* 64 (François Sagnard, *Clément d'Alexandrie, Extraits de Théodote* [SC 23; Paris: Cerf, 1948] 187), and *The Gospel of Philip* 115f. (trans. R. McL. Wilson [London: Mowbray, 1962] 43ff.

17. PTOLEMY, *Letter to Flora* 5, 8-10. 13-15

> Critical text: *Ptolémée, Lettre à Flora*, ed. Gilles Quispel, 2e ed. (SC 24 bis; Paris: Cerf, 1966) 62-66.

Writing in the second century, Ptolemy introduces Flora to Valentinian doctrines through an exegesis of the Scriptures. In ch. 4, he divides the Old Law into three parts: the commandments of God, those of Moses, and those of the elders of the people. Then, in ch. 5, he divides the commandments of God into three parts: the pure, eternally valid laws, those mixed with evil and injustice, and the typical, symbolic legislation. This last, he maintains (5, 2 and 6, 4), is now meant only to symbolize invisible realities.

a. The need to fast from evil-doing more than from bodily foods will likewise be the theme of much patristic preaching in the third and fourth centuries; see Arbesmann, *RAC* 7 (1969) 490-491.

b. Since the orthodox Christians observed the Pascha with fast and vigil on a definite day, Ptolemy and most other Gnostics probably rejected its ritual observance.

18. JUSTIN, *Dialogue with Trypho* 40, 1-3

> Edition: *Die ältesten Apologeten,* ed. Edgar Goodspeed (Göttingen: Vandenhoeck & Ruprecht, 1914) 137.
>
> English translation used here: *Saint Justin, Martyr, . . . Dialogue with Trypho,* trans. by Thomas B. Falls (FC 6; New York: Christian Heritage, 1948) 208-9.

The *Dialogue* was certainly written after 155, but may be based on disputations held in Ephesus A.D. 132-135.

a. This is probably an allusion to the rite of post-baptismal anointing, seen as the antitype of Exodus 12:7. The theme is carried out in the same fashion by Melito, *On the Pascha* 67 (text 22); Pseudo-Hippolytus, *Homily on the Holy Pascha* 15 (ed. Nautin, SC 27, 142-143); Eusebius, text 56, § 2. See Cantalamessa, *L'omelia,* 308ff.

b. More exactly: "the clay out of which God moulded Adam."

c. See also *Dialogue* 46, 2.

d. "Suffering" translates the Greek *pathos* and "undergo" translates *paschein.* Hence the phrase seems to anticipate the well-known equation of *pascha* with *paschein* (see texts 21 and 102).

19. JUSTIN, *Dialogue with Trypho* 111, 3

> Edition: Goodspeed, 227-228.
>
> English translation used here: Falls, 319-320.

a. The same identification of the Pascha with Christ, based on 1 Corinthians 5:7, is found in *Dialogue* 72, 1, and in Melito (see text 22, note a), in dependence on a Christian interpolation in Neh 6:19-21 (see Lactantius, *Divine Institutes* 4, 18, 22; *CSEL* 19, 355-56).

b. On the chronological problem posed by this affirmation and by Irenaeus, *Against the Heresies* II 22, 3; IV 10, 1 (cf. text 28), see Cantalamessa, *L'omelia*, 74-75 and notes.

20. MELITO OF SARDIS, *On the Pascha*, 1-10: Introduction

> Critical edition: Stuart George Hall, *Melito of Sardis: On Pascha, and Fragments*: Texts and Translations (Oxford: Clarendon, 1979) 3-7, from which we have taken the English translation and the arrangement in rhetorical cola.

Written perhaps between A.D. 160 and 170 in Asia Minor, this homily, in which the author attempts to express Christian doctrine in the style of the Second Sophistic period, may have been recited with the kind of cantillation customary in Scripture reading (E. J. Wellesz, *JThS* 44 [1943] 41-52). It was mistakenly entitled *On the Passion* by its first editor, Campbell Bonner, but the correct title is found in Papyrus Bodmer XIII (ed. M. Testuz, Geneva 1960). Authorship, dating, and the restoration of the text are discussed in Hall's *Melito of Sardis*, pp. xi-xxii.

a. *Hê men graphê tês Hebraïkês exodou* = "the Scripture from the Hebraic *Exodus*," that is, from the book entitled *Exodus* (see Hall, "Melito: Peri Pascha 1 and 2," 236-248). It does not mean "the Scripture about the Exodus of the Hebrews"; Melito does not comment on Exodus 13-14, the passage of the Red Sea, but on Exodus 12, the laws concerning Pesach and the sacrifice of the lamb.

b. *Diasesaphêtai* does not mean "interpreted" in the sense of being translated, as though the passage had been read first in Hebrew and then translated into Greek as was customary in the synagogues—contrary to Zuntz, *HThR* 36 (1943) 299-315. Nor does it refer to a preliminary literal explanation given by the reader, as Bonner suggested, *HThR* 31 (1938) 175ff., 36 (1943) 317ff. Nor need it signify a preliminary exegetical-theological interpretation, of the kind found in the second-century Asiatic Pseudo-Hippolytus, *On the Pascha* 16-42, as I suggested in *L'omelia*, 434-437, following Perler, *Méliton*, 131-132. Rather it refers to the "plain statement" of the mystery in the very words of Exodus 12, which Melito goes on to summarize in lines 3-5. The "understanding of the mystery," that is, "the explanation of the type and of its corresponding reality" (§ 46), will be given in §§ 2-45. (For *diasapheô* as "state plainly," see Hall, "Melito, Peri Pascha 1 and 2," 236-248.)

c. This line is found in the Latin and Georgian versions, not in the Greek.

d. This is the earliest occurrence of this expression. It is the equivalent of "the mystery of Christ" of Ephesians 3:4 and Colossians 4:3. Cf. text 22, § 65: "The mystery of the Pascha, which is Christ."

e. *Typos.*

f. *Eis gên* = "in (the) earth." This was probably found in the Greek manuscripts before they were damaged, according to Hall, *Melito of Sardis*, 2, since the Georgian version has the equivalent, though the Latin omits the phrase.

g. *Mê syntribeis*, according to the conjecture of Testuz adopted by Hall, based on John 19:36 and Exodus 12:10. The Georgian version has: "not eaten." Perler drops the negative and conjectures: *sphageis*, "slaughtered."

h. Three Latin manuscripts have "Lord"; one has "God."

i. The New Testament designates the paschal victim only by a term meaning "lamb" (*amnos* or *arnion*); later tradition, bringing in Isa 53:7, applies either *amnos* or *probaton* to Christ. Melito is the only one to make a distinction between the two terms: he reserves *probaton* (probably in the sense of sheep or goat) to denote Christ as man, and *amnos* to denote him as God or the Son of God (see § 7). Gregory of Nazianzus makes a similar distinction in oration 30, 21.

j. *Hê tou haimatos pompê* means "the rite of the blood." This is Hall's conjecture, following the Georgian version, "the shedding of the blood." The Chester Beatty papyrus reads: "the ritual of the lamb." Papyrus Bodmer XIII reads: *typos tou pascha pompê*, which Perler emends to *hê tou pascha pompê* means "the rite of the Pascha."

k. *En tôi neôi logôi* means "in the new word." The translation of the last four cola of § 6 is from Gerald F. Hawthorne, "A New Translation of Melito's Paschal Homily," in *Current Issues in Biblical and Patristic Interpretation: Studies in Honor of Merrill C. Tenney,* ed. Gerald F. Hawthorne (Grand Rapids, Michigan: Eerdmans, 1975). Hall translates them: "and the scripture from the law have reached as far as Christ, on whose account were all things in the ancient law, or rather, in the recent word."

l. Isa 2:3; cf. Mic 4:2.

m. § 8 is in Hawthorne's translation.

n. On the theme of Christ as Nomos and Logos, Law and Word, see Cantalamessa, *L'omelia*, 155–157.

o. On the meaning of this apparently modalist phrase, see Cantalamessa, *RSLR* 3 (1967) 16ff.

21. MELITO OF SARDIS, *On the Pascha*, 46:
The Mystery of the Pascha

> Critical edition and translation: Hall, *Melito of Sardis*, 22 and 24.

a. *Paschein* is the present infinitive, *pathein* the aorist infinitive of the same verb, which means "undergo" or "suffer." Here *paschein* is a pun on *Pascha*, as though it meant "to keep Pascha." The naive etymology (deriving a Hebrew from a Greek word) originated among the Asiatic Quartodecimans (but see also text 3, note a). Despite Origen's opposition (see text 37), it became widespread, especially among the Latins (see texts 95, 98, 100, 117, and Mohrmann, *EL* 66 [1952] 37–52). For the underlying paschal theology, see Cantalamessa, *La Pasqua della nostra salvezza*, 158ff.

22. MELITO OF SARDIS, *On the Pascha*, 65–69:
Redemption through Christ

> Critical edition and translation: Hall, *Melito of Sardis*, 34–37 (altered).

a. Cf. text 19. "The mystery of the Pascha" (mentioned also in text 20, § 2) is identified with Christ inasmuch as he constitutes its unique content from the very beginning: at first as model (*typos*) and ultimately as reality (*alêtheia*).

b. *pathê* means "sufferings," "passions."

c. The theme of the *passio* and the *compassio* is developed as a polemic against the Valentinians and against Theodotus in particular; see Cantalamessa, "Les homélies," 263–266.

d. *Esphragisen*: cf. Eph 1:13; 4:30; 2 Cor 1:22.

e. The foregoing four antitheses are borrowed from the Jewish Haggadah for Pesach (see text 6). On the relations between the Jewish Haggadah and the primitive Christian homiletic, see Cantalamessa, *L'omelia*, 428–447.

f. Cf. Exod 19:6; 1 Pet 2:5, 9; Rev 1:6; 5:10.

g. Cf. Exod 19:5.

h. As below, § 103 (text 24), *Pascha tês sôtêrias* describes Christ as the paschal lamb that saves—a fair summary of the whole document. The expression shows that by Melito's time at least, the Quartodeciman Pascha had a soteriological (and consequently a historical and commemorative) character. B. Lohse (*Passafest*, 118–121) maintains that originally it was purely eschatological—a fast for the Jews and a vigil with the Eucharist to express the expectation of the parousia. While the thought of Christ's death could hardly be absent from this primitive Pascha, it became the main content of the Quartodeciman feast only after the expectation of an imminent parousia had faded—namely, during the late second and the third centuries. (Trans.)

23. MELITO OF SARDIS, *On the Pascha*, 71: Redemption through Christ

Critical edition and translation: Hall, *Melito of Sardis*, 38–39.

a. Cf. Isa 53:7; Acts 8:32.

b. This unusual title for Mary is taken up by Romanos Melodos in Hymn 35, stanza 1 (*Romanos le Mélode, Hymnes,* ed. José Grosdidier de Matons, vol. 4 [SC 128; Paris: Cerf, 1967] 160), which is used in the Byzantine liturgy (*Triodion* for the Parasceve). It is also found in *Hymns to the Virgin* 9, 3, formerly attributed to Ephraem the Syrian; see *S. Ephraemi Hymni et Sermones*, ed. T. J. Lamy [Mechlin 1886] 2:520-642.

c. Cf. Exod 12:3-5.

d. Cf. Isa 53:7.

e. The lamb was to be slaughtered toward evening and totally consumed during the night (Exod 12:6, 8, 10). Following the Johannine chronology, Melito puts the death of Christ at evening on the fourteenth of Nisan, when the lambs were being slaughtered in the Temple.

f. Cf. John 19:36; Exod 12:10 (LXX), 46.

24. MELITO OF SARDIS, *On the Pascha*, 100-103: The Triumph of Christ

Critical edition and translation: Hall, *Melito of Sardis*, 56–59.

a. This phrase, which occurs twice, may also be translated: " 'I,' he says, 'am the Christ' " (Hawthorne, 173), or: " 'It is I,' he says, 'the Christ.' " (Trans.)

b. *Thriambeusas*. The same verb is used in Pseudo-Hippolytus, *On the Holy Pascha* 55, 1 (Nautin, *Homélies pascales*, 1:183); its source is perhaps Colossians 2:15.

c. Cf. Mark 3:27. In this, the first paschal catechesis, the descent into hell is seen as an integral part of Christ's victory and resurrection, and as his first act of salvation. See also Melito, fragment 13 (Perler, *Méliton de Sardes*, 238); Pseudo-Hippolytus, *On the Holy Pascha* 58 (Nautin, *Homélies pascales*, 1:186); Grillmeier, *ZKTh* 71 (1949) 5–14; Perler, *Méliton de Sardes*, 201–203.

d. *Pephyramenai* means "kneaded into a paste." Hall has "compounded."

e. Bonner sees here an Oriental influence (cf. Wifstrand, *VigChr* 2 [1948] 201ff.), but Melito is only taking up and developing the *Ego eimi* formula of the Fourth Gospel (John 8:12; 11:25; 14:26). He sounds a note of apotheosis and cultic epiphany (Blank, 89), thus underlining the Johannine character of his eschatology, which conceives salvation as already realized.

f. *To pascha tês sôtêrias* means "the paschal lamb that saves," a metaphor partially explained by the preceding and following clauses. (Trans.)

g. *Lytron*. Papyrus Bodmer XIII, followed by the Coptic version, has *loutron* mean "bath" (referring to baptism).

h. Cf. John 11:25; 14:6. The Chester Beatty papyrus omits: "I am your life."

i. The Chester Beatty papyrus has "Savior"; the Georgian version has "liberator of creatures."

j. The preceding five cola are in different order in different manuscripts. Blank, Perler, and Testuz adopt this reading: "I am your life, I am your resurrection, I am your light, I am your salvation, I am your king."

k. Papyrus Bodmer XIII and Chester Beatty put this colon at the end of the section, after "ages past"; the Georgian versions omit it.

l. Papyrus Bodmer XIII adds: "I will raise you up."

m. "There" is found only in Papyrus Bodmer XIII.

n. The Latin version omits everything from "I am leading" to "ages past."

25. MELITO OF SARDIS, Another Work *On the Pascha*, Quotation

Source: Eusebius of Caesarea, *Eccl. Hist.* 4, 26, 3

Critical text: Eduard Schwartz, *Eusebius Werke* 2/1 (GCS 9/1; Leipzig: Hinrichs, 1903) 382.

a. According to Perler, "Ein Hymnus," 25ff., Eusebius is referring to the recently recovered work *On the Pascha*, from which we have taken texts 20–24; but this is hardly probable, since this homily contains no discussion whatever of the date of the Pascha. Rather, Eusebius must be quoting from the lost treatise mentioned by Clement of Alexandria (see text 35).

b. Servillius Paulus is not known from the history of the second century; Rufinus here substitutes "Sergius Paulus." There was one "L. Sergius Paullus," who served as consul for the second time in 168; he may have been the proconsul of Asia in 166–168. See Perler, *Méliton de Sardes*, 23–24.

c. To judge from the ancient texts which echo this "discussion" (see Cantalamessa, *L'omelia*, 67–68), the controversy seems to have been confined to the Quartodeciman Churches, where someone wished to adopt the chronology of the Synoptics in place of that of John and celebrate the Pascha on the fifteenth of Nisan (cf. text 26).

d. Or: "fell at the right time." Perhaps this means that the Pascha that year fell after the spring equinox—a matter of grave concern to the Church a century and a half later (see texts 50–53). (Trans.)

26. APOLLINARIUS OF HIERAPOLIS, *On the Pascha*, Fragments

Source: *The Paschal Chronicle* (about A.D. 630).
Edition: *Paschalion seu Chronicon paschale* ed. Ludovicus Dindorf (Corpus Scriptorum Historiae Byzantinae, 16; Bonn: E. Weber, 1832) 1:13–14, repr. in *PG* 92, 79–81.

This lost treatise was written about A.D. 166. In *The Paschal Chronicle* the author's name is written "Apollinarios," but in Latin writers usually "Apollinaris."

a. The accord between Apollinarius and Hippolytus previously mentioned in the *Chronicle* (see text 46) does not concern the day of the Pascha, since Apollinarius is a Quartodeciman and Hippolytus an opponent of that usage (see text 11). Rather, they agree about the date of Christ's death, both accepting the Johannine date, the fourteenth of Nisan; see Cantalamessa, *L'omelia*, 70ff.

b. In all likelihood, this is the controversy at Laodicea mentioned in text 25.

c. Perhaps an allusion to the legal prohibition of executions on feast days.

d. That is, the Synoptics would contradict the Gospel of John (Duchesne, *RQH* 28 [1880] 9). However, the sentence could also be translated: "their opinion disagrees with the Law, and the Gospels seem to stand against them." (Trans.)

e. Apollinaris's position is that the true Pascha consists in the immolation of Christ in place of the lamb; since this occurred on the fourteenth of Nisan, the Pascha should be celebrated on that date. The adversaries, arguing, it seems, from Matthew, commemorated Jesus' paschal supper on the fourteenth and his death on the fifteenth.

f. The horns of the unicorn (mentioned in Ps 21:22 and Deut 33:17 in the LXX version) symbolize the cross, here and in Justin, *Dialogue with Trypho* 91, 2.

27a. AN UNNAMED QUARTODECIMAN (PSEUDO-HIPPOLYTUS), *Homily on the Holy Pascha*, 1-3

Critical edition: *Homélies pascales*, vol. I, *Une homélie inspirée du traité sur la Pâque d'Hippolyte*, ed. Pierre Nautin (SC 27; Paris: Cerf, 1950), 117-123. The original is extant in two recensions: (a) and (b). And most recently: Giuseppe Visonà, *Pseudo Ippolito, In sanctum Pascha. Studio, edizione, commento* (Studia Patristica Mediolanensia, 15; Milan: Vita e Pensiero, 1988).

Published in the seventeenth and eighteenth centuries among the spurious works of John Chrysostom (*Eis to pascha*, 6; *PG* 59, 735-746), since 1926 this homily has been variously attributed to Hippolytus of Rome, to an unknown follower of his (Pseudo-Hippolytus), or even to an unknown Monarchian. It was certainly used by Proclus of Constantinople (d. 446). In 1950 Nautin ascribed it to an unknown fourth- or fifth-century homilist who based his work on the lost treatise *On the Pascha* by a certain Hippolytus of the second or third century (cf. Nautin, *Lettres*, 203-207). But the homily is clearly sister to that of Melito and a product of the theology of Asia Minor in the second half of the second century; see Cantalamessa, *L'omelia*, 452-460.

As a hymn to Christ, the light and the life, this homily is a forerunner of the *laus cerei* (the *Exultet*), and contains several of its characteristic themes. For a detailed commentary, see Cantalamessa, *L'omelia*, 96-108.

a. In place of "spirit" the oldest manuscript (Cryptoferratensis B.a.LV, 8th-9th cent.) reads: "father."

b. Cf. Ps 109:3 LXX. Recension b has: "he who was begotten before the morning star, immortal and immense . . . ."

c. The "great shining day" here does not signify the Sunday of the Resurrection but, in accordance with the Quartodeciman conception, the day of Christ's death. See Apollinarius of Hierapolis in text 26: "The fourteenth is the true Pascha of the Lord."

d. The basic pattern of the entire homily (the ancient Pascha, model for the reality; the new Pascha, reality foreshadowed by the model) is expressed here in this distich. It is identical with that of Melito (see text 20).

e. The meaning of these antitheses is: *our* impassibility out of *his* suffering, *our* immortality out of *his* mortality, etc.

f. The coming of Christ upon the earth is represented under the Hellenistic image of an imperial visitation (*parousia*, here called *epidêmia*).

g. This concept of the typology is quite close to Melito's in *On the Pascha*, §§ 35-38. For an explanation of the affinity of the two works, see Cantalamessa, *L'omelia*, 45-65 and in particular 63.

h. The manuscripts read either *ho logos ho kratêr* or *logos ho kratêr*. Nautin conjectures *ho logos [kai] ho kratêr*, "the Word and the chalice." We follow Richard, 277, in reading *holos ho kratêr*.

i. Recension b adds: "was led as a sheep to slaughter."

j. Throughout this homily, "divine spirit" signifies the Word, or more precisely, Christ's divine nature, and only rarely the charism of biblical inspiration. On the pneumatology of this homily, see what I wrote in *L'omelia*, 171-185.

k. This celebration of the entire Christ-event, from his descent to earth to his passion, is comprehensible only as the product of an age when the Pascha still celebrated the whole Christian mystery and no other liturgical feasts existed. See *L'omelia*, 393-395.

l. *Apostolê*, the Father's sending of the Word in the incarnation; cf. Eusebius, *Eccl. Hist.* I 13, 20.

m. *Trophê*. The recension from which most editions derive (Nautin, *Homélies pascales*, vol. I [SC 27], 16-30) has *truphê*, "delight."

n. *Teletê*, one of the many terms that the homilist borrows from the language of the mystery religions. See Cantalamessa, *L'omelia*, 374. Cryptoferratensis B.a.LV (recension a) has *telê*, "consummations" or "consecrations."

27b. AN UNNAMED QUARTODECIMAN (PSEUDO-HIPPOLYTUS), *Homily on the Holy Pascha* 17, 1-3

Critical edition: Nautin, *Homélies pascales* 1 (SC 27), 145-149.

a. All the manuscripts omit "why" and have "thus" instead of "this," which is unintelligible.

b. *Ho tôn holôn technitês kai dêmiourgos theos.* All except the oldest manuscript have: *ho tôn kairôn kyrios kai dêmiourgos theos,* "the Lord of seasons and creator God."

c. This interpretation of Exodus 12:2, according to which the month of Pesach is the first month because in it the world began, is found already in Philo, *On the Special Laws* 2, 28, 150–152. Our homilist's assertion that the tradition was a secret, or rather a "private," one, that is, not contained in the inspired books, is justified by rabbinic statements: see Le Déaut, *La nuit pascale,* 218–237.

d. A similar conviction is expressed by Gregory of Nazianzus in oration 45, 14.

e. Two closely related manuscripts of the sixteenth or seventeenth century have "visible."

27c. AN UNNAMED QUARTODECIMAN (PSEUDO-HIPPOLYTUS), *Homily on the Holy Pascha,* 49–50

Critical edition: Nautin, *Homélies pascales* I (SC 27) 175–177.

a. The sentence alludes to the well-known equation of *Pascha* with *pathos,* found also in chapter 11 of this homily.

b. *Pathei pathous eleutherôse.* This may also mean: "by (his) passion he freed (us) from passion." (Trans.)

c. With these words the author takes the side of those who, following the Johannine chronology, maintained that, in the year of his death, Jesus did not eat the legal Pesach supper but let his death on 14 Nisan take its place. Cf. texts 26, 36, and 45.

d. Or: "passion."

e. That is, "from the tree." This Christological *testimonium* taken from Deut 28:66 is also found in Melito, *On the Pascha* 61 (Hall, *Melito of Sardis,* 32–33 with note 28). See also Jean Daniélou, *Études d'exégèse judéo-chrétienne* (Paris: Beauchesne, 1966), 53–75. The whole passage develops the idea of the Pascha as a return to Paradise.

f. That is, of the life-giving food on the tree, eaten by Christians in the paschal meal of the Eucharist. (Trans.)

27d. AN UNNAMED QUARTODECIMAN (PSEUDO-HIPPOLYTUS), *Homily on the Holy Pascha* 62, 1–4

Critical edition: Nautin, *Homélies pascales* I (SC 27) 181–191.

Up to this point the homilist has spoken of the Pascha as a feast; in the following passage he addresses the Pascha as a person, having Christ in mind. *Pascha*, therefore, in this passage might be translated: "paschal victim." (Trans.)

a. *Chorêgia*, the technical term in the classical world for the financing of a public festivity by a *chorêgos*. The Pascha is the feast of the whole world, for which Christ has paid with his blood.

b. The "man" who "ascended as God" is the humanity of the Savior and with it all of humanity. For a more detailed commentary on the entire hymn, see Cantalamessa, *I più antichi testi pasquali*, 130-132.

· c. Perhaps to answer them in antiphonal song, as in a theater (Nautin, *Homélies pascales* 1:190), or to fill out their numbers. (Trans.)

d. *Daidouchia* means "torch-bearing," another technical term from the Eleusinian mysteries. See Clement of Alexandria, *Protrepticus* 2, 22, 6-7.

e. I should prefer to translate: "O Pascha, . . . on whose account the lights of souls shall never be put out, but divinely and spiritually in all beings the fire of grace is transmitted to body and spirit and fed by the oil of the Anointed One." (Trans.)

28. IRENAEUS, *Against the Heresies* 4, 10, 1

> The Greek text, except for most of Book 1, is almost all lost. Critical edition of the Latin version of Book 4 by A. Rousseau (SC 100; Paris: Cerf, 1965) 492.

Written between 180 and 185, the work was originally entitled "The Unmasking and Refutation of the False Gnosis." In Book 4, Irenaeus uses the Scriptures to refute Gnostic, especially Valentinian, doctrines.

a. The widespread understanding of *Pascha* at this time was that it derived from *paschein*, "to suffer." (Trans.)

b. Everything seems to indicate that Irenaeus followed the Johannine chronology and put the death of Christ on 14 Nisan; for this would fulfill the immolation of the lamb which took place on that day, and to which the quotation from Deuteronomy 16:5-6 refers. In this case, his phrase, "eating the Pascha and suffering on the following day" (*Against the Heresies* 2, 22, 3) would indicate that he puts the Last Supper on the night of 13-14 Nisan and also recognizes it as a Pesach meal.

c. If one takes *extremitatem temporum* in its natural sense to mean "the end of the ages," then the typological interpretation (sunset as the hour of Christ's death) is here fused with an allegorical one (evening as the end of the ages). This idea is in fact found in Hippolytus, *Fragment on Genesis* (GCS 1/2, 71, 4); Pseudo-Chrysostom, *On the Pascha* 1, 9 (SC 36, 63); Pseudo-Cyprian (text 100); and Gaudentius of Brescia, *Sermons* 3, 12 (CSEL 68).

29. IRENAEUS, *The Demonstration of the Apostolic Preaching*, 25

The original was known only by its title, *Epideixis tou apostolikou kêrygmatos*, until the discovery, in 1904, of an Armenian translation from the late sixth century.

Edition: *Des hl. Irenaeus Schrift "Zum Erweise der apostolischen Verkündigung,"* ed. Karapet Ter-Mekerttschian and Erwand Ter-Minassiantz (TU 31/1; Leipzig: Hinrichs, 1907).

English translation used here: *St. Irenaeus, Proof of the Apostolic Preaching*, trans. Joseph P. Smith (ACW 16; New York: Newman Press, 1952) 64. Cf. *Irénée de Lyon, Démonstration de la prédication apostolique,* trans. L. M. Froidevaux (SC 62; Paris: Cerf, 1959) 70–71.

Chapters 1–42 are devoted to a presentation of the Christian faith (God, Trinity, Creation and Fall, Redemption), while Chapters 42–100 give proofs from the Old Testament.

a. The expression is the equivalent of the more usual "in a figure"; but Justin too uses the word *mystêrion* in this sense when he speaks of "the mystery of the sheep" (text 18).

b. One might expect that the word in the original Greek was *Pascha* or *paschein*, but elsewhere (*Demonstration* 4, 20, 1) the Armenian uses *P'aseak* or *P'asek* for *Pascha*, whereas here it uses *kirk'*, connected with *krel*, "suffer." Hence we can be fairly sure with Froidevaux, 71, that the original was not *Pascha* but a synonym for *paschein*—that is, *pathos*. In any case, it is clear that Irenaeus interprets *Pascha* as "suffering." (Trans.)

c. The implication is: the blood of the lamb gave the Israelites freedom from the tenth plague; the passion of Christ gives us freedom from God's wrath. Irenaeus agrees with Justin (*Dialogue with Trypho* 41, 1) in making the sufferings of Christ the cause or source of our freedom. Perhaps "salvation" or "protection" would have been a more appropriate word than "freedom," but Irenaeus is also thinking of the freedom from Egyptian slavery which followed upon the Pascha and the freedom from the servitude to the Devil or to sin which follows upon the passion. (Trans.)

30. IRENAEUS, *On the Pascha*, Indirect Quotation

Source: Theodoret of Cyrrhus (Pseudo-Justin), *Questions and Answers for the Orthodox*, 115

Critical edition: Otto, *Corpus Apologetarum* III/2 (Jena: 1881), 186–188, repr. in *PG* 6, 1364–65.

a. The tradition of not kneeling in the Easter season is constantly designated as apostolic: see the *Acts of Paul* (*Praxeis Paulou*, ed. C. Schmidt [Glückstadt and Hamburg: Augustin, 1936] 1, reprinted in Hennecke, *New Testament Apocrypha*, 2:370; Tertullian (text 92); Origen, Fragment of *On the Psalms* (*Hippolytus Werke* 1, 2., ed. Hans Achelis [Leipzig: Hinrichs, 1897], 138); Council of Nicaea, canon 20 (in *Conciliorum Oecumenicorum Decreta*, ed. J. Alberigo and others [3rd. ed.; Bologna: Istituto per le Scienze Religiose, 1973] 16); Eusebius (text 56, § 5); Epiphanius, *Exposition of the Faith* 22, 5ff. (GCS Epiphanius 3, 523).

b. The fifty days of the Pentecost are considered the equivalent of fifty Sundays: cf. Athanasius' description of the season as "the great Sunday" (text 58).

31. ARCHAEUS (or IRENAEUS), Fragment

Ed. by Angelo Mai, *Spicilegium Romanum* (Rome: 1840) 3:707; repr. in *PG* 5, 1490.

In the Arabic version, the fragment is attributed to a certain Archaeus: see Audollent, *Dictionnaire d'histoire et de géographie ecclésiastique* 3 (1912) 1528; Jordan, "Wer war Archaeus?" *ZNW* 13 (1912) 157ff. More probably it was written by Irenaeus, as the Syriac version says; see W. Harvey's edition of Irenaeus (Cambridge, 1857), 2:456. Perhaps, as O. Bardenhewer, *Geschichte der altkirchlichen Literatur* vol. 1, 2nd ed. (Freiburg: Herder, 1913), 417, asserted, it was written on the occasion of the paschal controversy (see text 10).

a. "But with the spirit," etc., takes this form in the Syriac version: "(his flesh) having become incorruptible and similar to spirit, he, full of glory, offered it to the Father when the heaven had been opened."

b. An allusion to Ps 24:7 and 9. For the application of this psalm to the ascension, see Irenaeus, *Proof of the Apostolic Preaching* 84 (trans. Joseph P. Smith, ACW 16, 99–100) and *Against the Heresies* 4, 33, 13 (ed. A. Rousseau, SC 100, 838).

32. *The Letter to Diognetus* 12, 9

>Critical edition: Karl Bihlmeyer, *Die Apostolischen Väter,* 2nd ed. Ausg. (Tübingen: 1956) 149.
>
>English translation used here: *The Epistle to Diognetus*, ed. Henry G. Meecham (Manchester: Manchester University Press, 1949) 91.

The *Letter* is generally dated in the second half of the second century and ascribed tentatively to various authors. But chapters 11 and 12 have a style different from the rest; Eduard Schwartz thought they belonged to one of the two lost treatises on the Pascha by Hippolytus of Rome (*Zwei Predigten Hippolyts,* 33.A.1, 47.A.1 [Munich: Beck, 1936]); others assign them to the end of Hippolytus' *Refutation of All Heresies* (*Philosophumena*). Section 9 is obscure; for a clear explanation of the many emendations and interpretations which have been offered, see L. B. Radford, *The Epistle to Diognetus* (London: S.P.C.K., 1908) 88-89.

a. Radford, 88, suggests this meaning: the gospel is proclaimed and the writings of the apostles are explained.

b. *To kyriou pascha*: the phrase refers here not to the imminent parousia, as Gry (*RB* 49 [1940] 92, note 2) and Joachim Jeremias (*TDNT* 5, 897, note 11) think, nor to the Eucharist, as suggested in *PGL*, 1048, but rather to the imminent feast of Pascha, or perhaps to the Pascha of Christ and the Church in general, as opposed to the Pesach of the Law. These lines are an ecstatic celebration of the eschatological event, similar to that of Melito (text 24) and to that of Hippolytus in his *Commentary on the Song of Songs* 25, 3-10 (*Traités d'Hippolyte sur David et Goliath, sur le Cantique des Cantiques et sur l'Antichrist, version géorgienne*, trans. Gérard Garitte [CSCO 264 / Scriptores iberici 16; Louvain: Secrétariat du CorpusSCO, 1965], 46-49).

c. Reading *kairoi* instead of the manuscript's *kêroi*, "wax candles"; this would refer to the festivals of the Christian year. But if the manuscript reading is correct, as Joachim Jeremias will have it (*TDNT* 5, 903, note 56), then the phrase means "and candles are brought in and decoratively arranged" (for the solemn beginning of the Easter vigil).

d. *Meta kosmou*. Credner conjectures: *metakosmia*, that is, the spaces between the worlds are arranged. Bunsen would supply *panta* so as to read: "all things are arranged in orderly fashion." The codices, with their reading *harmozetai*, favor a neuter plural subject, not *kêroi* or *kairoi*.

33. CLEMENT OF ALEXANDRIA, *Miscellanies* **2, 11, 51, 2**

>Critical edition: *Clemens Alexandrinus*, 2, *Stromata*, I-VI,

ed. Otto Stählin, 2nd ed. L. Früchtel (GCS 52; Berlin: Akademie-Verlag, 1960) 140.

English translation used here: in ANFa 2, 359.

Written in Alexandria towards the end of the second century, the *Miscellanies* is an apology for the Christian Gnosis as the highest form of culture.

a. I.e., "the tenths." The passage is derived from Philo (text 3).

b. *Diabasis*. This is the first instance of a Christian writer interpreting the Pascha as *humanity's* passing over. For the further history of this way of translating *Pascha*, see Huber, 120ff. In *Miscellanies* 7, 40, 2 we find *hyperbasis* (though Stählin conjectures *hypekbasis*).

34. CLEMENT OF ALEXANDRIA, *On the Pascha*, Fragment 25

Source: Eusebius of Caesarea, *Eccl. Hist.* 6, 13, 9.

Critical edition: *Eusebius Werke* 2, 2, ed. Eduard Schwartz (GCS 9/2; Leipzig: Hinrichs, 1908) 548.

35. CLEMENT OF ALEXANDRIA, *On the Pascha*, Fragment 26

Source: Eusebius of Caesarea, *Eccl. Hist.* 4, 26, 4.

Critical edition: *Eusebius Werke* 2, 1, ed. Eduard Schwartz (GCS 9/1; Leipzig: Hinrichs, 1903) 382–384.

a. The treatise *On the Pascha* of Melito of Sardis, previously mentioned by Eusebius (see text 25).

b. What this expression tells us about the respective positions of Melito and Clement is discussed in Cantalamessa, *L'omelia*, 79, note 22. The divergence between Melito and Clement does not consist in the Synoptic chronology's being defended by the one and the Johannine by the other, but in the fact that the former defends the Quartodeciman practice while the latter follows the more widespread practice of celebrating the Pascha on Sunday. Cf. Eusebius, *Eccl. Hist.* 5, 25 (text 10).

36. CLEMENT OF ALEXANDRIA, *On the Pascha*, Fragment 28

Source: *The Paschal Chronicle*.

Critical edition: *Paschalion seu Chronicon paschale* ed. Ludovicus Dindorf (Corpus Scriptorum Historiae Byzantinae, 16; Bonn: E. Weber, 1832) 1:14–15; repr. in *PG* 92, 81.

a. Clement defends the Johannine chronology of the passion, but seeks to bring that of the Synoptics into harmony with it by explaining that the Last Supper they report was a pre-paschal meal without the ritual lamb. His thesis is taken up by Eusebius, *On the Solemnity of Easter* 9-10 (see text 56). For the relationship between this discussion and the dispute at Laodicea in 164-166, see Cantalamessa, *L'omelia*, 67-81.

b. The coincidence of the day of the resurrection with the Jewish observance of the *'ômer* is, in the opinion of some, at the root of the observance of Easter on Sunday. See Rordorf, *ThZ* 18 (1962) 167-189.

37. ORIGEN, *On the Pascha*, 1

Edition: *Origène, Sur la Pâque: Traité inédit publié d'après un papyrus de Toura*, ed. Octave Guéraud, and Pierre Nautin (Christianisme Antique, 2; Paris: Beauchesne, 1979) 154-157.

This long-lost treatise, rediscovered in 1941, was probably written about A.D. 245, after Book 10 of the *Commentary on John* (Nautin, *Origène, Sur la Pâque*, 109).

a. The idea that the inspired Seventy had translated *pesah* with *pascha* because they foresaw the passion of Christ may have spread among Christians by Origen's time: see the scholia to Exodus 12:11 in Field, 1:100. But, according to Nautin, *Origène, Sur la Pâque*, 97-100, 110-111, with this treatise Origen wished to correct a certain Hippolytus, whose treatise *On the Holy Pascha* (texts 27a-d) had recently revived the Asiatic tradition of Melito and Apollinaris (see texts 21 and 26), which connected *pascha* with *paschein* and *pathos* (the passion). Origen knew this tradition: in *Homilies on Leviticus* 10, 1 he cites Melito *On the Pascha* 37.

b. The letter *het*. Since it has no Greek equivalent, it is not written in the Greek text, but we have supplied it with the symbol *h*. Origen vocalizes the Hebrew *psh* like the Aramaic *phasha'* and aspirates the initial *pe* as was done in Palestinian Aramaic. This aspiration is attested by the form *phasek*, found in Jeremiah 31:8 (LXX), in 2 Chronicles 30 and 35, and in Philo, Aquila, and Symmachus, and likewise by the form *phaska* in Josephus and *phese* in Aquila, Deuteronomy 16:1 (see Joachim Jeremias, *TDNT* 5, 896, with note 2). In the late Hellenistic period, *phi* came to be pronounced like Latin *f*, but the classical pronunciation *p + h* persisted through the fourth century A.D. (Haag, *Vom alten zum neuen Pascha*, 27)—otherwise Origen could not have said *pascha* was derived from *phasek* or from *phash*. (Trans.)

c. *Diabasis*. This is Origen's translation of *Pascha* also on p. 2, line 17, and p. 4, lines 18 and 22. The fact that in book 2 of this treatise (p. 45, line 14, and p. 47, line 33) *Pascha* is translated *hyperbasis* makes one doubt the attribution of the second book to Origen, since he never uses this translation elsewhere, and it is incompatible with his habitual explanation of Pascha as *diabasis*. See Nautin, *Homélies pascales*, 2:35, note 3.

d. "Not using" is based on the conjecture *chrêsthai* to complete the lacuna in the papyrus at this point. Nautin conjectures *ischeuein* instead, and translates the clause: "parce que les Grecques sont incapables, pour n'en avoir pas la vigueur, de dire *Fas* avec l'esprit rude plus fort en usage chez les Hébreux" (*Origène, Sur la pâque*, 154-155). However, a slur on the Greeks would be out of character for Origen, and *Fas* is surely the wrong way to read *phas*[*h*] (see note b above). (Trans.)

e. *Pascha* is the form used by the Septuagint translators of the Pentateuch at the beginning of the Hellenistic period and by subsequent Alexandrian translators of Joshua, 2 Kings, Ezra, Nehemiah, and Ezekiel as well. Rather than a further Hellenization of *phasek*, it is a Greek transcription of the Aramaic emphatic form *phashâ'*. The aspirate *chi* (which is more nearly equivalent to *het* than *kappa* is), is used in the second syllable; hence the initial aspirated *pe* becomes in Greek not the aspirate *phi* but simple *pi* (see text 70). (Trans.)

38. ORIGEN, *Commentary on John* 10, 18, 108-111

> Critical edition: *Origenes Werke* 4, *Der Johanneskommentar*, ed. Erwin Preuschen (GCS 10; Leipzig: Hinrichs, 1903) 189, revised by Cécile Blanc, *Origène, Commentaire sur saint Jean*, 2 (SC 157; Paris: Cerf, 1970) 446-449.

According to Nautin (*Origène, Sur la Pâque*, 108-111), Book 10 must have been written between A.D. 235 and 245.

Origen's fullest treatment of the Pascha, next to his treatise *On the Pascha* (see text 37), is found in this commentary, Book 10, ch. 13-19 (= §§ 67-118). Here he finds the spiritual meaning of the Old Testament descriptions of the Exodus and prescriptions for the Pascha. Eating the whole of the roasted lamb, for example, means understanding the Scriptures and all of creation under the influence of the Spirit (§§ 103-107), while the unleavened bread symbolizes the Christian's repentance and salutary trials (§ 102). These exercises prepare one to receive the manna, which he explains elsewhere (*Homilies on Exodus* 7, 4) as the Word of God incarnate and immolated as our paschal victim. The three foods given successively in the course of the Exodus—the lamb, the unleavened bread, and the manna—represent three phases of the spiritual life, but it is not said that they follow one another in that order. (Trans.)

a. *Propheteia* in the manuscripts. Preuschen would read instead: *trophê*, "food."

b. That is, in the group of students to which one belongs. Origen frequently says that the spiritual nourishment is to be taken in the form that suits one's degree of advancement in the spiritual life; see the texts cited by Henri Crouzel, *Origène et la "connaissance mystique"* (Paris: Desclée de Brouwer, 1961), 172-178, 470-474. Here he implies that instruction to the advanced students should be given apart from instruction to pagans or to more earthly-minded Christians. (Trans.)

c. Deuteronomy 16:7 prescribes boiling the paschal sacrifices, though this is specifically forbidden in Exodus 12:9. Origen notes this prohibition in § 92 and in § 105 gives an allegorical explanation of it. 2 Chronicles 35:13 perhaps indicates that at Josiah's renewal of the Pesach the sheep's flesh was roasted and only the bull's flesh was boiled. Postexilic Judaism seems to have returned to the exclusive use of sheep or goats for the Pesach: Rost, BHH 3 (1966) 1396. (Trans.)

d. The command not to break a bone of the lamb is found in v. 10 of the Septuagint, though it does not occur in the Hebrew until v. 46. The typological meaning of this and other prescriptions of Exodus 12 is given in the *Commentary on John* 10, 103-111 (SC 157, 444-50) and dealt with by Nautin, *Homélies pascales*, vol. 2 (SC 36), 43.

e. The Hebrew Pascha is the type, not of Christ's Passion or of any Christian rite such as the Eucharist or the liturgical celebration of the Pascha, but of the spiritual and interior eating of the Incarnate Word in understanding and affection (see text 43, preliminary note). This does not deny the validity of the Church's liturgical Pascha, but makes it entirely dependent on spiritual, interior actions and attitudes. The influence of Philo is perceptible here (see text 2 with note d). The difference between the three-stage typology, which is essentially allegorical, and the two-stage typology, which is essentially historical, is brought out by Huber, 89-108.

f. "Third" with respect to two other Paschas, that of the Law and that of the Gospel. Or else, "third" with respect to (1) the historical Pascha of the Old and New Testaments together and (2) the Pascha as celebrated by the Church. On the heavenly Pascha, see also Origen's *Series of Commentaries on Matthew* 86 in *Origenes Werke*, 11: *Origenes Matthäus-Erklärung*, II. *Die lateinische Übersetzung der Commentariorum Series*, by Erich Klostermann and E. Benz (GCS 38; Leipzig: Hinrichs, 1933), 2nd. ed. Ursula Treu (Berlin: Akademie-Verlag, 1976), 197-200; *Commentary on John* 10, 15, 87 ("feasts, of which the Pascha is one, are referred anagogically to the age to come"); *Homilies on Jere-*

miah 19, 15 at the end; and *Against Celsus* 8, 22 (see text 43). Compare also Gregory of Nazianzus, oration 45, 23 (text 71).

39. ORIGEN, *Homilies on Exodus* 5, 2

The original Greek is lost. Critical edition of Rufinus's ancient Latin version: *Origenes Werke*, 6: *Homilien zum Hexateuch in Rufins Übersetzung*, 1. *Die Homilien zu Genesis, Exodus und Leviticus*, ed. W. A. Baehrens (*GCS* 29; Leipzig: Hinrichs, 1920) 185–186.

This homily was composed after A.D. 244.

a. Cf. Exodus 13:20. The Septuagint reads *Othom*; the Massoretic Hebrew, *'etâm*; English versions, *Etham*. (Trans.)

b. In Hebrew, *'ôtâm* means: "their signs." (Trans.)

c. "The third day always turns out to be suited to mysteries" (*Homilies on Genesis* 8, 4).

d. Here we have one of the first theological interpretations of the paschal triduum. (For others, see texts 76 and 125.) In these three days, the Christian accomplishes the new, spiritual Exodus, which was prefigured in the Hebrew people, realized in the resurrection of Christ, and actualized in baptism.

e. "Our fathers were all under the cloud and all passed through the sea and all were baptized into Moses in the cloud and in the sea" (1 Cor 10:1-2).

f. Cf. Ephesians 2:4, 6: "But God . . . raised us up with him and made us sit with him in the heavenly places, in Christ Jesus." As in his book *Against Celsus* (text 43), Origen makes it Christ who raised the baptized up together with himself. Cf. Gregory of Nyssa (text 72). (Trans.)

40. ORIGEN, *Homilies on Exodus* 7, 4

Critical edition: Baehrens, *GCS* 29, 209.

According to Jewish law (Num 9:9-12), those who were unable to celebrate the Pesach in the month of Nisan were allowed to do so a month later. This second Pesach is seen as prefiguring the Pascha of the Church in connection with the Eucharist (the manna). Compare Hippolytus' reflections in text 44.

41. ORIGEN, *Homilies on Numbers* 23, 6

> The original Greek is lost. The critical edition of Rufinus's ancient Latin version: *Origenes Werke, 7: Homilien zum Hexateuch in Rufins Übersetzung, 2. Die Homilien zu Numeri, Josua und Judices*, ed. W. A. Baehrens (*GCS* 30; Leipzig: Hinrichs, 1921) 218.

As in text 38 and in Origen's *Series of Commentaries on Matthew* 85, here the Christian Pascha is practically identified with the understanding and acceptance of the deepest meaning of the Word of God. See Balthasar, *RSR* 26 (1936) 548ff.

a. Cf. text 2.

b. Or: "where the veil of the letter of the spiritual law is removed and mysteries of the world to come are laid bare." (Trans.)

42. ORIGEN, *Homilies on Jeremiah* 19, 13

> Critical edition: *Origenes Werke, 3: Jeremiahomilien, Klagelieder-Kommentar, Erklärung der Samuel- und Königsbücher*, ed. Erich Klostermann (*GCS* 6; Leipzig: Hinrichs, 1901), 169, revised by by Pierre Nautin, *Origène, Homélies sur Jérémie*, vol. 2, *Homélies XII–XX et Homélies latines* (*SC* 238; Paris: Cerf, 1977) 228–231.

a. This is also Casel's translation in "Art und Sinn," 34. In saying that the Church's Pascha is a symbol of Christ's Pascha, or of the Jewish Pascha which Christ observed, Origen certainly does not mean that it is a type or figure. Rather Origen would say that the Church's Eucharistic Pascha *is* Christ's Pascha, foreshadowed by the Jewish Pascha and in turn a foreshadowing of the heavenly Pascha. Casel states the matter correctly when he concludes (ibid.): "Origen distinguishes three things: the Old Testament celebration of the Pascha as type or shadow; the Church's liturgy as fulfillment of the type and as Christ-reality, but still mixed with earthly symbolism; finally the eternal heavenly celebration in which the Church's feast unfolds in its full reality." Hence a more literal translation would be preferable: "this feast (of) the Pascha, of which we perform the symbol (i.e. which we observe by our symbolic rite)." *Symbolon* is the external sign of one of the mysteries (Origen, *Commentary on John* 6, 6). Here it refers to the Eucharistic rite rather than to the whole paschal observance (Nautin, *SC* 238, 228, note 2). (Trans.)

b. Cf. Athanasius, text 60, and the exegesis of Mark 14:15-16 by Theophilus of Alexandria in his *First Paschal Epistle*, quoted by Cosmas Indicopleustes in the *Christianikê topographia* 10 (*PG* 88, 417): "When the disciples heard from Christ that the celebration was to take place in an upper room, the upper room of second deeds, they began running in spirit and proceeded to the Holy of Holies, into which Christ himself has entered for our sakes." (Trans.)

c. *Anabeis*. Celebrating the Pascha is understood as a moral ascent, *anabasis*, which is made possible for mortals by the descent, *katabasis*, of the Word. Cf. Origen, *Homilies on Numbers* 27, 3.

d. Origen has in mind the heavenly Pascha. As he says at the end of the homily (ch. 15), "May we be found worthy of that heavenly festivity and otherworldly Pascha." But he uses Eucharistic language because the Eucharist is its symbol (thus Casel, "Art und Sinn," 34).

43. ORIGEN, *Against Celsus* 8, 22

> Critical edition: *Origenes Werke*, 2: *Buch V-VIII Gegen Celsus, Die Schrift vom Gebet*, ed. Paul Koetschau (*GCS* 3; Leipzig: Hinrichs, 1899), 239-240. Also: *Origène, Contre Celse*, vol. 4, ed. Marcel Borret (*SC* 150; Paris: Cerf, 1969) 222-225.

In this work, published about 248, Origen, like Clement of Alexandria (*Miscellanies* 7, 35, 1ff.), shows himself sensitive to the Gnostic criticism of ritualism (e.g. text 17), and rather overdoes the spiritualization of the Christian festivals, including the Pascha, by minimizing to some extent their sacramental and ecclesial character and emphasizing their moral significance. But see Casel, "Art und Sinn," 32-34, and Cantalamessa, *La pasqua della nostra salvezza*, 178-183.

a. *Peri tôn par' hymin kyriakôn ê paraskeuôn.* Here and in the following sentence, the plurals of *kyriakê* and *paraskeuê* could be translated "Sundays" and "Fridays."

b. *Tês pentêkostês*: the whole period of fifty days.

c. On the idea of a continual Pascha, see also Origen, *Homilies on Genesis* 10, 3.

d. *Diabatêria*.

e. The Pentecost here appears as a time to celebrate the resurrection of believers with Christ and their mystical ascension into heaven with him (see Boeckh, *JLH 5* [1960] 23). In Origen's treatise *On the Prayer* 27, 14, it is given as seven weeks of ages, a symbol of eternity; in the fragment *On Psalm 150* (fragment 9 in *Hippolytus Werke* 1/2 [*GCS 1*] 138-140), it is said to be an anticipation of the joy and the feast of heaven.

The symbolic content of Pentecost is further specified by Origen as the remission of sins: *Homilies on Numbers* 5, 2; 25, 4; *Commentary on Matthew* 9, 3 (*SC* 162) 278ff. Cf. Athanasius, *First Festal Letter* (text 58).

44. HIPPOLYTUS OF ROME, *The Apostolic Tradition*, 33

Source: The orginal Greek, written about A.D. 215, is lost. For a critical reconstruction of the text, based on the fourth- or fifth-century Latin translation and on later African translations, see Bernard Botte, ed., *La Tradition apostolique de saint Hippolyte: Essai de reconstitution* (*LWQF* 39; Münster: Aschendorff, 1963) 78–80.

A title for this section is missing from the Latin version, but the Sahidic, Arabic, and Ethiopian translators have this: "That it is not right for anyone to taste anything in the Pascha before the hour in which it is right to eat."

a. Sahidic and Arabic versions omit: "pregnant or."

b. Good Friday and Holy Saturday, as in Africa (see text 96). On these days Christians fasted completely, not eating or drinking anything.

c. Sahidic and Arabic versions omit: "or in some necessity."

d. "For it is not the Pascha which we keep" is omitted by the Latin version but belongs to the text. Contrary to Botte (*La Tradition apostolique de saint Hippolyte*, 81), I understand it to mean the Pascha of the second month, which is the model (*typos*) of the Christian Pascha (see text 40). Christians who are prevented from keeping the Pascha at the regular time, therefore, are not asked to observe it a month later, as the Jews were, but only to fulfill the obligation of fasting, after the festive season of the Pentecost. In the *Canons of Hippolytus* (ed. R. G. Coquin, *PO* 31/1 [1966] 389) this was not understood, and the sentence was reworded to read: "After the Pentecost, let them fast *and keep the Pascha* with discipline."

45. HIPPOLYTUS OF ROME, *Against All the Heresies*, Quotation

Source: *The Paschal Chronicle*.

Critical edition: *Paschalion seu Chronicon paschale*, ed. Ludovicus Dindorf (Corpus Scriptorum Historiae Byzantinae, 16; Bonn: E. Weber, 1832) 1:12–13, reprinted in *PG* 92, 80.

The *Syntagma* or Treatise *Against all the Heresies*, written in Greek at Rome during the first quarter of the third century, is lost. See Cantalamessa, *L'omelia*, 25–33, 71ff.

a. It is conceivable that Hippolytus is here opposing Blastos (which is not the case later in the *Elenchos* or *Refutation of all the Heresies* 8, 18 [text 11]). In any case, the position he rejects coincides with that rejected by Apollinarius of Hierapolis (see text 26).

b. *Kai.* Duchesne, *RQH* 15 (1880) 10, note 4, proposes instead *hêi*, "on which."

46. HIPPOLYTUS OF ROME, *On the Pascha*, Quotation

Source: *The Paschal Chronicle.*

Critical editions: Dindorf, 1:13 (*PG* 92, 80 C); *Hippolytus Werke*, 1: *Exegetische und homiletische Schriften*, 2: *Hippolyt's kleinere exegetische und homiletische Schriften*, ed. Hans Achelis (*GCS* 1; Leipzig: Hinrichs, 1897) 270.

This lost treatise is mentioned by Eusebius, *Hist. Eccl.* 6, 22; see further Cantalamessa, *L'omelia*, 25–33, 71ff.

a. Hippolytus, just mentioned (text 45).

b. That is, neither in Luke 22:15, "I have desired to eat this Pascha with you," nor in the following verse, "I eat it no more."

c. This is Dindorf's or Migne's correction of the manuscript reading, "we eat."

d. If Christ held his supper on 13–14 Nisan (as the Fourth Gospel indicates), it could not have been the Pesach meal of the Jews, which was held on 14–15 Nisan. In this Hippolytus agrees with Apollinarius (text 26) and Clement of Alexandria (text 36).

47. HIPPOLYTUS OF ROME, *On Elkanah and Hannah*, Quotation

Source: Theodoret of Cyrus, *Eranistes*, Florilegium II, § 11.

Critical edition: Gerard H. Ettlinger, *Theodoret of Cyrus, Eranistes* (Oxford: Clarendon, 1975) 155.

a. The fragment quoted by Theodoret does not say anything about the third season.

b. That is, the true paschal lamb. Apollinarius of Hierapolis (text 26) uses the same phrase, *alêthinon pascha*, in the sense of an action: the true paschal sacrifice or immolation. In both authors, the essence of the paschal feast is the commemoration of the sacrificial death of Christ.

c. The essential content of the Pentecost is the mystery of the glorification of Christ and the anticipation of the future kingdom, without as yet any mention of the descent of the Holy Spirit. See Boeckh, *JHL* 5 (1960) 20ff.

d. On the offering of redeemed humanity to the Father (seen as the antitype of the offering of first fruits, Leviticus 23:10-14), see also Hippolytus, *Against Noetus* 4 (Hippolytus of Rome, *Contra Noetum*, ed. and trans. Robert Butterworth (London: Heythrop, 1977) 51-55, and Irenaeus, *Against the Heresies* 3, 17, 2 (ed. A. Rousseau and L. Doutreleau 2 [*SC* 211; Paris: Cerf, 1974] 330-333).

48. HIPPOLYTUS OF ROME, *Commentary on Daniel* 1, 16

> Critical edition: *Hippolytus Werke*, 1: *Exegetische und homiletische Schriften*, 1: *Die Kommentare zu Daniel und zum Hohenliede*, ed. G. Nathanael Bonwetsch (*GCS* 1; Leipzig: Hinrichs, 1897), 26-27. *Hippolyte, Commentaire sur Daniel*, ed. Gustave Bardy and Maurice Lefèvre (*SC* 14; Paris: Cerf, 1947), takes account of a manuscript discovered in 1911. For our selection, see 84.

This, the earliest orthodox Christian commentary on Scripture, was written about A.D. 204.

a. With Tertullian (text 93), this is the first explicit testimony to the link between the Pascha and baptism. (*The Apostolic Tradition* 20, to my mind, does not describe the paschal vigil but a baptismal vigil in general. We know from Tertullian that there were baptismal vigils throughout the Pentecost and beyond. See also Basil [text 68] and Gregory of Nazianzus, oration 40, 24.) Ambrosiaster, *Commentary on the Pauline Epistles*, on Ephesians 4:11 (ed. H. J. Vogels, *CSEL* 81/3, 100), says that at first the disciples baptized without paying attention to the day or to their own hierarchical status, but that now only priests baptize and only on certain days, unless the person is sick. However, Augustine, sermon 210, 2 (*PL* 38, 1048), attests to the fact that the link between the Pascha and baptism was not at all exclusive.

b. Allegorically representing the Church.

c. Represented allegorically by the two maids.

d. This rite of anointing after baptism is described in the *Apostolic Tradition* 21 (ed. Botte, *LWQF* 39, 50-52); its link with the Pascha is discussed in Cantalamessa, *L'omelia*, 306ff.

49. DIONYSIUS OF ALEXANDRIA, *Letter to Basilides*, 1

> Critical edition: *Dionysiou leipsana: The Letters and Other*

Remains of Dionysius of Alexandria, ed. Charles Lett Feltoe (Cambridge: University Press, 1904) 94–102.

English translation used here: C. L. Feltoe, *St. Dionysius of Alexandria, Letters and Treatises* (London: S.P.C.K., 1918) 76–81.

Eusebius, *Hist. Eccl.* 7, 22, 3, and Jerome, *About Illustrious Men* 69, mention various letters to Basilides, bishop of the Pentapolis. This letter was received by the Third Council of Constantinople (680) among the canonical letters.

a. Literally: "in concluding the Pascha." The Pascha is thought of chiefly as a fast.

b. Cockcrow (at the end of the third watch of the night, 3 a.m.: see Mark 13:35) is noted as the end of the paschal vigil already in the *Epistle of the Apostles* (text 14). See also *Didascalia* 21 [V 19]; the *Apostolic Constitutions* V 18, 1; Epiphanius, *Panarion* 75, 6, 2; *Exposition of the Faith* 22, 11.

c. Next, Dionysius reviews the gospel data about the hour of the resurrection (compare Pseudo-Gregory of Nyssa, *On the Resurrection of Christ* 2) and explains the expression *opse tôn sabbatôn* (Matt 28:1) as "far into the night."

d. A proverb meaning: "A miss is as good as a mile."

e. From 3 to 6 a.m.

f. The six-day fast is enjoined by the *Didascalia* 21 [V 18]; see text 86. Before this time (before the middle of the third century), the sources mostly speak of a two-day fast—Friday and Saturday (e.g., text 44), but Irenaeus (text 10, ch. 24, § 12) mentions a fast of more than two days. On the differing lengths of the paschal fast, see Arbesmann, *RAC* 7, 512ff.

g. Literally: "some continue the postponement without food on all the days." "Postponement" (*hyperthesis*) was the technical term for the prolongation of the fast beyond 3 or 6 p.m. See Arbesmann, *RAC* 7, 507ff.

50. ANATOLIUS OF LAODICEA, *Canons about the Pascha*, Quotation

Source: Eusebius, *Hist. Eccl.* 7, 32, 14–18.

Critical edition: *Eusebius Werke*, 2, 2, ed. Eduard Schwartz (*GCS* 9/2; Leipzig: Hinrichs, 1908) 722–724; *Eusebius* editio minor, ed. E. Schwartz, revised by Friedhelm Winckelmann (Berlin: Akademie-Verlag, 1955) 309.

English translation used here: J. E. L. Oulton, *Eusebius, The Ecclesiastical History* 2 (LCL; Cambridge: Harvard, 1932) 235–237.

Anatolius went back to the Metonic cycle of nineteen years (Schwartz, *Ostertafeln*, 65ff.), which was more accurate than either cycle of sixteen years (Eusebius, *Eccl. Hist.* 6, 22; reproduced in *DACL* 6, 2423ff.) or the eight-year cycle which Dionysius of Alexandria proposed after denouncing the practice of celebrating the Pascha before the spring equinox.

a. March 22. Anatolius calculates the equinox as occurring on March 19.

b. *Kat' autên*, an unintelligible phrase. In any case, the sentence refers to those who regarded the fourteenth day, if it fell on the day before the equinox, as the paschal full moon. This was apparently Tricentius' mistake (see text 51). See also Grumel, *REByz* 18 (1960) 163ff., and Grumel, "La date," 217ff.

c. Musaeus is otherwise unknown. Anatolius wishes to say that the Jews kept the Pascha after the equinox at the time of Christ and deviated from the correct reckoning only later; this opinion is shared by Peter of Alexandria (*The Paschal Chronicle*, ed. Dindorf, 4: cf. text 51) and by the Pseudo-Chrysostom, *Homily on the Holy Pascha*, 7, 15–16 (ed. Floëri and Nautin, *Homélies pascales* 3 [*SC* 48] 125).

d. Actually Aristobulus lived in the time of Ptolemy Philometor, in the second and not the third century B.C. Eusebius, in the *Preparation of the Gospel* 7, 14 and 8, 10, gives fragments of his work *On the Mosaic Law*.

e. *Ta diabatêria.*

51. TRICENTIUS, Quoted by PETER OF ALEXANDRIA in a Fragment of *On the Pascha*

Source: Peter of Alexandria's treatise on the Pascha, excerpted in *The Paschal Chronicle*.

Critical edition: *Paschalion seu Chronicon Paschale,* ed. Ludovicus Dindorf (Corpus Scriptorum Historiae Byzantinae, 16; Bonn: E. Weber, 1832), 1:7; reprinted in *PG* 92, 74.

Peter, writing from Alexandria about A.D. 300, answers a certain Tricentius who had defended the Antiochene tradition of keeping the

Pascha "with the Jews," that is, on the Sunday after 14 Nisan, even if the latter date comes before the spring equinox. Cf. the *Diataxis* as quoted by Epiphanius (text 65, § 2): "This is what the apostles decree: 'You shall not calculate, but celebrate the feast whenever your brethren from the Circumcision do. Keep it together with them.' " (Trans.)

a. Every few years a thirteenth month (second Adar) had to be added to the lunar year to make it agree with the solar year. After the destruction of the Second Temple, this was no longer done by the priests and with ocular observation of the appearance of the new moon, but according to a nineteen-year cycle. The intercalary month prevented the paschal full moon (14 Nisan) from coming before the equinox. In the solar calendar of the Egyptians, the equinox was on 29 Phamenoth (25 March), later moved to 25 Phamenoth (21 March). The first full moon thereafter might be any day from 30 Phamenoth to 29 Pharmuthi. But if the 14 Nisan coincided with 29 (25) Phamenoth, the Alexandrians, claiming that the solar year was not yet complete, insisted on waiting another month for the paschal full moon.

b. This expression does not mean that Tricentius was a Quartodeciman (see Huber, 63, note 12). The Pascha was called the "Commemoration of the Passion," even by those who celebrated it on Sunday, until the middle of the fourth century (e.g., texts 52 § 8, 82, and 100).

c. Tricentius points out that his tradition is older than that of the Egyptians.

d. *Dis.* The Paris manuscript, however, reads: "on the sixteenth."

e. Peter goes on to say that all the great men of the Old Testament and Christ himself kept the Pascha after the vernal equinox. The Chronicler then quotes Athanasius to the effect that it was only after the destruction of Jerusalem under Vespasian that the Jews became careless about this point. Actually Philo and Josephus, whom Athanasius quotes to prove this, are not concerned about it at all, and the Jews seem to have been satisfied if Pesach was held about the time of the vernal equinox (thus Holl, *Gesammelte Aufsätze*, 2:222).

52. CONSTANTINE THE GREAT, *Letter to the Churches*, 18

Source: Eusebius, *Life of Constantine* 3, 17–20.

Critical edition: *Eusebius Werke*, 1: *Über das Leben Constantins, Constantins Rede an die heilige Versammlung, Tricennatsrede an Constantin*, ed. Ivar A. Heikel (*GCS* 7; Leipzig: Hinrichs, 1902) 85–86. Or: *Athanasius Werke*, 3, 1, ed. G. Opitz (Berlin-Leipzig: 1935) 55–56.

The emperor's letter to the Churches of the Roman world was written at the conclusion of the Council of Nicaea in 325.

a. This had already been decreed for the West at the Council of Arles in 314 (text 104).

b. The Christians, who had always followed the Jews in setting the date of the Pascha (texts 50–51), were perplexed when the latter, at the beginning of the third century, began to allow 14 Nisan to come before the equinox and thus from time to time celebrate the Pascha twice in a single solar year: see Grumel, *REByz* 18 (1960) 163ff.

c. Throughout this letter we find the idea that *pascha* means *pathos*, without any allusion to the resurrection, and the paschal festival on Saturday-Sunday is called the Day of the Passion. In the *Discourse to the Assembly of the Saints* attributed to Constantine, the paschal festival is again called simply the Day of the Passion, but it is described as "a prelude to the resurrection and a restoration of bodies formerly in pain" (*Eusebius Werke*, 1 [*GCS 7*] 154; *PG* 20, 1253A) and apparently refers to Good Friday. This new way of thinking of the feast of the Passion makes the attribution of this discourse to Constantine very doubtful. (Hanson, *JThS* 24 [1973] 505–511, on other grounds ascribes it to an unknown critic of Julian the Apostate after 362.) The distinction between the Day of the Passion and the Day of the Resurrection first becomes clear in 364 with Gregory of Nazianzus' oration 1 (cf. text 69). Huber, 186–197, sees this as a result not only of the liturgical process of historicization but also of the systematic theological exaltation of the resurrection over the crucifixion in accord with the anti-Arian emphasis on the divine omnipotence of Christ and effort to deny his human weakness.

53. THE FIRST COUNCIL OF NICAEA, *Decree on Easter*, Report

> Source: John the Scholastic, *Synagôgê kanonôn seu Collectio quinquaginta titulorum* (about A.D. 550).
>
> Edition: Joannes Baptista Pitra, *Spicilegium Solesmense*, vol. 4 (Parisiis: Firmin-Didot, 1858; repr. Graz: Akademische Druck- und Verlagsanstalt, 1963), 541.

According to Athanasius, *Letter to the African Bishops* (*PG* 25, 537–93; R. W. Thomson, *Athanasiana syriaca* vol. 1–3; *CSCO* 257f., 272f., 324f.) the Council of Nicaea was convoked to settle two matters: Arianism and the day of the Pascha, the latter because "the Syrians, Cilicians, and those who dwell in Mesopotamia dissented from us and kept the Pascha at the same time as the Jews." Modern historians, however, regard this decree as merely a summary of Constantine's *Letter to the Churches*; it does not appear among the canons of Nicaea—probably because, as Huber (65–68) suggests, Rome would not abandon its computation based on an eighty-four-year cycle in favor of the Alexandrian computation, based on a nineteen-year cycle. The two sees came to terms year by year until after 455, when the bishop of Rome ceased to urge his view. (Trans.)

a. Constantine's part in resolving the problem of the Pascha is seen in his *Letter to the Churches* 1–12 (cf. text 52), in Eusebius, *On the Paschal Solemnity* 8, and in Epiphanius (text 64).

b. The decree is not only aimed at the Quartodecimans, as was thought up to 1880, when Duchesne published "La question de la Pâque au Concile de Nicée," but also at the Protopaschites, who took the date of paschal week from the Jews (see texts 50, 51, 86 with note b, and 87 with notes k, n, and o). The latter were also condemned by imperial decrees: see *Codex of Theodosius* 16, 6, 6 and 16, 10, 24. Protopaschites and the followers of Sabbatios are discussed by Aubineau, *SC* 187, 348–352.

c. Though the Oriental bishops at the council subscribed to the decree, it encountered strong opposition throughout the rest of the fourth century and constituted the paschal problem par excellence: see Huber, 75–88.

54. PSEUDO-CHRYSOSTOM, *Homilies on the Holy Pascha*, 1, 1–4: The Excellence of Our Pascha

> Edition: *Homélies pascales 2, Trois homélies dans la tradition d'Origène*, ed. Pierre Nautin (*SC* 36; Paris: Cerf, 1953) 55–57.

The homily, one of seven called "the Bugles," was attributed to Chrysostom; see J. A. de Aldama, *Repertorium Pseudo-chrysostomicum* (Paris: 1965), No. 409. Nautin, in his edition, 33ff., attributes it to an imitator of Origen at the end of the fourth century. I am sure it is earlier, and its dependence on Origen remains to be determined.

a. Some manuscripts read: "are transcending."

b. This section strongly resembles Melito, *Homily on the Pascha* 4 (text 20) and 36–38. Perhaps the homilist knew Melito's work through Clement of Alexandria, *On the Pascha*, fragment 33 (*Clemens Alexandrinus, Werke*, 3, ed. O. Stählin, [Leipzig: Hinrichs, 1909] 218, and Origen, *Homilies on Leviticus* 10, 1 (*SC* 287, 128–32).

c. That is, in relation to the reality foreshadowed in the ancient Pascha.

d. The explanation of the word *pascha* with *hyperbasis* is taken from

Aquila (see text 1a, note d), as we see from homily 3 (ed. Nautin, *SC* 36, 111, 12ff). Origen usually interprets *pascha* as *diabasis* = "the crossing" (by the people). Here we have one of the few instances where a Christian author adopts the "theological" explanation of Exodus 12:23 and 27 (cf. texts 4 and 114 with note b).

55. PSEUDO-CHRYSOSTOM, *Homilies on the Holy Pascha*, 1, 6–7: The Beginning of a New Life

Edition: Nautin, *Homélies pascales* 2 (*SC* 36), 59–61.

a. That is, the reality, the predicted Savior, the new dispensation (as in text 54, note c).

b. Similar symbolism can be found in Pseudo-Hippolytus, *Homily on the Holy Pascha* 19 (ed. Nautin, *SC* 27, 149–51).

c. This is the moral interpretation of Exodus 12:2, derived, it seems, from Origen (see Nautin, *Homélies pascales*, 2 [*SC* 36] 36f.) and found also in Chromatius of Aquileia, *Sermon 17*, 3 (ed. J. Lemarié [*SC* 154], 172).

d. The saving event of the Pascha is made real in the present. This is the basis of the "today" of the liturgy and of Gregory of Nazianzus' "yesterday I died with Christ, today I rise with him" (text 69).

56. EUSEBIUS OF CAESAREA, *On the Paschal Solemnity*

Source: Catena on Luke compiled by Nicetas of Serrae (eleventh century).

Edition and Latin translation by Angelo Mai, reprinted in *PG* 24, 693–706.

a. *Metabasis*.

b. *Ta diabatêria*. Eusebius follows Philo (see text 2) and Origen (see text 37) in viewing the Hebrew Passover as the *passage* or Exodus from Egypt, but he also regards it, together with the Christian Pascha, in the light of Exodus 12, that is, as sacrifice and banquet (see below, ch. 2, 3, 7, 8, and 10), and refers to the Christian Pascha as "the feast of the saving Passion" (*Eccl. Hist.* 2, 17, 21).

c. *Tais logikais sarxi*.

d. The idea of interpreting the flesh of the lamb as the Word of God comes from Origen (see text 41).

e. A very old typological interpretation, found already in Justin (see text 18).

f. *(Kairos) tetêrêmenos.* Cf. Symmachus' translation of *lêl simmurîm* (Exod 12:42) as *nyx paratetêrêmenê*, "night reserved" (text 5 with note a). (Trans.)

g. Cf. Genesis 1:11-19; 2:1. On the Pascha as anniversary of creation, see text 27b with note c. The Fathers elaborated this theme into truly lyrical celebrations of spring as the setting for the Pascha; the best examples are mentioned by Michels, *JLW* 6 (1926) 1-15; Hugo Rahner in *Paschatis Sollemnia*, 68-75; Cantalamessa, *La pasqua della nostra salvezza*, 196-198; Huber, 142-143.

h. *Kyklôn periodois*, referring to the solar and lunar cycles by which the date of the Pascha is determined. (Trans.)

i. *Hê tessarakontêmeros askêsis*, one of the first explicit mentions of Lent. (The fifth canon of Nicaea I mentions *tessarakostê*, but this may refer to the fortieth day after Easter: see Salaville, *EOr* [1910] 65ff. and 32 [1929] 257ff.) Ascetical exercises in preparation for Easter are also mentioned in Eusebius' *Eccl. Hist.* 2, 17, 21.

j. *Eis alêston aiôna* = "for an unforgettable age," that is, continuously throughout the year (see below, ch. 7). This is the Origenian theme of the continual Pascha (text 43). Chrysostom seems to have known the Eusebian treatise on the Pascha: cf. text 74. (Trans.)

k. The same theological interpretation is found in Hippolytus, text 47.

l. Chrysostom, in *Homilies on Acts* 4, 1, modifies this idea. For him the *day* of Pentecost is the time to put in the sickle, and so the coming of the Holy Spirit on this day was the beginning of the harvest of souls.

m. The syntactical relationship of "churches" to "brought together" is unclear. (Trans.)

n. On this tradition, see text 30.

o. Origen writes: "The number six indicates, it seems, labor and trouble; but the number seven, repose" (*Commentary on Matthew* 14, 5).

p. See Huber, 163. Here and in *Life of Const.* 4, 64 Eusebius depends on Philo, *On the Spec. Laws,* 2, 176.

q. Statements about the weekly Eucharistic Pascha are characteristic of this period, in which every effort was being made to detach the Christian Pascha from that of the Jews, both as to date and as to content. See also Gregory of Nazianzus, oration 40, 30 (*PG* 36, 401); Didymus, *On the Trinity* II 16 (*PG* 39, 721); Chrysostom, text 74; Pseudo-Pionius, *Life of Polycarp* 2 (Lightfoot, 434-438).

r. The same interpretation of Exodus 12:11 is found in Aphraates, *Demonstration* 12, 9 (ed. Parisot, 525-528; trans. Bert, TU 3, Heft 3-4, 191), but with "the sword of the Spirit, which is the word of God" (Eph 6:17) rather than the staff in hand.

s. *Aei tên erêmian tou anthrôpeiou biou metadiôkomen*. Perhaps this means: "we always seek the desert of the humane life, the solitude where one can live a truly human life." (Trans.)

t. The ten "always" clauses in ch. 7 explicate the typology of the Exodus narrative, as did ch. 4 above. In Eusebius, the Pascha as yet shows no signs of the historicization that it was to undergo later in the fourth century; it is still ruled by the typological idea (the correspondence between the old and the new Pascha) and by the idea of the saving mystery. See Huber, 186–89; Casel, "Art und Sinn," 67–69 and passim.

u. Objecting to the decree of Nicaea against keeping the Pascha at the same time as the Jews; see texts 52, 53, and 64.

v. Compare Chrysostom, *Orations against the Jews* 3, 3 (*PG* 48, 866): "Christ kept the Pascha with them, not in order that we should keep it with them, but that he might introduce the truth by means of a figure."

w. Eusebius, better acquainted with Jewish customs and more careful of the data furnished by the Gospels than Clement of Alexandria (compare text 36), reconciles the Synoptic and Johannine chronologies by supposing that Jesus ate his paschal supper on the legal date (on the evening following 14 Nisan, which was the Parasceve and the first day of unleavened bread, and which fell that year on a Thursday), while the high priests put off their Parasceve until Friday. The Gospels do not rule this out; they say merely that Jesus died on the Parasceve (Matt 27:62; Mark 15:42; Luke 23:54; John 19:14, 31, 42) without mentioning the day of the month. Indeed the Synoptics seem to demand some such solution; for Mark has Jesus eating the Pascha on the evening after "the first day of unleavened bread" (Mark 14:12; Matt 26:17; cf. Luke 22:7), which was the Day of Preparation, "on which the paschal lamb had to be sacrificed" (Mark 14:12; Luke 22:7), and then being buried towards evening the next day, which was again the Day of Preparation (Mark 15:42; Luke 23:54; cf. Matt 27:62). Eusebius' ingenious solution made no impression on his younger contemporary Aphraates, who follows the Asian tradition in putting Jesus' death on the fourteenth and his resurrection on the sixteenth (see text 87, § 12). (Trans.)

x. This would be after sunset, that is, after the end of the day, according to traditional Jewish reckoning. But Eusebius follows the Roman and Greek custom, according to which a calendar day ends at midnight (see von Orelli, *RE* 19 [1907] 312–313). (Trans.)

57. ASTERIUS THE SOPHIST, Homily 11: *Sixth Homily on Psalm 5, On Monday in the Octave of Easter 6, 4*

Edition: *Asterii Sophistae Commentariorum in Psalmos quae*

supersunt ed. Marcel Richard (*Symbolae Osloenses*, 16; Oslo: Brøgger, 1956) 77.

This text may be seen as a preliminary to the *Exultet* and Easter preface. Its sources are discussed in Auf der Maur, 102ff. The genre of the *improperia*, which became part of the Good Friday liturgy and which has roots in the Jewish Haggadah and in Melito, also has Asterius for a forerunner (homily 28, 6; ed. Richard, 226-27; see Auf der Maur, 125ff.).

a. Each of the following epithets in the original begins: "O night!"

b. This is the rubric above the psalm in the LXX. The Hebrew, properly translated is: "For the choirmaster. For flutes. Psalm. Of David."

58. ATHANASIUS OF ALEXANDRIA, *Festal Letter* 1 (for 329), 10

The original Greek is lost, but we have a faithful Syriac translation. Critical edition: W. Cureton, *The Festal Letters of Athanasius* (London: Society for the Publication of Oriental Texts, 1848).

German translation of the Syriac: F. Larsow, *Die Fest-Briefe des Heiligen Athanasius, Bischofs von Alexandria* (Leipzig-Göttingen 1852).

Our translation is based on the Latin translation of an Italian version made by an anonymous Maronite monk; the Latin accompanied the Syriac in Angelo Mai, and is reprinted in *PG* 26, 1366 A.

a. Monday of Holy Week, March 31.

b. The week of the Pascha recapitulates the week of creation, a variation of an idea that we meet in Philo and elsewhere. See texts 27b, 63, and 72.

c. Saturday of Holy Week. Athanasius puts the end of the fast on Saturday or "on the evening of Saturday," which is a translation of *opse tôn sabbatôn* (Matt 28:1; cf. text 49, note c). In fact he means the hour before dawn on Sunday: see Casel, "Art und Sinn," 44.

d. A common interpretation in the Alexandrian school: see Philo, *On the Special Laws* 2, 176; Clement of Alexandria, *Miscellanies* 6, 11; Origen, *Homilies on Numbers* 5, 2; 25, 4; *Commentary on Matthew* 11, 3; Daniélou, *The Bible and the Liturgy*, 324-327.

e. Cf. *Festal Letter* 4 (for 332). This eschatological interpretation of the Pentecost is the more ancient: cf. texts 47; 56, § 4; and 93. Boeckh, *JLH* 5 (1960) 33ff. and 40ff., gives the origins of the theme of the Pentecost as the Lord's Day, that is, a single great Sunday.

f. Following Origen's three-stage typology, Athanasius considers the only perfect and definitive Pascha to be that of heaven, e.g. in *Festal Letter 24* (for 352) and *26* (for 354); cf. Merendino, 22ff. In *Festal Letter 4* 3, Athanasius uses the two-stage typology which we find in Melito (see text 20), in which the "eternal and heavenly" Pascha is the liturgical Pascha of the Church, in opposition to that of the Jews.

59. ATHANASIUS OF ALEXANDRIA, *Festal Letter* 5 (for 333), 4

Critical edition of the Syriac version: W. Cureton.

Critical edition of the Coptic version: L. Th. Lefort, *CSCO* 150.

Letter 5 is the richest in paschal theology. Here the Pascha is seen as immolation (ch. 1) and as Eucharistic banquet (ch. 4, "We have eaten the Pascha of the Lord," and ch. 5, "The Pascha is heavenly food"), which produces in the faithful Christian "the passage from death to life." It is the "commemoration of salvation" and the "waiting for the Lord," historical and eschatological at the same time.

60. ATHANASIUS OF ALEXANDRIA, *Festal Letter* 6 (for 334), 13

Critical edition of the Syriac version: W. Cureton.

Critical edition of the Coptic version: L. Th. Lefort, *CSCO* 150.

61. ATHANASIUS OF ALEXANDRIA, *Festal Letter* 14 (for 342), 6

Critical edition of the Syriac version: W. Cureton.

Critical edition of the Coptic version: L. Th. Lefort, *CSCO* 150.

a. "Pentecost," for Athanasius, does not always mean the period of fifty days, as it does in *Festal Letter* 3, 6 and 4, 5; more often it means the fiftieth day, as above in text 58, in *Festal Letters* 13, 7 and 24 (Lefort, *CSCO* 151, 13), and *On His Flight* 6 (*SC* 56, 139).

b. In Athanasius, Pentecost becomes more and more clearly the feast of the Spirit: *Festal Letter* 3, 6; cf. Gregory of Nazianzus, *Oration* 41, 4–5. But the Spirit is still thought of in a Christological sense, as the "spiritual" presence of Christ among his disciples: see Boeckh, *JLH* 5 (1960) 1ff.

62. ATHANASIUS OF ALEXANDRIA, *Festal Letter* 42 (for 370), Excerpt

Source: Cosmas Indicopleustes, *Christianikê topographia* 10, 8.

Edition: *PG* 26, 1440 *B* and *SC* 197, 247.

English translation used here: Burgess, revised by Payne Smith, in *Select Writings and Letters of Athanasius, Bishop of Alexandria*, ed. Archibald Robinson (*NPNF* 2d series, vol. 4; repr. Grand Rapids: Eerdmans, 1978), 552.

Here the Christian Pascha is essentially the commemoration of the sacrifice of Christ that is celebrated in the Eucharist; thus also *Festal Letter* 5, 1 and 13, 7 ("Let us celebrate the Pascha, in which Christ was slain").

63. CYRIL OF JERUSALEM, *Catechesis* 14, 10

Critical edition: G. C. (W. K.) Reischl and J. Rupp, *Cyrilli Hierosolymitani opera quae supersunt omnia* 2 (Munich, 1860), 118.

English translation used here (with modifications): *The Works of Saint Cyril of Jerusalem* 2, trans. Leo P. McCauley and Anthony A. Stephenson (*FC* 64; Washington, D.C.: Catholic University of America Press, 1970), 37–38.

a. *Diorthôsis*. Cyril enriches the cosmological theme of the Pascha as anniversary of the creation by adding the Irenaean theme of the Pascha as recapitulation. See Cantalamessa, *La pasqua della nostra salvezza*, 192ff.

b. The Good Thief: see *Catechesis* 13, 31.

64. EPIPHANIUS OF CONSTANTIA, *Panarion* 70, 9, 2-3

Critical edition: *Epiphanius Werke*, 3: eds. Karl Holl, Hans Lietzmann, and Walter Eltester (*GCS* 37; Leipzig: Hinrichs, 1933) 241.

Constantia was the Byzantine name of Salamis, the capital of Cyprus. The *Panarion* or "Medicine Chest" was written there between 375 and 378.

a. Contrary to B. Lohse, *Passafest*, 16–18, the followers of Audius were not Quartodecimans, for they always celebrated the Pascha on Sunday. But this had to be the first Sunday after the Pesach of their Jewish contemporaries—whose manner of computing the date was rejected at Nicaea (see texts 52 and 53). This rejection was the basis of their grievance against Constantine. For the history and doctrines of the Audians, see Puech, *RAC* 1, 910–915.

65. EPIPHANIUS OF CONSTANTIA, *Panarion* 70, 10, 1–6

Critical edition: Holl-Lietzmann-Eltester, *GCS* 37, 242–243.

a. According to Schwartz, *Ostertafeln*, 108–109, the fragment comes from an older, perhaps Quartodeciman, edition of the *Didascalia* (cf. texts 85 and 86).

b. The exact construction is unclear, but the sense is plain.

c. See Eusebius, *Eccl. Hist.* 4, 5, 2. The changes which came about with the entry of the Gentile community in 135 are mentioned in *Panarion* 70, 9, 9. There is no reason, however, to assert that this was the moment when Jerusalem abandoned the original Quartodeciman practice to celebrate the Pascha on Sunday (see text 10, note b).

d. Holl found a gap in the manuscript text at this point.

e. Cf. *Didascalia* 21, ed. Funk [V 20, 10], in text 86; cf. also text 87, chs. 8 and 12.

66. EPIPHANIUS OF CONSTANTIA, *Exposition of the Faith* 22, 10–14

Critical edition: Holl-Lietzmann-Eltester, *GCS* 37, 523–524.

This "Treatise on the Faith of the Catholic and Apostolic Church" (*De Fide*) was written about 377 and appended to the *Panarion*. (Trans.)

a. Holl would read "only" where the manuscripts read "then."

b. On the six-day fast, see texts 49 and 86.

c. *Synaxeis epitelousi*. The synaxis or assembly often included the celebration of the Eucharist, but this might not be true of the services held on the weekdays of Lent and Holy Week. (Trans.)

d. This may refer to some churches in Syria, as may be inferred from Aphraates (text 87, note g).

e. At Jerusalem, two Masses were celebrated on Calvary on Holy Thursday afternoon (text 116, § 35). Augustine (letter 54, 4–6) is aware of both customs—that of celebrating two Masses, one in the morning and one in the evening, and that of celebrating only one, in the evening. These rites were introduced into the Holy Thursday observance in order to commemorate the institution of the Eucharist.

f. This was still the practice in Egypt and elsewhere, and it probably goes back to the beginning of Christianity. The *Epistle of the Apostles*, for instance, mentions the observance of the Pascha in memory of Christ's death with a fast and vigil lasting till cockcrow (text 14). Whether this took place in the night after the fourteenth or in the night between Saturday and Sunday, the context seems to exclude any other observance of the Pascha than this one.

67. AERIUS, Quotation and Report

Source: Epiphanius of Constantia, *Panarion* 75, 3, 4–8.

Critical edition: Holl-Lietzmann-Eltester, *GCS* 37, 335.

In 360, Aerius quarreled with his fellow ascetic, Eustathius, bishop of Sebaste, whom he accused of being too interested in material things. He attracted many dissidents in lesser Armenia to his schism and was still living in 375, when Epiphanius wrote.

a. Or: "are eager to fast."

b. The same refusal to celebrate the Pascha liturgically or to fast on prescribed days is found in the Gnostics of the second century (see text 17). The asceticism (*apotaxia*) of Aerius may have had other Gnostic features, such as the encratism, or exaggerated asceticism, known to have been practiced by the followers of Eustathius (see Salaville, *DThC* 5, 1571–1574), but Epiphanius does not list encratism among Aerius' defects. Only Filastrius of Brescia (*Diversarum hereseon liber* 72; ed. Marx [*CSEL* 38; Vienna: Tempsky, 1913] 38) ranks the Aerians among the Encratites. In 381 and 383 the emperor Theodosius condemned the Apotactics and Encratites as Manichaeans (see Bareille, *DThC* 1, 1646).

c. "Xerophagy," observed in Holy Week, and consisting of abstinence from all foods except bread, salt, and water (cf. texts 66 and 86).

d. Probably referring to the sufferings of the fasters rather than to those of Christ. (Trans.)

68. BASIL OF CAESAREA, Homily 13: *Exhortation to Holy Baptism*, 1

Edition: J. Garnier, Maurist (Paris 1721–1730); reprinted in *PG* 31, 424D–425A.

This homily was preached when Basil was bishop of Caesarea in Cappadocia (370–379).

a. Easter was also the privileged day for baptism in Jerusalem about

350: see Cyril of Jerusalem, *Catecheses* 18, 32 (*PG* 33, 1053), and thirty years later, Egeria (text 116, § 38). For Constantinople in 404, see Palladius, *Dialogue on the life of Chrysostom* 9 (*PG* 42, 33). For Syria in the fourth century, see text 87, ch. 13. In Thessaly baptism was given exclusively "in the days of the Pascha" according to Socrates, *Eccl. Hist.* 5, 22 (ed. Hussey-Bright [Oxford: Clarendon, 1893] 241). Elsewhere it was conferred also on the Epiphany and Pentecost, and during the Pentecost (text 48, note a).

b. Note the development which has taken place in the concept of the Pascha: in Tertullian (text 93) the Pascha is the day of baptism because the Pascha is the celebration of the passion; here, because the Pascha is the celebration of the resurrection. See Cantalamessa, *La pasqua della nostra salvezza*, 174ff.

69. GREGORY OF NAZIANZUS, Oration 1: *First Oration on the Pascha*, 3–4

> Critical edition: *Grégoire de Nazianze, Discours 1–3*, ed. Jean Bernardi (*SC* 247; Paris: Cerf, 1978) 74–77.

Gregory delivered this oration on the first Easter after his ordination to the priesthood in 362 (Bernardi, *SC* 247, 11–17).

a. The image is borrowed from Melito, *On the Pascha* 30 (ed. Hall, 16–17): "The death of the sheep was found to be a wall for the people." It is a biblical image: see, for example, 1 Samuel 25:16.

b. *Phyrama*. Actually Gregory's Bible says that in the Exodus from Egypt, the Hebrews took with them their *phyramata* (lumps of dough) without leaven (Exod 12:34 LXX). Gregory probably has in mind Paul's exhortation to the Christians to be what they really are, a new lump, unleavened (1 Cor 5:7). On the other hand, Pseudo-Hippolytus glides from 1 Corinthians 5:7 to Matthew 7:6 (in § 40) to make his metaphor: "We have received the new dough of his holy mixing, kneaded and fermented by a stronger power, his holy Spirit": *On the Holy Pascha* 39–40; ed. Nautin (*SC* 27), 160–161. (Trans.)

c. Cf. Rom 6:4-8. Nicetas of Heraclea (eleventh century) comments that "yesterday" may be taken to refer to Lent (*tessarakostê*) and "today" to the paschal feast (*PG* 36, 953C). But it is more likely that Gregory only wishes to contrast Good Friday and Holy Saturday with Easter Sunday. In any case, here, as in Basil (text 68), we see how the Church has begun to distribute the content of the Pascha over several days. The term *Pascha* continues to designate the fast, vigil, and Eucharist of the night before Sunday, but in this liturgy the moment of the Cross is now greatly attenuated in favor of the Resurrection (see Huber, 190).

70. GREGORY OF NAZIANZUS, Oration 45: *Second Oration on the Pascha*, 10

Edition: A. B. Caillau and R. Clémencet, Maurists (Paris 1778-1840); reprinted in *PG* 36, 636-637.

This oration was composed between 383 and 395.

a. In this passage, Gregory depends on Origen: see text 37, with note b. Gregory's typological interpretation of Exodus 12 in ch. 11-21 also seems to be derived from Origen's recently recovered treatise *Peri Pascha*: compare it with Procopius of Gaza's *Commentary on Exodus* (*PG* 87/1, 561ff.), which clearly depends on Origen's *Peri Pascha* (see Guéraud, *Journal of Egyptian Archaeology* 40 [1954] 63ff.).

b. Cf. text 2. In his letter 120 (*Gregor von Nazianz, Briefe*, ed. Paul Gallay [*GCS* 53; Berlin: Akademie-Verlag, 1969] 90), Gregory characterizes the day of the Pascha as *diabatêrion* and "mystery of the heavenly goods." His spiritualist, Origenian interpretation then passed into ascetical and monastic literature. Dorotheus of Gaza, for example, in his *Instructions to his Disciples* 16 (*Dorothée de Gaza, Oeuvres spirituelles*, ed. L. Regnault and J. de Préville [*SC* 92; Paris: Cerf, 1963] 460), quotes Evagrius of Pontus, who says in *Advice to the Monks* (Hugo Gressmann, *Nonnenspiegel und Mönchsspiegel des Euagrios Pontikos* [*TU* 39/4; Leipzig: Hinrichs, 1913] 156): *Pascha kyriou, diabasis apo kakias*, "The Pascha of the Lord is a transition from evil."

c. Pascha resembles *paschein* ("to suffer") and thus is associated with its cognate synonym *pathein* and the substantive *pathos* ("passion"). (Trans.)

71. GREGORY OF NAZIANZUS, Oration 45: *Second Oration on the Pascha*, 23

Edition: Caillau-Clémencet, reprinted in *PG* 36, 653C-656.

a. The three-stage typology seen here is based on Origen's triad of shadow, image, and truth (see texts 38 and 58, note f). This is itself patterned after the "shadow," "image," and "future goods" of Hebrews 10:1.

b. In the context, this must mean: "What we learn from the Logos in the present dispensation will never grow old and out of date (though it must be augmented and perfected in the future kingdom)." (Trans.)

72. GREGORY OF NYSSA, *On the Three-Day Interval between Our Lord's Death and Resurrection*

> Critical edition: E. Gebhardt in *Gregorii Nysseni Opera* 9, 1, *Sermones* (Leiden: Brill, 1967) 274. There is an English translation of this work by S. G. Hall on 31–50 of *The Easter Sermons of Gregory of Nyssa; Translation and Commentary*, eds. Andreas Spira and Christoph Klock (Patristic Monograph Series, 9; Cambridge, Mass.: Philadelphia Patristic Foundation, 1981).

This oration was pronounced during an Easter vigil in Gregory's later years (386–395). Note *The Easter Sermons of Gregory of Nyssa*, trans. Andreas Spira and Christoph Klock (Patristic Monograph Series, 9; Cambridge: Philadelphia Patristic Foundation, 1981).

a. Cf. Genesis 2:3. The celebration of the mystery of the Sabbath is typical of the Cappadocians and of the Greek writers in general; see, for example, texts 73 and 76, § 35.

b. According to Athanasius (text 58, with note b), the six days preceding Holy Saturday symbolize the six days of creation.

c. *Tên tês katapauseôs hêmeran*. Compare the *Epistle of Barnabas* 15, 8–9 (trans. Kirsopp Lake [LCL; London: Heineman, 1912] 394–397): "God says, 'The present Sabbaths are not acceptable to me, but that (Sabbath is acceptable) which I have made, on which, having given rest to all things (*katapausas ta panta*), I will make a beginning of an eighth day, that is, a beginning of another world.' This is why we keep the eighth day with rejoicing: on it Jesus rose from the dead and appeared (to his followers) and went up to heaven." (Trans.)

d. More exactly: "through the dispensation regarding his death."

e. Pseudo-Athanasius, *Sermon on the Holy Pascha* (*PG* 28, 1073C–1076A) describes Christ's resurrection as *anaklêsis tôn pantôn* ("the recall of all things from exile"), and depicts the risen Creator calling the universe to be re-created (*pros anaktisin*).

f. Cf. text 76, § 36.

73. AMPHILOCHIUS OF ICONIUM, Oration 5: *For Holy Saturday*, 1

> Critical edition: *Amphilochii Iconiensis Opera*, ed. Cornelis Datema (*CCh.SG* 3; Turnhout: Brepols, 1978) 133.

A cousin of Gregory of Nazianzus, Amphilochius was bishop of Iconium from 373 to 394; he was an opponent of Arianism and of exaggerated (Manichaean) asceticism.

a. The descent into Hades is the beginning of Christ's triumph over death and anticipates in a way the resurrection: see Schulz, *ZKTh* 81 (1959) 1–66.

b. The same dichotomy of "yesterday" and "today," which Gregory of Nazianzus used (text 69) to detach Christ's resurrection from his death, is used here to detach the descent into Hades from the death. The same thing is done by Pseudo-Epiphanius, *Homily for the Great Sabbath* (*PG* 43, 440C and 441 A), who sees the Descent as the realization of the salvation of the world—something which Gregory of Nazianzus (oration 45, 1) and the Physiologus (§ 16; *PG* 43, 517–539) had seen rather in the resurrection. On the centrality of the Descent in the Greek and Byzantine view of the Pascha, see Huber, 197–203.

74. JOHN CHRYSOSTOM, *Orations Against the Jews* 3, 4

Edition: Bernard de Montfaucon, Maurist; reprinted in *PG* 48, 867.

This oration, delivered early in 387, warns the Christians of Antioch against celebrating the Pascha "with the Jews" as the Protopaschites did, contrary to the decree of Nicaea.

a. The four days of the week on which the Divine Liturgy is celebrated in the Greek Church—Wednesday, Friday, Saturday, and Sunday—are mentioned by Basil, letter 93 (*PG* 32, 484; *Saint Basile, Lettres*, ed. Yves Courtonne 2 [Paris: Les Belles Lettres, 1957] 203.

b. Didymus of Alexandria, *On the Trinity* 3, 21 (*PG* 39, 905D), asks, "Why, then, do we celebrate the Pascha in faith every year, nay, every day, or rather every hour, partaking of his Body and Blood?" He is thinking of Communion in the home.

c. Instead of the Pascha *every year*, we have the Pascha *every time* we have the Eucharist. This radical reduction of the Pascha to the Eucharist is found also in Eusebius, text 56, § 7, where the Sunday Eucharist is presented as a weekly Pascha; also Augustine, text 130, says that the Pascha is celebrated every day in meditation on the passion and resurrection, and in daily Communion but without attenuating the importance of the yearly celebration.

d. "Awesome" (*phriktos*) is Chrysostom's favorite epithet for the Christian mystery and for the Eucharist in particular: see, for example, *Homilies on John* 10, 3 (*PG* 59, 77). The term is found in other Antiochene writers, for example, Theodore of Mopsuestia and the *Apostolic Constitutions*, and derives from Cyril of Jerusalem.

75. PSEUDO-CHRYSOSTOM, *Homily on the Holy Pascha* 7, 3-4: A Complex Mystery

> Critical edition: Fernand Floëri and Pierre Nautin, *Homélies pascales* 3, *Une homélie anatolienne sur la date de Pâques en l'an 387* (Paris: Cerf, 1957; *SC* 48) 113-115.

This sermon, preached on April 21, 387, is devoted to explaining why Easter is being held so late: the fourteenth of the first lunar month being a Sunday, the feast of the Resurrection is deferred for a week so as not to coincide with the Pascha, the day of the passion.

a. Epiphanius, *Panarion* 50, 1, 5-8 (*PG* 41, 881 D - 885 B), mentions that some contemporary "Quartodecimans" kept the Pascha on a fixed date—March 25 (or 23), which they considered the anniversary of Christ's death (see also *Panarion* 50, 15; Huber, 85-86; and Loi, *EL* 85 [1971]).

b. *Mystêrion*, the mystery in a ritual sense.

c. *Theôria*, the mystery in an intellectual sense. Augustine (text 124) gives the same reason for the movable date of the Pascha, namely, representation of the multiple meanings in the mystery.

d. On the coincidence of the three elements—equinox, full moon, and triduum—see also Epiphanius, *Panarion* 70, 11, 1f.

76. PSEUDO-CHRYSOSTOM, *Homilies on the Holy Pascha* 7, 35-36: The New Beginning

> Critical edition: Floëri and Nautin, *SC* 48, 145-147.

a. Our homilist does not say: "the Passion is commemorated at the equinox," as he would if the day of the Passion were movable in the solar calendar. For him, the day of the passion is March 25, which is also the equinox. It is not necessarily the day of the Pascha, however; this is determined by the moon. (Trans.)

b. *Anakephalaiôsis*. The central theme of the whole homily is the Pascha as recapitulation and re-creation (*anaktisis*). The very original idea of a return of "the most pure time" of the beginnings (cf. § 28) is found also in Procopius of Gaza, *Commentaries on Exodus*, Exodus 12:15 (*PG* 87/1, 575 A), and it is not impossible that it is found in Origen. See also Gaudentius of Brescia (text 118).

c. *Paraskeuê*.

d. *Diorthôthênai, diorthôsis* = "straighten," "set on his feet again."

e. A similar interpretation of the mystery of Holy Saturday is found in Gregory of Nyssa (text 72). The connection between our homilist and

Gregory of Nyssa is brought out in detail by Nautin, *Homélies pascales* 2 (*SC* 36) 84ff.

f. *Tên ek tou pathous eleutherian*. Cf. Irenaeus, text 29: "the name of this mystery is *pathos*, source of liberation." (Trans.)

g. The typological nexus between the first day of creation and the Sunday of the Resurrection is found already in Justin, *First Apology* 67. Gregory of Nazianzus, oration 44, 5, sees the idea of recapitulation in every Sunday, which as first day of the week is also eighth day of the past week.

77. PSEUDO-CHRYSOSTOM, *Homilies on the Holy Pascha* 7, 39: The New Paschal Sacrifice

Critical edition: Floëri and Nautin, *SC* 48, 149.

a. *Amnos*, which Nautin substitutes for the manuscript reading *anthropos* ("man").

b. *Pathos*. Throughout the homily, especially in §§ 34, 48, and 50, *pascha* = *pathos*, an equation which survived from the Asiatic tradition after the disappearance of the Quartodecimans.

c. For our homilist, the essence of the liturgical Pascha of the Church, insofar as it "imitates the true Pascha," which is the historical Pascha of Christ, is found in the Eucharist: see §§ 38, 40, and 48, and Cantalamessa, *La pasqua della nostra salvezza*, 225–226. The same is true for the late fourth-century Pseudo-Pionius (*Life of Polycarp* 2, 3; ed. Lightfoot, *Apostolic Fathers*, 434), for whom the Pascha and the Pentecost consist in the offering of bread and wine, "the new mystery of the passion and resurrection."

d. *En toutois tois typois*: later commonly called *antitypoi* (see text 83 with note c), the elements of bread and wine, even when consecrated, are still signs and figures, not the final reality. (Trans.)

78. DIDYMUS OF ALEXANDRIA, *Commentary on Zechariah* 5, 88

Critical edition: *Didyme l'Aveugle, Sur Zacharie* 3, ed. Louis Doutreleau (*SC* 85; Paris: Cerf, 1962) 1016–1018.

Didymus the Blind dictated this mostly allegorical commentary in 387.

a. *Tên diabatêriôn heortên*: the Pascha as *diabasis* remains the dominant concept at Alexandria. Cyril of Alexandria, *Commentary on Luke* 22, 8 (*PG* 72, 904B) calls it *diabasis*, and Pseudo-Cyril, *On the Pascha* (*PG* 77, 1208B), defines it as *diabatêrion*.

b. Here, as in Athanasius (text 59), the three interpretations of *pascha* as passage, suffering, and Eucharist are united and harmonized. Cf. Didymus, *On the Trinity* 3, 21 (*PG* 39, 905 B-D).

79. *Apostolic Constitutions* 5, 20, 1-2. 4. 14

> Critical edition: *Les Constitutions Apostoliques* 2, ed. Marcel Metzger (*SC* 329; Paris: Cerf, 1986), 274-277, 282-283.

Entitled "The *Diatagai* (or *Diataxeis* or *Diatagmata*) of the Holy Apostles through Clement," this document is a reworking of the *Didachê*, the *Diataxis*, and the *Didascalia*, done in Syria about 380.

a. Note the prominence given to the "feast" of the octave day (see the Introduction, part V, 1, "The Traditions of the Greek Church"). In the prescriptions that the author adds to those of the *Didascalia*, in book 8, 33, 3, the week after Easter is even treated as the equal of the Great Week (Holy Week): "The one is of the resurrection; the other, of the passion." The entire fortnight is declared a holiday for the servants, so that they can be instructed in their faith during these days. This prescription is found also in imperial legislation of 389 and 392. Later, the synod in Trullo (692) and, in the West, the Councils of Aachen (809), Mainz (813), Meaux (846), and Engelheim (949) call for the festal observance of a full week after Easter, though not necessarily before (Funk, *Didascalia et Constitutiones Apostolorum* 1:298, note 14, and 539, note 3).

b. Some manuscripts read: "and of the lance with which he was wounded in the side."

c. That is, from Easter Sunday, the first Sunday of the solar year, which begins with the spring equinox. (Trans.)

d. *Analêpsis*, i.e., the ascension. The Greek term is based on Acts 1:2 and 2:2, *anelêmphthê* = "he was taken up."

e. Note the fixing of the commemoration of the Ascension (called "the limit of the dispensation pertaining to Christ" in 8, 33, 4) on the fortieth day, and the emergence of a special commemoration of the descent of the Holy Spirit on the fiftieth day, with the implicit devaluation of the fifty days as a single feast.

e. Like the week after Easter, the week after Pentecost was celebrated as a feast in the fourth century. (Trans.)

80. SEVERIAN OF GABALA, Fragment

> Source: The Greek Catena on the Acts of the Apostles.
> Critical edition: *Catenae Graecorum Patrum in Novum*

Testamentum 3: *Catena in Acta SS. Apostolorum e Cod. Nov. Coll.*, ed. John Anthony Cramer (Oxford 1838; reprinted Hildesheim: G. Olms, 1967) 16.

Drawing upon late Jewish tradition, which we find reflected in the Book of Jubilees and the Qumran literature, Severian (about 400) sees the day of Pentecost as the feast of the Giving of the Law for the Jews and of the Holy Spirit (the new law) for the Christians: see Kretschmar, *ZKG* 66 (1954-1955) 209-53. In the West, the same idea is expressed in so many words by Augustine: see text 133.

81. THEOPHILUS OF ALEXANDRIA, *Festal Letter for 401* 20, 4

Source: Jerome, *Letters* 96, 20, 4.

Edition: *Sancti Eusebii Hieronymi Epistulae*, Part 2 (Letters 71-120), ed. Isidorus Hilberg (*CSEL* 55; Vienna: Tempsky, 1912) 181.

a. In 401, these dates corresponded to March 9, April 8, and April 13 in the Julian calendar.

b. Some manuscripts read: *reliquas*; others: *alias*.

c. The structure of the celebration of the Pascha in Alexandria seems not to have changed since the days of Athanasius. Moreover, "the festivity of Pentecost" still means the entire period of fifty days.

82. THEODORET OF CYRRHUS, *Cure for the Greek Illnesses* 9, 24

Critical edition: *Théodoret de Cyr, Thérapeutique des maladies helléniques*, ed. Pierre Canivet (*SC* 57; Paris: Cerf, 1958) 343.

This apology against pagan thought was written perhaps at Antioch and probably before the council of Ephesus (431); so Canivet, 1:28-31.

a. Passion and resurrection are still united as the single content of the Pascha, while it remains known as "the day of the Passion": see also Theodoret's *Festal Letters* 63 and 64 (ed. Y. Azéma, *SC* 98, 142-143). At about this time in other places the two mysteries are found distributed between Good Friday and Easter Sunday. For example, in 449 the Council of Ephesus (*ACO* 2, 1, 1; p. 187, line 15) says: "The day of the saving passion has come, and the sacred night, and the feast of the Resurrection."

b. An allusion to the persecution of Diocletian in 303. Cf. Eusebius, *Eccl. Hist.* 8, 3: here too the Pascha is called "feast of the Passion."

83. EUTYCHIUS OF CONSTANTINOPLE, *Sermon on the Pascha and the Eucharist*, 2

> Edition: Angelo Mai, *Bibliotheca nova patrum*, 4:54; reprinted *PG* 86/2, 2393 B.

Eutychius was patriarch of Constantinople from 552 to 565 and from 577 to 582.

a. *Mystikon pascha* is an expression for the Supper used also in the *Quaestiones ex concordantia evangelica* 34 (*PG* 93, 1421 D, in a work called *Collectio difficultatum et solutionum*—but see G. Bardy, *RB* 1933, 226–229) attributed to Hesychius of Jerusalem, and by John Philoponus, *On the Pascha* (*Disputatio de Paschate*, ed. C. Walter [Jena, 1899] 209). (The belief that Christ himself partook of the Eucharist was common among the Syrians; Marcion too had interpreted Luke 22:15 [see text 12, note d] in this sense.)

b. The ancient Johannine tradition of Pascha-as-passion, attested yet again in Procopius of Gaza, *On Exodus* 12, 2 (*PG* 87, 561 B), survives in the Synoptic version of the Pascha as immolation or mystic passion (i.e., as Eucharist), inherited from the Syrians. Eutychius, in ch. 4 of this sermon (*PG* 86/2, 2397 A), defines the Supper as "first-fruits and mystical pledge of the historical reality of the Cross."

c. The paschal lamb was the type; the Eucharistic species, the antitype (see *PGL*, s.v. *antitypos*, 7 b). Christ "mixed himself into" the bread before breaking it.

84. *The Paschal Chronicle*

> Critical edition: *Paschalion seu Chronicon paschale* ed. Ludovicus Dindorf (Corpus Scriptorum Historiae Byzantinae, 16; Bonn: E. Weber, 1832), 1:424–425. Reprinted in *PG* 92, 1057.

This chronicle of world events from Adam to A.D. 629 was written in the first half of the seventh century, very probably in Constantinople.

a. The identification of the Pascha with the Sunday of the Resurrection is rather late in patristic writing and did not remain unopposed, even in the West—for example, text 140 with note a.

b. See this Chronicle, ed. Dindorf, 228; *PG* 92, 552–53.

c. The Devil, according to Hebrews 2:14.

d. *Hyperbasis*, a word traditionally reserved for the passage of God (e.g., texts 4, 54, and 114 with note b), is used here like *diabasis*, to denote an action of human beings.

85. *Diataxis of the Apostles*, Fragment

Source: Epiphanius, *Panarion* 70, 11, 3.
Critical text: Holl-Lietzmann-Eltester, *GCS* 37, 244.

This sentence seems to be the basis for many statements in the *Didascalia*, ch. 21 (see text 86). Schwartz, *Ostertafeln*, 108–109, concludes that the *Diataxis* ("ordinance," "constitution") in which Epiphanius found this sentence was probably an early (Quartodeciman?) version of the *Didascalia*. In any case, it corresponds exactly to the program for the Quartodeciman Pascha: a fast on the fourteenth, continuing through the night, followed by a feast on the fifteenth. It also suggests that the Christian feast lasted a whole week (the seven days of Unleavened Bread).

a. The traditional rationale given for the paschal fast is: "the days will come when the Bridegroom is taken away from them; in those days they will fast" (Mark 2:20): see Tertullian, text 96; *Didascalia* 21 (ed. Funk [5, 13–16, 19–20]; Vööbus' trans., 188); Epiphanius, *Exposition of the Faith* 22 (*PG* 42, 825 B - 828 A); *Apostolic Constitutions* 5, 18 (ed. Metzger, 2:270–271). The present passage in the *Diataxis*, plus ch. 21 in the *Didascalia* (ed. Funk 5, 13–16, 19–20; Vööbus' trans., 188–196, 199, 201), and the corresponding passages of the *Apostolic Constitutions*, are the only instances in the tradition where atonement for the Jews is given as a reason. (*Didache* 1, 3, and Pseudo-Barnabas 7, 5, should not be adduced as instances.)

b. For the interpretation of the week of Unleavened Bread as a time of mourning, see also Aphraates, *Demonstration* 12, 8. (Trans.)

c. Actually bitter herbs were ritually eaten with the matzah only at the Passover meal itself.

86. *Didascalia Apostolorum*, 21

Critical edition: Arthur Vööbus, *The Didascalia Apostolorum in Syriac* (Louvain: Secrétariat du CorpusSCO, 1979), ch. XI–XXVI, text: *CSCO* 407 / script. syr. 179, 211–215; translation *CSCO* 408 / script. syr. 180, 196, 198–200, 202.

English version used here: *Didascalia Apostolorum: The Syriac Version Translated and Accompanied by the Verona Latin Fragments*, by Richard Hugh Connolly (Oxford:

Clarendon, 1929) 187–192. Subdivision numbers in square brackets are taken from F. X. Funk's edition, *Didascalia et Constitutiones Apostolorum*, vol. 1 (Paderborn: Schöningh, 1905), where they serve to indicate the identity of sentences in the *Didascalia* with those in the *Constitutiones*.

The *Didascalia* (teachings) was written for Gentile Christians in northern Syria in the first decades of the third century. The Greek original is lost, but we have a Syriac version made in the same century.

a. In the Syrian writers, "the People" means the Jews.

b. Again, below [5, 20, 10]: "When that people keeps the Passover, do you fast." After the calendar disputes of the fourth century (see texts 52 and 53), the author of the *Apostolic Constitutions* changed this prescription so as to enjoin the opposite: "Be not concerned to celebrate the feast at the same time as the Jews" (5, 17).

c. An interpolation, according to Holl (*Gesammelte Aufsätze*, 2:210): the original only prescribed fasting on Wednesday and Friday, the days on which Jesus was arrested and crucified. Nevertheless, after Dionysius of Alexandria (text 49), this is one of the earliest witnesses to the extension of the paschal fast to the whole of Holy Week (see Arbesmann, *RAC* 7, 513–514). For other witnesses to the author's unusual chronology of the passion, see Jaubert, *The Date*, 69–76.

d. Cf. text 44.

e. Until cockcrow, the traditional time for breaking the paschal fast.

f. Cf. below [5, 6] and [5, 20, 12]. "The third hour in the night" must be either 3 a.m. or the time between 2 and 3 a.m., taking midnight as the division point between the days, after the Roman and Greek custom. This must have been the way of reckoning familiar to those for whom the *Didascalia* was written, since, in [5, 14, 19], the author is at pains to explain and justify the biblical reckoning of the whole night to the following day. The Roman and Greek way of reckoning is certainly presupposed by the *Testament of our Lord Jesus Christ* (from Syria at the beginning of the fifth century) when it moves the end of the fast from cock-crow to midnight (2, 12; ed. and trans. Ignatius Ephraem Rahmani [Mainz: Kirchheim, 1899], 135). In the latter document, the purpose was probably to avoid fasting on Sunday, even for the Pascha—though the *Didascalia* [5, 20, 12] had made an exception for this one Sunday. (Trans.)

g. This structure for the vigil (with a few variations, namely, mention of the Law among the Scriptures to be read, of the administration of baptism, and of a homily to the people) is found again in Syria towards the end of the fourth century: *Apostolic Constitutions* 5, 19, 3; ed. Metzger, 2:270–273.

87. APHRAATES, *Demonstration* **12:** *On the Pascha*, **6–8, 12–13**

> Syriac text with Latin trans.: Ioannes Parisot in *Patrologia Syriaca*, vol. 1 (Paris: Firmin-Didot, 1894), col. 515–524, 533–540. Our chapter numbers are taken from this edition.
>
> German trans.: *Aphrahat's des persischen Weisen Homilien*, trans. Georg Bert (*TU* 3, 3/4; Leipzig: Hinrichs, 1888) 188–190, 194–195.

The following notes, except g, l, m, and p, are largely the contribution of the translator, James M. Quigley.

In this treatise, written in the year 344 for someone (perhaps a Quartodeciman) with "difficulties about the date of the Pascha" (ch. 12), Aphraates explains how his church faithfully observes the Pascha on 14 Nisan (whatever the day of the week), by beginning the paschal fast on that date, but also is true to the gospel narrative by celebrating the passion on the following Friday (whatever day of the month it might be).

a. *B-lilyâ ntîrâ*, "in the 'night of observance' " (Exod 12:42; see text 5, note a).

b. The Jewish Passover was eaten in the night after the fourteenth of Nisan, but Aphraates puts Jesus' Passover meal in the night leading to the fourteenth, which his tradition held as the day of Jesus' death.

c. That is, he celebrated the Pascha in such a way as to change it into the reality which it had foreshadowed.

d. Ephraem too makes Judas depart without receiving "the bread which saves from death"; the morsel he receives has been dipped in water so as to negate its covenant meaning, which is the real presence of Christ's body (*Commentary on the Diatessaron* 19, 3, for which see Louis Leloire, *S. Éphrem, Commentaire de l'Évangile concordant, Version arménienne* [*CSCO* 137 / script. arm. 1; Louvain: Secrétariat du CorpusSCO, 1953] 269–270, and Louis Leloire, *Éphrem de Nisibe, Commentaire de l'Évangile Concordant ou Diatessaron* [*SC* 121; Paris: Cerf, 1966] 332). But in the *Hymns on the Unleavened Bread* 14 and 18, this morsel was taken from the paschal meal before the institution of the Eucharist (Beck, *CSCO* 413, 5–6) and was only a type of Christ's body. A century or so later, in Pseudo-Ephraem, *Sermons for Holy Week* 4, 173–197 (Beck's trans., *CSCO* 413, 57–58 with note 53), the blessing which is washed out of the bread through dipping is the real presence of Christ's body. Funk, *Didascalia et Constitutiones Apostolorum*, 272, lists Tatian, Victor of Capua, Ammonius, and Hilary as agreeing with Aphraates that Judas did not partake of the Eucharist, while Chrysostom, Jerome, Augustine, and Theodoret say that he did.

e. The Syriac text must be translated either: "he who has eaten his body and drunk his blood," or: "he who has eaten his own body and drunk his own blood." Neither concept accords with the context. The Armenian version puts us on the right track; it reads: "when his body has been eaten and his blood has been drunk" (see *La version arménienne des oeuvres d'Aphraate le Syrien*, trans. Guy Lafontaine, vol. 3 [Louvain: Peeters, 1980; *CSCO* 424 / Script. arm. 12] 91). Hence we accept Burkitt's emendation of the Syriac from *'kl* (has eaten) to *'kyl* (is eaten): cf. Connolly, *Didascalia*, 266. The idea that Jesus could be counted among the dead when his body had been eaten and his blood drunk is found also in Ephraem, *Commentary on the Diatessaron* 19, 4 (in Leloir's trans. of the Armenian, *SC* 121, 333–334), where it is moreover explained that Jesus could be considered dead once he had broken his body and given it to the disciples because he gave them his body to eat as a memorial or sacrament of his death and then passed into their bellies just as he would later go into the earth. Somewhat more elegantly, Gregory of Nyssa (*On the Three-Day Interval*, ed. Gebhardt, 287–288) explains it as follows: "He who gives his disciples his own body to eat declares that the sacrifice of the lamb has already been carried out; for the body of the sacrificial animal would not be edible if it were still alive."

f. *'arûbtâ* (cf. Hebrew *'ereb*, "evening") means "eve of the Sabbath," that is, Friday. It is Aphraates' word for the gospel term *paraskeuê*, "preparation," which Mark 15:42 defines as "the day before the Sabbath," but which in John 19:14 means the day before the Pascha. Aphraates follows John literally in putting Jesus' death on "the Paraseceve of the Pascha," but he understands this datum as the Friday of the Pascha rather than as the Preparation Day for the Pascha.

g. When he sets the institution of the Eucharist at the same hour as the resurrection, Aphraates may be reflecting a liturgical datum. It is possible that, already in his time, the Syrian Church held two vigils in the paschal week. The first, the traditional Syrian Pascha, in the night between Thursday and Friday, would have commemorated the institution of the Eucharist together with Christ's death, and would have included the administration of baptism, which the Syrians connected with Christ's washing his disciples' feet and with his passion (see *Demonstration* 12, 10). A second vigil would then have been held in the night between Saturday and Sunday to celebrate the resurrection (and to observe the Pascha on the same day as the rest of the Church). Something of the sort is indicated by the fact that only thirty-three years later Epiphanius (text 66) reported that some Churches kept two vigils, one before Good Friday, the other before Easter Sunday. The only Church known to have done this is the Syrian, and this custom can be traced back at least to the beginning of the fifth century: see F. C. Burkitt, "The Early Syriac Lectionary System," *Proceedings of the British Academy* 10 (1921-1923) 323f. The Chaldean liturgy still keeps the vigil between Holy Thursday and Good Friday: see Juan Mateos, *Lelya-Sapra: Essai d'interprétation des matines chaldéennes* (Orientalia christiana analecta 156; Rome: Pontificio Istituto Orientale, 1959) 219 and 228. By the seventh century among the Nestorians the first vigil had been shortened to a vesper service after sunset, but this ended with a Eucharistic liturgy and the breaking of the Lenten fast: "Isôbabh [d. about 660] says about the last Thursday [of Lent, Holy Thursday]: 'After sunset they begin the evening (office) and follow it with the mysteries' " (Anonymi auctoris *Expositio Officiorum Ecclesiae Georgio Arbelensi vulgo adscripta*, ed. R. H. Connolly, vol. 1 [*CSCO* 64 / script. syr. 25; 1911; reprinted Louvain: Durbecq, 1954] 62; Latin trans. by R. H. Connolly, 1 [*CSCO* 71 / script. syr. 28; 1913; reprinted ibid. 1954] 52). Subsequently, it seems, the Eucharistic liturgy was moved to midday on Thursday, and it was the patriarch George (ninth century) who put it back in the evening, so that the tenth century author could report: "On Friday we break the fast, wherefore on Friday [that is, in the night following Thursday] we add the mysteries of the Pascha to the evening office. Friday and Saturday, therefore, belong to the passion, and they are not days of the fast but of the crucifixion" (ibid., ch. 13; *CSCO* 64, 62; *CSCO* 71, 51). The Syriac *Didascalia*, however, prescribes a strict fast for the Friday and Saturday of Holy Week: see text 86 [5, 18]. This was the paschal fast, distinct from the forty-day fast of Lent.

h. Gregory of Nyssa also reckons the three days and three nights of Matthew 12:40 as beginning with the institution of the Eucharist and concluding with the end of the Sabbath: see *On the Three-Day Interval*, ed. Gebhardt, 288. The author of the *Didascalia*, however, reckons the first day as "the hours when our Lord was crucified" (apparently the time between the third and sixth hour on Friday as mentioned in Mark 15:25, 33—cf. *Apostolic Constitutions* 5, 14, 14; ed. Metzger, 2:257), and the third night he counts as "the three hours of the night after the Sabbath, in which our Lord slept" (ch. 21 [5, 14]; Vööbus' trans., 190). This is the solution adopted by Origen, Ephraem, and Epiphanius (Drobner, 106-107). The purpose of these admittedly artificial reckonings at first seems to have been to fix the proper times for beginning and ending the absolute fast, undertaken in imitation of the apostles, who fasted "for a testimony of the three days" (text 86 [5, 18]) "when the Bridegroom was taken from them," and when Jesus himself ate and drank nothing (*Demonstration* 12, 12). But Drobner detects a different purpose in Gregory of Nyssa, namely, to counter the doctrines of Eunomius and

Apollinarius of Laodicea by stressing the full divinity and humanity of Christ, who, as Lord of time, was able to divide days and nights as he chose, and, as God made man, was able to lay down his soul and take it up again when he chose (Drobner, "Three Days and Three Nights in the Heart of the Earth," in Spira and Klock, 263–278).

i. Aphraates insists that Jesus was crucified on the fourteenth, but here (ch. 8) he identifies the Day of the Passion, and below (ch. 12) the Day of Crucifixion with the fifteenth. This is not a natural day of twenty-four hours but a liturgical entity—the Pascha celebrated from noon on Friday to cockcrow on Sunday. It is called *'arûbtâ, "Parasceve,"* because it begins on Friday, but it is counted as the fifteenth because it occupies the middle ground between the trial on the fourteenth and the resurrection on the sixteenth.

j. Alluding to the bitter herbs eaten with the unleavened bread at the Passover meal. Cf. text 85.

k. There follow eight instances of the fulfillment of Old Testment types, showing how the Christian Pascha differs from that of the Jews. Next we have a section criticizing the Jews for the commonplace reasons that (a) they keep the Pascha outside of Jerusalem, contrary to the Law, and (b) all their feasts are illegitimate since the abrogation of the Covenant and its replacement by Christianity. There is, however, no criticism of the Jewish calendar, and Aphraates seems content to keep the Pascha always in the same month as the Jews. But see note o below.

l. *Yawmâ d-peshâ d-haseh d-pârûqan.* The combination, "Pascha of the Passion," indicates the persistence of the (Quartodeciman) concept of the Pascha as the feast of the Passion. It may also be taken to imply awareness of a rival concept and distinct feast, that of the Pascha-of-the-Passion-and-Resurrection celebrated by the Great Church on the eve of Sunday. In this treatise Aphraates gives no indication of how his church observed this other Pascha or how it celebrated the resurrection. The compound series of nouns, "Day of the Pascha of the Passion of our Savior" recurs in almost identical form in a contemporary Syrian document preserved only in Latin translation, the treatise *De solstitiis et aequinoctiis,* by Bernard Botte as an appendix to his study, *Les origines de la Noël et de l'Épiphanie* (Textes et études liturgiques, 1; Louvain: Abbaye de Mont-César, 1932; reprinted ibid. 1961) 99. The unknown author, in asserting that the death of Christ occurred on the anniversary of his conception, March 25, the day of the equinox and of the Pascha, calls it *dies paschae passionis domini et conceptionis eius.*

m. Cf. *Didascalia* 21 [5, 13]; Vööbus' trans., 191: "It is not lawful to you to fast on the first of the week, because it is my resurrection."

n. The observance of the week of Unleavened Bread, beginning with the Jewish Pascha on 14 Nisan, on whatever weekday this happened to fall, together with the beginning of the paschal fast, is also prescribed in the *Didascalia* (text 86 [5, 20]). Thus, and with the title "Day of the Pascha of the Passion" for the fourteenth, the Syrian Church honored the Quartodeciman tradition. But, by having the solemnity of the Lord's death always on the following Friday and Saturday, it was able to keep the Pascha with the other Churches and still preserve its content as a feast which emphasized the death of Christ more than the resurrection. In this arrangement, the Syrian Church of the early fourth century agreed with the Audians.

o. *Men 'edan l-'edan*: Bert translates: "from beginning to end," referring to the seven-day festival of the Unleavened Bread. But *'edan* also means an annual occasion, and it is more probable that Aphraates is referring in a vague way to dates for the Pascha. (This is surely the meaning of the phrase in ch. 8 above: "from year to year.") If "at the proper time" then means that each Pascha should fall in a distinct solar year, coming always after the spring equinox, he would, with this phrase, distance himself from the Protopaschites, who were envisaged by Constantine's *Letter to the Churches* (see text 52 with note b) and by the paschal decree of Nicaea (see text 53 and Duchesne, *RQH* 28 [1880] 5–42). The Protopaschites had recently been excommunicated by various synods in the East, including the Council of Antioch in 341 (see Bardy, *Dictionnaire de droit canonique* 1, 597), for "celebrating the Pascha with the Jews" rather than with the other Churches of the Empire. But Aphraates is far from clear on this point. Only with the *Apostolic Constitutions* (ed. Funk, 5, 17; ed. Metzger, 2:266–269) around 380, does a Syrian writer unequivocally reject the Jewish paschal computus.

p. *Rûsmà l-metal*: an allusion to the rite of anointing, which in Syria preceded the immersion rather than following it (see J. Ysebaert, *Greek Baptismal Terminology: Its Origins and Early Development* [Graecitas Christianorum Primaeva, 1; Nijmegen: Dekker en van de Vegt, 1962] 338, 364–365). On the baptismal anointing at Easter, see text 48 with note d. Bert, 194–195, sees this phrase rather as the equivalent of *reddere symbolum*, referring to the repetition of the Creed by the one about to be baptized.

q. Probably the consecration of the Eucharist rather than of the baptismal water (Bert, 195).

r. Towards the beginning of the fourth century, in the Church of Caesarea in Palestine, at least, every Friday was a fast in honor of the passion (Eusebius, *On the Paschal Solemnity* 12; *PG* 24, 705C). The *Diataxis*, according to Epiphanius, *Panarion* 75, 6, 1, had prescribed fasting every Wednesday and Friday except during the Pentecost, and later, around 380, the *Apostolic Constitutions* 5, 20, 18 (ed. Metzger, 2:284–285) prescribe fasting every Wednesday and Friday except on feasts of the Lord. See Arbesmann, *RAC* 7, 509–510.

88. EPHRAEM THE SYRIAN, *Hymns on the Crucifixion* 3, 1–2

> Critical edition: *Des heiligen Ephraem des Syrers Pascha-hymnen (De azymis, de crucifixione, de resurrectione)*, ed. and trans. Edmund Beck (Louvain: Secrétariat du CorpusSCO, 1964); *CSCO* 248 / script. syr. 108, 49–50; *CSCO* 249 / script. syr. 109, 40.

Ephraem seems to have written the *Hymns on the Crucifixion* in Nisibis before he migrated to Edessa in 363.

a. The sun is always "full," but on the fifteenth of the lunar month, the moon is equally full. This has symbolic meaning for Ephraem; e.g. *Hymns on the Crucifixion* 4, 15: "The heavenly bodies too served him on the day of the passion: they were both full, a symbol of his fullness." The fact that in the middle of the month one rises as the other sets means that there is no time of darkness, and the hours of the night are as full of illumination as those of the day (Eusebius: "The moon was created full, as was fitting" (*PG* 5, 1368), and "God, having made sun and moon gave them each an equal share in the period of day and night" (Cyril of Jerusalem, text 63). Furthermore, the position of the sun and moon opposite each other in the sky can be given several symbolic interpretations (see *Hymns on the Crucifixion* 6 and 7). (Trans.)

b. In his *Commentary on Exodus* 12, 3 (trans. by Tonneau; *CSCO* 153, 121), Ephraem sees the paschal meal of the Hebrews as a figure of both the passion and the Eucharist. See also Pseudo-Ephraem, *Sermons for Holy Week* 4, 7 (ed. Beck, *CSCO* 412, 28).

c. This two-stage typology, which is strong in Aphraates (*Demonstration* 12, 5–6), is characteristic of Ephraem's paschal hymns. Even in the concluding strophe of the *Hymns on the Unleavened Bread* (5, 23; cf. Beck's trans., *CSCO* 249, 11), where the redemption is expressed as having three phases:

> The figure in Egypt, * the reality in the Church,
> the sealing of the rewarding * in the Kingdom,

the typology is still in two stages: the Old Testament type and the New Testament fulfillment.

89. CYRILLONAS, *First Homily on the Pascha*

> Edition: G. Bickell, "Die Gedichte des Cyrillonas nebst einigen anderen syrischen Ineditis," *Zeitschrift der Deutschen Morgenländischen Gesellschaft*, 27 (1873) 569, 571, 575–576.
>
> German trans.: *Ausgewählte Schriften der syrischen Dichter Cyrillonas, Baläus, Isaak von Antiochien und Jakob von Sarug*, trans. S. Landersdorfer (Bibliothek der Kirchenväter, 2nd ed., 6; Munich: Kösel, 1913) 30–39.

This homily, entitled *On the Crucifixion*, but actually recounting the institution of the Eucharist, was written towards the end of the fourth century in Syria or northern Mesopotamia (see Huber, 131–132). It is a *mêmrâ*, a sermon in meter; in the first part, there are seven accents to the line. (Trans.)

a. In the manuscript, the following verses, which have but five accents to the line, are captioned: "of Mar Balai," referring to another obscure Syrian poet of the early fifth century. Landersdorfer ("Baläus," *BKV* 6, 5–6) shows that this caption merely identifies the meter, which is typical of Balai. (Trans.)

b. In the manuscript, the following verses, which have but four accents to the line, are captioned in the same second hand: "of Mar Jacob," referring to Jacob of Sarug (451–521) and the meter typical of his *mêmrê*. (Trans.)

90. PSEUDO-EPHRAEM, *Sermons for Holy Week* **2, 605–629**

> Critical text and German translation: *Ephraem Syrus, Sermones in Hebdomadam Sanctam*, ed. and trans. by Edmund Beck (Louvain: Secrétariat du CorpusSCO, 1979); *CSCO* 412 / script.syr. 181, 19; *CSCO* 413 / script. syr. 182, 41.

Rhythmical discourses written by an unknown sixth-century Monophysite imitator of Ephraem (according to Beck, *CSCO* 413, 12), these sermons paraphrasing the passion narrative of the Gospels were read in the night offices of Holy Week.

a. Cf. Luke 22:15-16. The orator displaces "this Pascha" from v. 15 to v. 16 so as not to say directly that Jesus ate the Jewish Passover. For Aphraates (text 87, ch. 6) and Ephraem (*Hymns on the Unleavened Bread* 6, 10; *Hymns on the Crucifixion* 3, 2), however, Jesus ate the Pascha so as to fulfill it. (Trans.)

b. Cf. verses 567–568: "This leavened Pascha * abolished the unleavened Pascha." The Syrian Church used leavened bread in the Eucharist.

Ephraem had polemicized vigorously against those who wished to use unleavened (*Hymns on the Unleavened Bread* 13, 18, and 19).

c. The beatific vision consists in "eating" the same Pascha "over there" as is eaten "here" in the Eucharist. Thus the Pascha has only two stages—the Jewish type and the Christian reality: cf. text 88, note c, and Beck, *CSCO* 413, 41, note 133.

d. Cf. Irenaeus, *Against the Heresies* 3, 17, 2; *SC* 211, 333.

e. A similar concept of the Eucharist, with Stoic overtones, is found in Pseudo-Hippolytus, *On the Holy Pascha* 8 (see Cantalamessa, *L'omelia*, 330-331).

91. TERTULLIAN, *On the Prayer* 18, 3-7

> Critical edition: Gerard Frederick Diercks (Bussum 1947), reprinted in *Quinti Septimii Florentis Tertulliani opera* (*CChr.SL* 1; Turnholt: Brepols, 1954) 267.
>
> English translation used here: Emily Joseph Daly in *Tertullian: Disciplinary, Moral, and Ascetical Works* (*FC* 40; New York: Fathers of the Church, 1959) 174.

This homily on the Lord's Prayer and on prayer in general was written around A.D. 200, before Tertullian became a Montanist: see Ernest Evans, *Q. Septimii Florentis Tertulliani de oratione liber* (London: S.P.C.K., 1953) xi.

a. *Operationem tuam* = "your (good) work."

b. *Die Paschae.* According to Schümmer, 51ff., Holy Saturday is meant.

92. TERTULLIAN, *On the Prayer* 23, 1-2

> Critical edition: Diercks, *CChr.SL* 1, 271-272.
>
> English translation used here: Daly, *FC* 40, 182.

a. Cf. *On the Crown* 3, 4 (ed. Kroymann, *CChr.SL* 2, 1043), *On Fasting* 14, 2 (eds. A. Reifferscheid and G. Wissowa, *CChr.SL* 2, 1273), and the authors referred to in text 30, note a.

b. *Spatio pentecostes* = "the duration of the Pentecost." In Tertullian, *pentecostes* usually retains the meaning of the whole period of fifty days, beginning with the breaking of the fast during the paschal vigil— e.g., text 93 and *On Idolatry* 14, 7 (eds. A. Reifferscheid and G. Wissowa, *CSEL* 20, 47 = *CChr.SL* 2, 1115). In *On the Crown* 3, 4, however, the special meaning of "fiftieth day" already makes its appearance with the words, "eadem immunitate a die Paschae in Pentecosten usque gaudemus." See Introduction, § VII.

93. TERTULLIAN, *On Baptism* 19, 1-3

Critical edition: J. G. Ph. Borleffs, *Q. S. Fl. Tertulliani libri de patientia, de baptismo, de paenitentia* (The Hague 1948), reprinted in *Quinti Septimii Florentis Tertulliani opera* (*CChr.SL* 1; Turnholt: Brepols, 1954) 293-294.

This treatise may be dated in the years around A.D. 200.

a. The paschal vigil is meant: see text 94.

b. So also texts 48 and 68.

c. *Pascha* and *passio* are brought together, hinting at the well-known equation, *pascha = paschein / pathos.*

d. The same concept of baptism is found in fourth-century Syria: Aphraates, *Demonstration* 12, 10, calls it "the sacrament of our Savior's passion."

e. *Laetissimum spatium.* The early editors Mesnart (Paris 1545) and Gelenius (Basel 1550) would read: *latissimum spatium.*

f. *Frequentata est. Frequentare* sometimes means "to cherish the memory of" or simply "to observe or celebrate" (*Oxford Latin Dictionary*, ed. P. G. W. Glare [Oxford: Clarendon, 1982] 734). Casel, 18, and Boeckh, *JLH* 5 (1960) 14, 44, and 45, translate "is repeated," which, in reference to Jesus' resurrection, makes no sense. (Trans.)

g. *In pentecoste.* On the expectation of the parousia during the Pentecost, see text 15 and Boeckh, *JLH* 5 (1960) 13ff., 33ff.

h. *In die festo paschae*, translating the Greek *en heortêi phasek.* The Greek translator must have read *bmw'd psh* ("on the feast of Pesach") where the correct text (Jer 31:8) has *bm 'wr wpsh* ("with them the blind and the lame"). Le Déaut, *La nuit pascale*, 121, considers it a targumic gloss on the text which found its way into the Greek text, replacing part of the verse as it stands in the Hebrew. It is incorrect, therefore, to divide Tertullian's text as Kroymann, Casel, and others do: "cum dicit . . . in die festo, paschae diem significat" = "when he says . . . on the festal day, he means the day of the Pascha."

i. Thus Basil (text 68) and Augustine, sermon 210, 2 (*PL* 38, 1048).

94. TERTULLIAN, *To his Wife* 2, 4, 2

Critical edition: Aemilius Kroymann (*CSEL* 70; Vienna: Hoelder, and Leipzig: Becker, 1942) 117; reprinted, *CChr.SL*

1; Turnholt: Brepols, 1954, 338; revised by Charles Munier, *Tertullien, A son épouse* (*SC* 273; Paris: Cerf, 1980) 137.

In the guise of a letter to his wife, Tertullian admonishes Christian widows not to remarry, but if they do, not to marry pagans.

a. *Sollemnibus* = regular, annual ceremonies, or solemn ceremonies: see Schümmer, 53.

b. *Paschae* = "of the paschal vigil," as in *On the Crown* 3, 4 and *On Baptism* 19, 1 (text 93).

95. TERTULLIAN, *Against Marcion* 4, 40, 1

Critical editions: Kroymann (*CSEL* 47; Vienna: Tempsky, 1906) 559; revised and reprinted in *Quinti Septimii Florentis Tertulliani opera* (*CChr.SL 1*; Turnhout: Brepols, 1954) 655–656. Cf. *Tertullian Adversus Marcionem*, ed. and trans. Ernest Evans (Oxford: Clarendon, 1972) 490–492.

Writing about 208, Tertullian argues that the God of the Old Testament is the good God, the God of Jesus Christ, because Christ was careful to fulfill the Old Testament prophecies in every detail.

a. That is, in reference to the passion of the Lord. We may conclude, then, that Tertullian interprets "the Pascha of the Lord" to mean "the passion of the Lord"; cf. text 98.

b. Contrary to what he wrote in *Against the Jews* (text 98), Tertullian follows the Synoptic chronology and admits that Christ ate the legal Pesach meal. Thus also Irenaeus, *Against the Heresies* 2, 22, 3: "eating the Pascha and suffering on the following day"; and the Pseudo-Cyprian, *Computus for the Pascha* 9 (*CSEL* 3/3, 256): "He ate the Pascha . . . and suffered the next day." Tertullian was probably unaware of the problem of differing chronologies in John and the Synoptics and simply used the gospel words which suited his polemic on each occasion—here, to counter Marcion's thesis that Christ did not eat the Jewish Pascha (a thesis listed by Epiphanius, *Panarion* 42, 11, 15; *Elenchus* 61).

c. Cf. *Against Marcion* 5, 7, 3 (*CChr.SL* 1, 682): the Pascha is "the type of Christ on account of the resemblance of the saving blood of the sheep to that of Christ." The Pascha proves the unity of the two Testaments.

96. TERTULLIAN, *On Fasting* 2, 2.

Critical edition: *Q. S. Fl. Tertulliani de ieiunio aduersus psychicos*, eds. August Reifferscheid and Georg Wissowa (*CSEL*

20; Vienna: Tempsky, 1890) 275; reprinted in *Quinti Septimii Florentis Tertulliani opera* (*CChr.SL* 2; Turnholt: Brepols, 1954) 1258.

As a Montanist (after 207), Tertullian criticized the laxity of the Catholics in regard to fasting.

a. Good Friday and Holy Saturday, which this work lumps together under the name *Pascha*, as in the phrase, "except for the Pascha" in 13, 1 (*CChr.SL* 2, 1271), meaning, "besides those days in which the Bridegroom is taken away." In Tertullian, therefore, *pascha* covers various liturgical and chronological elements, all coming before the Sunday of the Resurrection. But already with Cyprian (circa 250), *pascha* begins to mean Easter Sunday, if not the whole Pentecost: see letters 21, 2; 43, 1 and 7; 56, 3 (ed. Hartel [*CSEL* 3/2; Vienna: Gerold, 1906] 530f., 591f., 649). See Koch, *ZWTh* n.s. 20 (1914) 297ff.

97. TERTULLIAN, *On Fasting* 14, 2–3

Critical edition: Reifferscheid-Wissowa, *CSEL* 20, 292–293 = *CChr.SL* 2, 1272–1273.

a. *Sollemnia*.

b. Tertullian is defending Montanist practice against criticism from Catholics, but does he know the difference between them and the Gnostics (see text 17) in this matter? They implicitly cite Galatians 4:9-10 against the observance of "days and months and seasons and years."

98. PSEUDO-TERTULLIAN, *Against the Jews* 10, 18

Critical edition: *Q. S. F. Tertulliani adversus Iudaeos*, ed. H. Tränkle (Wiesbaden: F. Steiner, 1963) 30.

a. *Novorum*: this might mean: "of young crops," "of young lambs," or "of new years." One would expect instead: "in the middle of the first month of the year." The vagueness and inaccuracy of Tertullian's phrase may be due to the fact that this is an early work, not intended for publication in its present form (Tränkle, 95).

b. "Hanc sollemnitatem hujus diei . . . manducaturos praecanebat."

c. In Matthew 26:17 and Mark 14:12 ("the first day of Unleavened Bread, when they sacrificed the Passover lamb"), the Supper is put on the evening of the fourteenth and Christ's death on the fifteenth. Tertullian, however, follows John in putting Jesus' death on the fourteenth "at eventide," following which the Jews ate their paschal meal "with bitterness." Thus also Justin (text 19) and Irenaeus (text 28).

99. PSEUDO-TERTULLIAN, *Against All the Heresies* 8, 1

Critical edition: Kroymann, *CSEL* 47, 225 = *CChr.SL* 2, 1410.

Following Harnack, E. Schwartz (*Sitzungsberichte der bayrischen Akademie der Wissenschaften, Philosophische-Philologische-Historische Klasse* 1936, Heft 3, 38–45) thinks this was written in Greek by Pope Zephyrinus (199–217), revised in an anti-Origenist sense, and translated into Latin by Victorinus of Pettau (martyred under Diocletian, about 303).

a. Blastos, together with Florinus (Eusebius, *Eccl. Hist.* 5, 15; 5, 20, 1ff.), came to Rome under Eleutherius or Victor from Asia Minor—which explains his Quartodeciman practice (cf. text 10, ch. 24, § 14), even though this does not seem to have been the principal aim of his "schism." Marcel Richard, *OrSyr* 6 (1961) 198ff., thinks it was his schism that provoked the paschal controversy under Victor.

b. The Quartodecimans held nothing in common with the Jews besides the date of the Pascha, but from the Council of Nicaea on, they and all who kept "the Pascha with the Jews" were accused of Judaizing: see B. Lohse, *Das Passafest*, 94–98.

c. Kroymann finds a lacuna in the codices and suggests filling it with *Nisan* or *Aprilis*, but this is completely unnecessary.

100. PSEUDO-CYPRIAN, *Computus for the Pascha*, 2

Critical edition: *S. Thasci Caecilii Cypriani opera omnia*, ed. Guilelmus Hartel (*CSEL* 3/3; Vienna: Gerold, 1868) 250.

This anonymous writing from A.D. 243 attempts to correct Hippolytus' *Demonstration of the Times of the Pascha* with quotations from Scripture. See George Ogg, trans., *The Pseudo-Cyprianic De Pascha computus*, translated with brief annotations (London: S.P.C.K., 1955).

a. See text 28, note d. "In Egypt" here means "under the dominion of Satan."

b. The author seems to follow the Synoptic chronology; in chapter 9 he says: "he ate the Pascha . . . and suffered the next day" (cf. Tertullian, text 95, note b). With that, he moves away from the previous Western computus: see Huber, 49f. But it is hard to be sure, because the authors use the various gospel indications, probably without ever asking themselves about the different chronologies.

c. The same definition is found in Tricentius (text 51), whose problematic seems to be shared by the author here and in the rest of the text.

101. COUNCIL OF ELVIRA, Canon 43

Critical edition: *Concilios visigóticos e hispano-romanos,* ed. José Vives (España cristiana, Textos 1; Barcelona and Madrid: Consejo superior de investigaciones cientificas, 1963) 9.

This disciplinary council was held in Spain either between 300 and 303 (L. Duchesne) or in 309 (H. Grégoire).

a. In the Codex Toletanus I, this clause reads: "so that after the Pascha we should all celebrate not the fortieth but the fiftieth as the day of Pentecost." An ancient epitome of these canons summarizes canon 43 thus: "After the Pascha let the fiftieth, not the fortieth (day), be kept" (Mansi 2, 26A). These two witnesses interpret the council as condemning the abandonment of the feast of Pentecost on the fiftieth day for the feast of the Ascension on the fortieth day. Perhaps, however, as Huber, 159–160, and Cabié, 182ff., suggest, the council merely wished to reinstate the custom of considering the Pentecost as a period of fifty days, without a special feast on the fiftieth day.

102. LACTANTIUS, *Divine Institutes* 4, 26, 40

Critical edition: Samuel Brandt, *L. Caeli Firmiani Lactanti . . . Divinae Institutiones et Epitome Divinarum Institutionum* (*CSEL* 19; Vienna: Tempsky, 1890) 384.

Written before 311, Book 4 shows that Christ was the first to bring true wisdom from heaven.

a. This would make better sense if it read: "the very people who perform the sacrifice of the sheep call it *pascha* from the word *paschein.*" In any case, see texts 18 and 21. (Trans.)

103. LACTANTIUS, *Divine Institutes* 7, 19, 3

Critical edition: Brandt, *CSEL* 19, 645.

Written about 313, book 7 treats of the Last Things.
a. See texts 13 and 113.

104. FIRST COUNCIL OF ARLES, Canon 1

Critical edition: C. Munier, *Concilia Galliae A. 314 – A. 506* (*CChr.SL* 148; Turnhout: Brepols, 1963) 5, 9.

a. In 314, summoned by Constantine.

b. Bishop of Rome, 314–335.

c. The Jewish method of setting the date of the Pascha had been abandoned by most Churches. It became the custom instead that the bishop of Alexandria should notify the bishop of Rome of the next date of Easter so that he in turn could notify the bishops of the West. See Huber, 66.

105. ZENO OF VERONA, *Treatise on the Pascha* 1, 57

> Critical edition: B. Löfstedt (*CChr.SL.* 22; Turnhout: Brepols, 1971) 132.

Zeno, bishop of Verona 362–371 or 372, in this sermon makes the day of the Pascha, "the great day" (§ 58), not only the turning point of the year, but also the celebration of the passion with the resurrection, and of the baptismal passage of the catechumens to the condition of Christians hoping for eternal life. (Trans.)

a. Some manuscripts read: *in stabili cursu*; others: *instabilis cursus*.

b. "Through" requires an object. Perazzini suggested: *ambages* = "roundabout ways," "ambiguities."

c. The baptismal font. In a reverse metaphor, Melito, fragment 8, 3 (Perler, *Méliton*, *SC* 123, 232) had called the ocean, "the baptistery of the sun."

d. *Novelli* = "young plants or animals." It is a frequent poetic designation of the newly baptized. *Competentes* just above is an ecclesiastical term for candidates for baptism.

e. Zeno has applied solar symbolism (sunset, sunrise) to three classes of events: (1) historical: the death and resurrection of Christ; (2) mystical: the immersion in, and emergence from, the baptismal font; (3) eschatological: the future resurrection. He goes on to develop the third application in the next chapter of the sermon.

106. AMBROSE OF MILAN, *On Cain and Abel* 1, 8, 31

> Critical edition: Carolus Schenkl (*CSEL* 32/1; Vienna: Tempsky, 1897) 366.

Written about 377, this passage is an attempt to blend the Philonic idea of Pascha-as-passage with the idea, traditional in the West, of Pascha-as-passion. Ambrose does the same in text 107. In his *Explanation of Twelve Psalms*, Ps 43, § 37 (ed. M. Petschenig, *CSEL* 64, 288–289), he connects the paschal lamb, the passion of Christ, and the

Eucharist in the typological pattern which is also to be found in Gregory of Elvira (text 117, § 20).

a. *Pascha Domini*, the Old Latin translation of Exodus 12:11, following the tradition seen in the Codex Alexandrinus: see text 1a, note d.

b. Cf. Philo, *On the Sacrifices of Abel and Cain* 17, 63 (*LCL*) 2:141–42.

c. That is, because the reality foretold in the symbol of the slaughtered lamb is the Lord's passion.

107. AMBROSE OF MILAN, Letter 1, to Justus, 9–10

> Critical edition: Otto Faller, *Sancti Ambrosii opera*, Part 10, *Epistulae et Acta*. 1, *Epistularum libri I–VI* (*CSEL* 82/1; Vienna: Hoelder-Pichler-Tempsky, 1968) 7.

Writing about 380, Ambrose again attempts to blend the ideas of passage and passion in his explanation of the Pascha. In chapter 9, the Pascha is the lamb eaten by the Hebrews; as a sacrificial victim it typifies Christ in his passion. In chapter 10, it is the feast commemorating the passage of the Hebrews, which is an allegory of the soul's passage from vice to virtue, a passage achieved in an exemplary way by Christ in his passion.

a. Citing Philo, *Who is the Heir?* 40, 192 *LCL* 4:379. "Good compassion" represents Philo's *eulogos eupatheia* (text 3, note a), but Christianized in the sense of Paul's "suffering with Christ" (Rom 8:17). Ambrose has a tendency to express concepts from Philo in Pauline terminology. In *Hexameron* I 4, 14 (*CSEL* 32, 12), for example, he speaks of the (baptismal) passage of souls from vices to virtue as a passage from "the leaven of malice and wickedness" to "truth and sincerity" (cf. 1 Cor 5:8).

108. AMBROSE OF MILAN, *Exposition of the Gospel according to Luke* 10, 34

> Critical edition: M Adriaen, *Expositio evangelii secundum Lucam; Fragmenta in Esaiam* (*CChr.SL* 14; Turnhout: Brepols, 1957) 355.

The *Exposition* was compiled in 389 from Ambrose's homilies.

a. Here the content assigned to the yearly feast of the Pascha is the commemoration of the work of redemption and in particular of the death of Christ (the resurrection forms part of the Pentecost). This is also the case in *De Sacramentis* 2, 6 (*CSEL* 73, 32–34) and in the Good Friday hymn *Hic est dies verus Dei* (in A. S. Walpole, *Early Latin Hymns*

[Cambridge: University Press, 1922] 77–82), which bears the ancient title *In die Paschae* (see Guido Maria Dreves, *Hymnographi Latini: Lateinische Hymnendichter des Mittelalters*, 2. Folge [*Analecta Hymnica Medii Aevi*, 50; Leipzig: Reisland, 1907] 16). More frequently, however, the content of the feast appears to be the moral one. For example, *Hexameron* 1, 4, 14 (*CSEL* 32, 12): "Each year we celebrate the Pascha of Jesus Christ, that is, the passage of souls from vices to virtue."

b. Despite the opposition here between spring and summer, *Pentecostes* for Ambrose still seems to designate the entire period of fifty days, as it does for Hilary of Poitiers, *Treatise on the Psalms*, Instruction 12 (ed. A. Zingerle [*CSEL* 22; Vienna: Temsky, 1911] 11). Its content is still the archaic one: glorification of Christ and anticipation of the kingdom.

109. AMBROSE OF MILAN, *On the Sacraments* 1, 4, 12

Critical edition: Otto Faller, *Sancti Ambrosii opera*, part 7: *Explanatio symboli*, etc. (*CSEL* 73; Vienna: Hoelder-Pichler-Tempsky, 1955) 20.

Published about 391, this work is based on stenographic notes taken during Ambrose's catechesis.

a. The typological structure used most by Ambrose when he writes or speaks about the Pascha is the correspondence between the passage of the Red Sea and baptism, e.g. *Hexameron* 1, 4, 14 (*CSEL* 32, 12) and *On the Sacraments* 1, 6, 20–22 (*CSEL* 73, 24). The paschal sacrament par excellence for Ambrose is baptism rather than the Eucharist, because in baptism the concept of Pascha as passage is stronger than that of Pascha as passion.

b. Here Ambrose puts the Christological and sacramental significance into the moral perspective of Philo (passage from vices to virtue): see Huber, 125–126.

110. The Paschal Proclamation: *Exultet*

Critical edition: Bernard Capelle, in *Miscellanea Giovanni Mercati* (*StT* 121; Vatican City: Typis Polyglottis Vaticanis, 1946) 1:225–228.

English translation used here: *The New Holy Week Book . . .* in the New English Version prepared under the auspices of the English National Liturgical Commission (London: Burns & Oates, 1966) 94–96.

For conjectures about the late fourth-century author of this piece, see the articles by Capelle, Bonifatius Fischer, and Huglo in the bibliography.

a. *Mysteria divina.* Mohrmann, *EL* 66 (1952) 274–281, has shown that here the phrase is equivalent to *ministeria divina,* meaning the heavenly spirits in the service of God (see Ezek 1:4-28).

b. *Claritatem* = "brightness." The English translator may have been thinking rather of the way in which the Easter fire is lit, by striking fire from flint.

c. *Levitarum* = "deacons."

d. *Praecipiat* = "command." Some codices read: *perficiat* = "bring it about."

e. The paschal proclamation is a development of the genre *laus cerei,* connected with the rite of lamplighting during the evening office: see Hippolytus, *Apostolic Tradition* 25. The rite is attested for the paschal vigil as early as the second century: see Eusebius, *Eccl. Hist.* 6, 9, 2-3. It is a legacy from the Jewish synagogue liturgy: on its origins, see Schuberth, *JLH* 12 (1967) 94–100.

f. Literally: "And with your spirit."

g. In the author's time, the paschal vigil still celebrated the death of Christ as much as his resurrection (which is mentioned below: "On this night Christ . . . rose victorious from the grave.")

h. *Hodie.* More probably, it means "nowadays" in contrast to the *primum,* "long ago," of the Exodus commemorated in the previous few lines.

i. An echo of Philo's and Ambrose's definition of the Pascha as "passage from vices (sin) to virtue": see text 2, § 147, and texts 3 and 109. The sentence as a whole seems to refer to baptism during the paschal vigil.

j. A few phrases seem to be missing here.

k. Capelle, 230–232, has demonstrated the Ambrosian origin of the theology of the *renovatio in melius* expressed in these daring phrases. See Ambrose, *Explanation of Twelve Psalms,* Ps 39:20 OL: "Happy the fall which is repaired for the better"; and *On Jacob and the Blessed Life* 1, 2: "Fault more fruitful than innocence."

l. This and many other expressions are found in the *preconium paschale* of the *Missale Gothicum* (Cod. Vat. Reg. lat. 317, No. 270) attributed to Ambrose: see Gamber, 159ff.

m. "Sed iam columnae huius praeconia novimus." The paschal candle is compared to the column of fire which went before the Hebrews in the Exodus (Exod 13:21).

n. Some codices add here the praise of the bee, a favorite idea of Ambrose's, taken from Vergil's *Georgics* 4, 56–57, 198, 201.

o. *Humanis divina*, omitted in some codices.

p. The expression "Morning-Star" is drawn perhaps from Ps 109:3 OL, "From the womb before the morning-star have I begotten thee." The psalm-verse is applied to Christ by Justin, *Dialogue with Trypho* 45, 4; 63, 3, and, in a paschal context, by Melito, *On the Pascha* 82 (ed. Hall, 44–46).

q. The theme of Christ, the light that never sets, is very old: see Cantalamessa, *L'omelia*, 102.

r. *N.* = the name of the current pope. Later missals add prayers for the bishop, the temporal ruler, etc., and the piece concludes *Per dominum nostrum Iesum Christum* etc.

111. AMBROSIASTER, *Old and New Testament Questions* **96, 1**

> Critical edition: *Ambrosiaster, Quaestiones Veteris et Novi Testamenti* ed. A. Souter (*CSEL* 50; Vienna and Leipzig: 1908) 170–171.

This "imitator of Ambrose," whose real name is not known, wrote in the time of Pope Damasus (366–384).

a. "Immolatio pascha hoc Domini est." See text 1a, note h.

b. This refers to Jerome, the only Latin writer who explained *Pascha* as the passage of the Destroying Angel (see text 114). On this controversy about the meaning of *Pascha*, see Cantalamessa, *Aevum* 44 (1970) 219ff.

112. AMBROSIASTER, *Commentary on the Thirteen Epistles of Paul,* **on 1 Corinthians 5:7**

> Critical edition: Henricus Joseph Vogels (*CSEL* 81/2; Vienna: Hoelder-Pichler-Tempsky, 1968) 56.

a. This is stated more clearly in *Old and New Testament Questions* 116, 1: "The Pascha gets its name from 'passion.'" The equation of *Pascha* with *immolatio* comes from the constant confrontation of 1 Corinthians 5:7, "Pascha nostrum immolatus est Christus," with Exodus 12:27, "Immolatio pascha hoc Domini est."

b. That is, first comes the immolation of the lamb (typifying the Savior), then the sign made with its blood that ensures salvation.

113. JEROME, *Commentary on the Gospel of Matthew* **4, on Matt 25:6**

> Critical edition: *Eusebius Hieronymus, Commentarius in evangelium Matthei* ed. D. Hurst and M. Adriaen (*CChr.SL* 77; Turnhout: Brepols, 1969) 236–237.

a. See texts 5, note k; 13, note b; and 15, note b.

b. *Nostrarum frontium.* This phrase, of course, belongs not to the list of events in Egypt but to the Christian interpretation of those events, to a sentence that Jerome thought it superfluous to write. (Trans.)

c. Strobel, *ZNW* 49 (1958) 157–196, sees a vestige of this apostolic tradition in Luke 17:20, but this is not certain. The same applies for the *Epistle of the Apostles* (text 15) in spite of Lohse, 78ff.; I consider the *Gospel of the Hebrews* (text 13) the only explicit witness to such a tradition before Lactantius (text 103).

114. JEROME, *Commentary on the Gospel of Matthew* **4, on Matt 26:2**

> Critical text: Hurst-Adrien, *CChr.SL* 77, 245.

Jerome is commenting on the words, "You know that after two days the Pascha is coming."

a. Jerome is attacking the views of Ambrosiaster, as I have shown in *Aevum* 44 (1970) 227ff.

b. In his treatise *On Hebrew Names* (ed. P. de Lagarde; *CChr.SL* 72, 140 and 148), Jerome explains *phase* as *transitus sive transgressio* and *pascha* as *transcendens vel transgressio*. This corresponds to the *hyperbasis* of Aquila and Josephus (see text 1a, note c, and text 4 with note c) and has its basis in Exodus 12:23 and 27. For a Greek author who accepts this explanation, see text 54.

c. Jerome found this meaning (*phase* = "protection") in Isaiah 31:5. See his *Commentary on Isaiah* 10, 31, 5 (*CChr.SL* 73, 403).

d. The commentary on Exodus was never written.

e. Here Jerome returns to the Philonian (moral) meaning of *transitus*. Cf. his letter 78, 1 to Fabiola (ed. I. Hilberg [*CSEL* 55; Vienna: Temsky, and Leipzig: Freytag, 1912] 51): "transitum . . . eo quod de peioribus ad meliora pergentes, tenebrosam Aegyptum relinquimus."

115. JEROME, *On the Sunday of Pascha*

> Critical edition: *S. Hieronymi presbyteri Tractatus sive Homiliae in Psalmos, in Marci Evangelium aliaque varia argu-*

menta . . . ed. Germanus Morin, 2nd ed.; (*CChr.SL* 78; Turn-
holti: Brepols, 1958) 545.

This text was produced by someone taking notes during Jerome's homilies to his monastic community at Bethlehem, where he lived from 386
to 419 or 420.

a. This celebrated verse had been in use in the Jewish Pesach as a liturgical anticipation of the parousia of the Messiah (see Jeremias, *Eucharistic
Words*, trans. N. Perrin, 255–262). This psalm was apparently not applied to the parousia of Christ in the second and third centuries, but it
enjoyed wide usage in the catechesis and Christian paschal liturgy of the
fourth and fifth centuries; Huber, 5–8; Aubineau, *SC* 187, 320ff.

b. For Zeno of Verona (text 105), the day of the Pascha is "the parent
of the year."

c. Already in Pseudo-Barnabas 15, 8f., the Sunday of the Resurrection is called "the eighth day" and "the beginning of a new world."
For the theology of the eighth day, from Pseudo-Barnabas to Augustine,
see Daniélou, *The Bible and the Liturgy*, 255–281.

d. E.g., Ps 6 LXX: *hyper tês ogdês* = "for the sake of the eighth";
Hebrew: *'al-hasseminît*, meaning perhaps: "for the octachord."

116a. EGERIA, *Travels in the Holy Land*, 35–39

Critical edition: *Itinerarium Egeriae* eds. A. Franceschini and
R. Weber (*CChr.SL* 175; Turnhout: Brepols, 1965) 78–83.

English translation used here: John Wilkinson, *Egeria's
Travels to the Holy Land*, revised ed. (Warminster, England:
Aris & Phillips, 1981) 134–139.

Egeria may have visted the Holy Land in 383 (see text 116b, note b).
The journal she kept was published toward the end of the fourth or beginning of the fifth century.

a. Holy Thursday.

b. A rotunda with a cupola constructed over the Holy Sepulcher.

c. Basilica erected by Constantine over the ditch where the cross was
found.

d. See text 66, note e.

e. Name derived from *Elaiôn* = olive grove. The church there enclosed
the grotto of the mysteries: see Eusebius, *Life of Constantine* 3, 41;
Tricennial Oration (*De laudibus Constantini*) 9, 17; Emmanuele Testa,
"Le grotte dei misteri giudeo-cristiane," *Liber annuus* 14 (1963–1964)
65–144.

f. John 13:16-18:1, according to the Armenian Lectionary, No. 39 (ed. Renoux, *PO* 36/2). This document was composed in Jerusalem about 417–439.

g. Name derived perhaps from *en bomôi* = "on the summit."

h. The Eleona, according to Thibaut, 32. But more probably it is the church "at the roots of the mount" of Olives: Eusebius, *Onomasticon* (ed. Klostermann, 75); Vincent-Abel, *Jérusalem*, 2:1007ff.

i. The Armenian Lectionary, No. 40, confirms this gospel as Matthew 26:31-56.

j. That is, to the Sanctuary of the Cenacle. In this church the Christians had placed the column of the scourging: Jerome, letter 108, 9.

k. The ceremonies of the Adoration of the Cross spread from Jerusalem to the rest of the Christian world, changing the primitive physiognomy of Good Friday, which had been aliturgical.

l. The' Armenian Lectionary, No. 43, confirms this gospel as John 19:17-37.

m. At Jerusalem, we see, Holy Saturday is still an aliturgical day. There is no hint of a commemoration of the Descent among the Dead, though this is done elsewhere, e.g. in Cappadocia: see text 73.

n. *Vigiliae paschales.* The plural comes from the military use of the word: there were four *vigiliae* or watches during the night. On the structure of the Paschal Vigil at Jerusalem, see Renoux, *PO* 35/1, 84ff.

o. The newly baptized, whatever their age (cf. Augustine, sermon 208, 1; 1 Pet 2:1).

p. In chapters 45–47 Egeria gives a lengthy description of those "who are baptized for Pascha" and of the mystagogical catechesis, which, as in the West, was imparted to them during the octave. See Ambrose's *On the Mysteries* and *On the Sacraments* and Augustine's sermons *Ad infantes* (ed. Poque, *SC* 116, 82ff.).

q. Does this allude to the postbaptismal anointing or to confirmation? Compare Cyril of Jerusalem, *Mystagogical Catechesis* 3 (ed. August Piédangel, trans. Pierre Paris [*SC* 126; Paris: Cerf, 1966] 120-32).

r. The following sentence is my translation, not Wilkerson's. (Trans.)

s. Again, in ch. 47, § 1, *dies paschae* will mean: "from Easter to the octave." The first testimony to a celebration of the octave comes from Asterius the Sophist in the first half of the fourth century. Bit by bit this octave takes the place of the compound octave 7 x 7 + 1, the ancient Pentecost. Note how, in Egeria (cf. also ch. 20, § 6; ch. 42, § 1; ch. 47, § 1), *Pascha* begins to have the meaning of "the Sunday of the Resurrection," which will become its predominant meaning from the fifth century on. See, for example, Caesarius of Arles, sermon 204 (*CChr.SL* 104, 819), and text 140.

116b. EGERIA, *Travels in the Holy Land*, 42–43

> Critical edition: Franceschini-Weber, *CChr.SL* 175, 84–85.
> English translation used here: Wilkinson, 141–142.

a. The Armenian Lectionary (*PO* 36/2, 337–338) shows that at Jerusalem at the beginning of the fifth century, the feast of the Ascension was held forty days after the Pascha. This had been the case in other places for some time: Chrysostom, *PG* 50, 463; Gregory of Nyssa, *PG* 46, 690. The history of the term *quadragesima* (see text 123, note c) seems to confirm that it stands here for the Ascension (see Bastiaensen, *Observationes*, 132ff., Renoux, *PO* 35, 1, 72). According to others (Cabié, Huber, J. G. Davies, *The Peregrinatio Egeriae and the Ascension: VigChr* 8, 1954, 93–100) *quadragesima* is merely a chronological expression with no reference to the feast of the Ascension, which in Egeria's time was still celebrated fifty days after Easter together with Pentecost. (See also the following note.)

b. In Bethlehem that day (May 18) the feast of the SS. Innocents was probably celebrated, which in the year 383 fell precisely forty days after Easter. (See P. Devos, *Egérie à Bethléem, Analecta Bollandiana* 86, 1968, 87–108.) This doesn't necessarily exclude that in Jerusalem the Ascension was celebrated forty days after Easter, in the *quadragesima*.

c. *Missa* doesn't mean here dismissal (*missio*), but has already the sense of service, Mass: see Chr. Mohrmann, *VigChr* 12, 1958, 67ff.

117. GREGORY OF ELVIRA, *Treatises [of Origen] on the Books of Holy Scripture* 9, 9. 16. 20. 22

> Critical Edition: *Gregorii Iliberritani episcopi quae supersunt*, ed. Vincentius Bulhart (*CChr.SL* 69; Turnholt: Brepols, 1967) 72 and 74–75.

Gregory (died after 392) was bishop of Elvira in southern Spain. The work excerpted here is one of twenty sermons attributed to Gregory; the attribution to Gregory is not certain. Most of them treat passages from the Old Testament. The title "of Origen" is surely not from Gregory; when these treatises were published in 1900 they were attributed to Origen. See F. J. Buckley, *Christ and the Church according to Gregory of Elvira* (Rome: Gregorian, 1964).

a. Like the Ambrosiaster (see text 111 f.) the author reacts against the Alexandrian, anthropological interpretation. See my article in *Aevum* 44 (1970) 223f.

b. The same development is found in treatise 7. It is taken over from Melito (see Perler in *SC* 123, 172f. and 191f.). But it is commonplace in this era. See Zeno, *Tractatus* 1; Gaudentius of Brescia (text 118); and Daniélou, *Sacramentum* 152ff.

c. The same concept is found in Tertullian, *De baptismo* 9, 1.

d. If Christ's *Pascha* was his passion on the historical plane, then on the liturgical plane the Church's *Pascha* is realized in the Eucharist. See also tractate 9, 1: "Thus the mystery of the Pascha . . . which is now celebrated in the bread of the Lord's body." And cf. Hilary of Poitiers, *Commentary on Matthew* 30: "Without him [that is, Judas] the Pascha is accomplished, when the chalice has been taken and the bread broken."

e. This rich expression, too, may be inspired by Melito (see text 22, note c).

118. GAUDENTIUS OF BRESCIA, Tractate 1: *On Exodus* 3. 10. 13.

Critical edition: A. Glück, *Tractatus* (*CSEL* 68; Vienna and Leipzig: Hoelder, 1936) 19–21.

Gaudentius, bishop of Brescia in northern Italy, died after 406. Twenty-one of his sermons are extant; ten of them were delivered during Easter week.

a. The tradition of Pascha as the recapitulation of the seven days of creation (which may depend on text 76) was introduced among the Latins by the Ambrosiaster (*Quaestiones Veteris et Novi Testamenti*, 55). It is combined with the tradition about Christ's death on the twenty-fifth of March. Cf. Loi, *EL* 85 (1971) 8ff.

b. The typological comparison of Moses' rod with the wood of the cross is a *testimonium* known as early as Justin (*Dialogue with Trypho* 86, 1).

c. See text 117 and note b there. Just as Ambrose does, Gaudentius sees the spiritual significance of the Exodus exclusively in baptism. (See also text 109).

119. GAUDENTIUS OF BRESCIA, Tractate 2: *On Exodus* 2, 25–26

Critical edition: A. Glück, *CSEL* 68, 29–30.

a. Here Pascha is the Passover of Christ into the appearances of bread and wine. This is a unique attempt to unite the interpretation of Pascha as *transitus* ("passing over") and the traditional Eucharistic interpretation of Pascha as *passio* ("suffering"). Elsewhere (*Tractate* 2, 31), apparently in dependence on Ps-Chrysostom (see text 77) Gaudentius defines the Eucharist as image and exemplar of the passion.

b. The author uses a vivid, if rather tasteless, comparison: the "flesh of Christ" is not to be taken so literally that it might be cooked in the stew-pot of the heart. (Trans.)

c. The same connection between fire, the Spirit, and the Eucharist is found in Pseudo-Hippolytus, *On the Pascha* (see text 88).

120. CHROMATIUS OF AQUILEIA, Sermon 16:
   On the Great Night, 1

> Critical edition: J. Lemarié, Chromace d'Aquilée, Sermons, vol. 1 (*SC* 154; Paris: Cerf, 1969) 258–62. English translation (with unmarked omissions) in A. Hamman, *The Paschal Mystery: Ancient Liturgies and Patristic Texts*, ed. Thomas Halton (Montreal: Palm, 1969) 135–38. This translation by J.T.L.

Chromatius was bishop of Aquileia (near the modern Trieste in northwest Italy) from 387 to 407. More than fifty of his sermons are extant. They were rediscovered only in the twentieth century.

a. The same quotation is found in Augustine (text 131); that text shows a close affinity with this passage from Chromatius. The application of Psalm 3:6 to the death and resurrection of Christ is very ancient. It became the introit for the old Mass of Easter in the Latin liturgy. See *1 Clement* 26, 2; Justin, *First Apology* 38, 5; Justin, *Dialogue with Trypho* 97, 1; Irenaeus, *Against the Heresies* 4, 33, 13; and Irenaeus, *Demonstration of the Apostolic Preaching* 73. The fusion of Psalm 3:6 and Jeremiah 31:26 is attested in Irenaeus, *Against the Heresies* 4, 31, 2.

b. A Christological motif that goes back to Melito (text 22, § 66). For the relation between the incarnation and the paschal mystery in Chromatius see Jossua, *Le salut*, 145ff. On the theme of Christ's sleeping in his humanity and keeping watch in his divinity see A. Grillmeier, *Der Logos am Kreuz* (Munich, 1956).

c. In Chromatius, the paschal vigil still celebrates the whole mystery of Christ as a unity. The theme of the cross has a central position here, along with that of the resurrection (see also sermon 17, 1f. [*SC* 154, 268f.]). Moreover, the descent into hell (attributed to the divinity, in harmony with the schema "Word and flesh") forms a part of the mystery of this night and is not celebrated separately, as had already occurred among the Greeks (see text 73).

121. CHROMATIUS OF AQUILEIA, Sermon 17A: *On the Pascha*, 1

Critical edition: J. Lemarié, *SC* 154, 276-78.

a. The Latin word for "feed" here is *pascere*, the root of the English word "pastor" (one who feeds sheep). The same unusual connection between *pascha* and *pascere* is found in Augustine (text 134) and in Pseudo-Augustine, Sermon Mai 154, 2 (*PLS* 2, 1252): "For whoever pass over, these are fed." (Text 114 connects *pascha* with *transcensio*, the word here translated "passing over.") This gives "celebrating Pascha" the sense of being fed with the Eucharist.

b. A Eucharistic interpretation, connected with the tradition of *pascha* as *passio* (see text 117, § 20).

122. MAXIMUS OF TURIN, Sermon 54: *On the Holy Pascha*, 1

Critical edition: A. Mutzenbecher, *Collectio sermonum antiqua nonnullis sermonibus extravagantibus adiectis* (*CChr.SL* 23; Turnhout: Brepols, 1962) 218.

English translation by Boniface Ramsey, *Maximus of Turin: Sermons* (*ACW* 50; New York: Paulist, 1989). English translation of this sermon also in Hamman, *Paschal Mystery*, 193-95; Hamman also has translations of two other sermons on Easter by Maximus (36 and 57). This translation is by J.T.L.

Maximus, bishop of Turin, died between 408 and 423; he was a distinguished preacher, better known for a poetic and mystical bent than for theological reflection. About one hundred of his sermons are extant.

a. The *praeconium* of the *Missale Gothicum* (see text 110, note f), which is attributed to Ambrose, says of the night of the Pascha: "a night in which . . . of those made old You restore mature infants." On St. Maximus' catechesis see Huber, *Pascha*, 182f.

123. PAULINUS OF NOLA, Poem 27: *On the Feast of St. Felix*

Critical edition: *Sancti Pontii Meropii Pauline Nolani Carmina* . . . ed. Guilelmus de Hartel (*CSEL* 30; Vienna: Tempsky, 1894) 264-265.

English translation: *The Poems of St. Paulinus of Nola*, trans. P. G. Walsh (*ACW* 40; New York: Newman Press, 1975) 272.

a. See also Paulinus, letter 31 (*CSEL* 30, 274) where *Pascha* is presented as the day in which the mystery of the Cross is celebrated. According to his contemporary Filaster of Brescia, *Book on the Heresies* 140 (*CCL* 9, 304), the third Christian feast is Pascha "when he suffered"; also Prudentius, *Apotheosis* 347, still associates *Pascha* with *passio*. But this doesn't mean that these authors ignore the resurrection. For Filaster, *Haer.* 140, Easter is also the day in which Jesus "suffered, was raised up and appeared."

b. Note the same effort to balance the daily *Pascha,* the Eucharist, with the yearly festival, as in Augustine (text 130).

c. Pentecost has lost its ancient christological content and it is seen as the feast of the descent of the Holy Spirit (see text 133). Paulinus seems to ignore the feast of the Ascension on the fortieth day, while Augustine (letter 54, 1) speaks of the *quadragesima Ascensionis* as a feast "known in all the earth." For Filaster, see Huber, 179.

124. AUGUSTINE OF HIPPO, Letter 55 to Januarius 1, 2

> Critical edition: *S. Aurelii Augustini Hipponiensis episcopi epistulae*, part 2 (Letters 31–123), ed. Aloisius Goldbacher (*CSEL* 34/2; Vienna: Tempsky, 1898) 170.

The letter was written in the year 400.

a. Cf. text 75 and note a. Augustine's correspondent, Januarius of Gaul, like the Easterners, put the death of Christ on March 25, while others in the West usually put it on March 23 (for example Lactantius, *Divinae Institutiones* 4, 10, 18).

b. On the meaning of *sacramentum* see sermon 272 (*PL* 38, 1246–1248) and C. Couturier, "Sacramentum et mysterium dans l'oeuvre de St. Augustin," in *Études Augustiniennes*, ed. Henri Rondet (Paris: Aubier, 1953) 161–332.

c. It was probably the obscurity of this phrase which led copyists to vary the text in their efforts to make it more intelligible. (Cantalamessa follows Goldbacher's punctuation, and takes *adtestent in* as passive. But Henri Chirat, *Dictionnaire Latin-Français des auteurs chrétiens* knows only deponent meanings. If the word is deponent, the comma should be moved from *adtestent in* to *significationem*. Augustine uses *adtestor* with the dative; here it governs *ad* with the accusative. Trans.)

d. Augustine's favorite text for expressing the paschal mystery. Cf. *Sermo Guelferbytanus* 4, 2 (in *Miscellanea Agostiniana*, ed. G. Morin, 1:456, repr. in *PLS* 2, 549) and 5, 1 (text 132).

e. Only with Augustine do we arrive at a perfect balance between the passion and the resurrection in the definition of the paschal mystery. In *De catechizandis rudibus* 23, 41, 3 (ed. J. B. Bauer, *CChr.SL* 46 [1969]

166) he contrasts the first, Mosaic, Pascha with "the passion and resurrection of the Lord, which is the true Pascha"; he does the same in sermon Denis 7 (in Morin, *Miscellanea Agostiniana* 1:32–34).

125. AUGUSTINE OF HIPPO, Letter 55 to Januarius 14, 24

Critical edition: A. Goldbacher, *CSEL* 34/2, 195

a. The Greeks have exactly the same interpretation of the triduum, except that in the case of Saturday, the accent is on the descent into hell rather than on the burial. See Origen (text 39) and Pseudo-Chrysostom (text 76).

126. AUGUSTINE OF HIPPO, *Exposition of Psalm 120* (Sermon Preached on the Feast of St. Crispina, Martyr), 6

Critical edition: *Sancti Aurelii Augustini Enarrationes in Psalmos CI–CL*, eds. Eligius Dekkers and Iohannes Fraipont (*CChr.SL* 40; Turnholt: Brepols, 1956) 1791.

a. Jerome is meant: see my article in *Aevum* 44 (1970) 232.

b. Cf. *De Civitate Dei* 16, 34 (*CChr.SL* 48, 549); translated by William McAllen Green, St. Augustine, *The City of God*, vol. 5 (*LCL*; Heinemann: London, 1965) 199: "Foretelling that he should pass over from this world to the Father through the sacrifice offered in his passion." Thus Augustine achieved the difficult synthesis of two traditions— the archaic tradition of *Pascha* as *passio* and the Alexandrian tradition of *Pascha* as *transitus*. Cf. *Aevum* 44 (1970) 232. Aponius (text 136) imitates Augustine.

c. The concept of *Pascha* as passage, it is plain, has a historical content when applied to Christ and a mystical or sacramental one when applied to man. The anthropological meaning Philo gives it is very rare in Augustine; the only example I know is letter 55, 16.30 (*CSEL* 34, 2, 205): "vocantur autem ad requiem alterius vitae, quo ab ista vita transitur quod pascha significat, omnes . . . ."

127. AUGUSTINE OF HIPPO, *Tractate 55 on the Gospel of John*, 1 (on John 13:1-5)

Critical edition: Radbodus Willems, *Sancti Aurelii Augustini in Iohannis Evangelium Tractatus CXXIV* (*CChr.SL* 36; Turnholt: Brepols, 1954) 463–464.

English translation by John Gibb and Janes Innes, *Lectures or Tractates on the Gospel According to St. John* (*NPNF* 2, 7; repr. Grand Rapids: Eerdmans, 1974) 299.

a. Augustine is referring to the previous Latin tradition and in particular to Ambrosiaster (see text 111f.). Though not deriving philologically the term *Pascha* from *passio,* Augustine sympathized with the theological idea lying behind it: see *Sermo Mai* 15, 2, 3 ("Ipsius nos passione Pascha celebramus"), *De cat. rud.* 20, 34, 4; sermo 210, 2 ("anniversaria Domini passio . . . quod Pascha dicitur").

b. Ed. Par. 1555, *propterea quia tunc*: "because the first celebration . . . ."

c. This typological explanation is common since Justin (see text 18, note a).

d. Augustine first (and, according to some modern exegetes, correctly) sees in John 13:1, the intention of the evangelist to give a Christian interpretation of the term *Pascha.* The idea of *passage* is expressed by John with *metabaino* (not with *diabaino* as in Philo 41), but *metabasis* appears to be equivalent to *diabateria* also for Eusebius (see text 56, note a).

128. AUGUSTINE OF HIPPO, Sermon 220: *On the Vigil of Pascha*

Edition: *PL* 38, 1089.

More than five hundred of his sermons survive. Many of his sermons on the paschal season are available in English translations. Sermons 219 to 265, for the vigil of Easter, Easter Sunday, the Easter season, and the feast of the Ascension, are translated by Mary Sarah Muldowney, *Saint Augustine: Sermons on the Liturgical Seasons* (FC 38; New York: Fathers of the Church, 1959). Hamman, *Paschal Mystery,* translates sermons 34, 219, 233, 235, 356; sermons Morin-Guelferbytanuus 5, 8, 12, 13, 16, 17; and sermon Denis 2. Suzanne Poque has an extended essay on Augustine's understanding of Easter in *Augustin d'Hippone. Sermons pour la Pâque* (*SC* 116; Paris: Cerf, 1966) 9–153. She also provides a bibliography. This sermon is translated by Muldowney in *FC* 38, 173–74. (Trans.)

a. Throughout this passage Augustine contrasts the feast (*solemnitas*) with the truth (*veritas*), meaning by truth the knowledge of history.

b. This sermon contains Augustine's clearest formulation of the relationship between the historical event (the "once") and its liturgical and sacramental celebration ("each year")—that is, between the Pascha of

Christ and the Pascha of the Church. (See also *Sermo Wilmart* 4 [PLS 2, 717f.], letter 98, 9 [CSEL 34, 2, p. 530f.].) For the concept of "celebration" see sermon 267, 1, where Augustine proposes the etymology of *solemnitas* as "ab eo quod solet in anno," that is, as derived from "occurs by custom each year."

129. AUGUSTINE OF HIPPO, Sermon Wilmart 4, 3

> Critical edition: G. Morin, *Miscellanea Agostiniana* (Rome 1930) 1:685.

a. Augustine has established a rare equilibrium among the three essential elements of the paschal celebration: memorial, presence, and expectation. One of his imitators is even clearer. He writes: "The Pascha that we celebrate renders the past present and is extended to the future by the resurrection" (Pseudo-Augustine, Sermon Caillau-St. Yves 1, app. 3 [*PLS* 2, 1020]). Augustine's preoccupation with stressing "what has already happened," that is, the historical event, as the basis both of the liturgy and of eschatology, is noteworthy. See also Pseudo-Augustine, Sermon Caillau-St. Yves 1, 38 (*PLS* 2, 986): "No one should so hope for his coming that he denies that he has already come."

130. AUGUSTINE OF HIPPO, Sermon Wilmart 9, 2

> Critical edition: G. Morin, *Miscellanea Agostiniana* (Rome 1930) 1:693.

a. For Augustine, too, the Church's Pascha is essentially realized in the Eucharist. (See Augustine, *Against the Letter of Petilian* 2, 37: "Pascha, . . . which we receive in the body and blood of the Lord.") But, unlike the Greeks (see texts 56, § 7; 74), this does not compromise the special significance of the yearly celebration (the *solemnitas*); "as often as you do this" does not annul the concept of "each year" (see also text 128), as the following text shows. (See also text 123.)

131. AUGUSTINE OF HIPPO, Sermon Morin-Guelferbytanus 4, 2

> Critical edition: G. Morin, *Miscellanea Agostiniana* (Rome 1930) 1:456. (The great Benedictine scholar Germain Morin discovered thirty-three previously unknown sermons by Augustine in a manuscript preserved in Wolfenbüttel in Germany; hence they are called "Morin-Guelferbytanus"; "Guelferbytanus" is the Latin form of "Wolfenbüttel." He first published these sermons in Munich in 1917. Trans.)

a. In this sermon, the vision of the vigil as the commemoration of Christ's "sleeping" in death prevails. It is based on the Christological theme of death-and-life. See also sermon Guelf. 5, 4: "He who died so that we might live has slept so that we might keep watch." The same theme and the same quotation of Psalm 3:6 occur in Chromatius of Aquileia; see text 120.

b. Besides the commemorative significance, the vigil also has an eschatological meaning. It anticipates the coming of Christ. See sermon Guelf. 6: "Let us keep vigil, so that with watchful hearts we may hope and await his coming." More often it is an image of eternal life. See sermon Wilmart 4, 3; 7, 1; and sermon 362, 29. The vigil also has an ascetical aspect, linked to 2 Corinthians 11:27 and Matthew 26:41; see sermon 7, 2 and sermon Morin-Guelf. 5, 2.

132. AUGUSTINE OF HIPPO, Sermon Morin-Guelferbytanus 5, 1–2

> Critical edition: G. Morin, *Miscellanea Agostiniana* (Rome 1930) 1:457–58.
>
> English translation in Hamman, *Paschal Mystery*, 148–52. See also *SC* 116, 210–22. This translation by J. T. L.

a. In opposition to the "daily celebration of Pascha"; see text 130.

b. The vigil commemorates Christ's death and resurrection together, although the passion was already celebrated on Good Friday by a homily and readings; see Augustine's sermons "On the Passion of the Lord." Nevertheless in this sermon (see also § 4), in contrast to the preceding one, emphasis on the vigil tends to shift in anticipation towards the pure joy of the resurrection. See Mohrmann, *EL* 66 (1952) 51f.

c. See sermon 219: the paschal vigil is "the mother of all holy vigils." There is an analogous concept in Chromatius of Aquileia (text 120) and Jerome (text 115).

d. See sermon 252, 12: "For the forty days preceding let us keep vigil." It appears that for Augustine the paschal vigil, and not Holy Thursday, as Callewaert holds (*Sacris Erudiri* [2nd ed.; Steenbrugge: Sint Petersabdei, 1960] 462ff.), marks the end of the forty-day fast. See Frank, *ALW* 9 (1965) 1ff.

133. AUGUSTINE OF HIPPO, Sermon Mai 158, 4

> Critical edition: G. Morin, *Miscellanea Agostiniana* (Rome 1930) 1:383.

a. The mystery of Pentecost (see also §§ 1–2 of this sermon) consists in the correspondence between the figure (that is, the giving of the Mosaic Law on the fiftieth day; see Exodus 19:1ff.) and the reality (that is, the giving of the Holy Spirit, the new law). So too Augustine, *City of God* 16, 43; and letter 55, 30. For an analogous interpretation among the Greeks, see text 80. "Pentecost" is thus restricted to the "fiftieth day." See Augustine, *Against Faustus the Manichee* 32, 12, a feast of the "coming" or "birthday" of the Holy Spirit; thus sermon Mai 158, 2; sermon Frangipane 1.

134. PSEUDO (?)-AUGUSTINE, Sermon Denis 7, 1

Critical edition: G. Morin, *Miscellanea Agostiniana* 1 (Rome 1930) 1:32–33.

English translation by Denis J. Kavanaugh, *Saint Augustine: Commentary on the Lord's Sermon on the Mount with Seventeen Related Sermons* (*FC* 11; New York: Fathers of the Church, 1951) 327–30. This translation by J. T. L.

a. At Hippo, the "alleluia" was reserved exclusively for the days of Pascha (see Augustine, letter 55, 32). Its significance was both sacramental and eschatological; it was the song of the new man (see Augustine, sermon Mai 82; Guelf. 8, 2; *Enarr. in Psalmos* 106, 1) that anticipates "our future activity" (letter 55, 28).

b. On the authenticity of this sermon—whether it is Augustine's—see what I wrote in *Aevum* 44 (1970) 20. The pairing of *pascha* and *passio* ("suffering"), albeit based not on etymology but on content, is present in Augustine (see text 127). The pairing of *pascha* and *pascere* ("to feed"), in a Eucharistic sense, is found in Chromatius of Aquileia (see text 121).

135. LEO THE GREAT, Sermon 49: *On the Fast of Lent*, 1

Critical edition: Antonius Chavasse, *Sancti Leonis Magni . . . Tractatus* (*CChr.SL* 138A; Turnhout: Brepols, 1973) 285.

English translation by Charles Lett Feltoe in *NPNF* II, 12, 160–62. This translation by J. T. L.

Leo the Great was pope from 440 to 461. He succeeded in defending Italy against barbarian attacks, and influenced the Council of Chalcedon (451). Almost one hundred of his sermons are extant, and many letters.

a. For the Pascha as the single celebration of the whole Christian mystery, see Leo, sermon 46, 1: ". . . on the paschal feast, in which all mysteries of our religion come together.'' See also sermon 48, 1 and 72, 1 (where ''the whole paschal mystery'' means the account of the passion and resurrection). For Leo, too, the dominant aspect is not the resurrection, but the cross. See sermon 48, 4; further, in 48, 1, ''the day of Pascha'' is ''the cross of the Lord.'' In explaining the significance of *pascha*, Leo follows Augustine. According to sermon 72, 6, *pascha* means ''passing over from this world to the Father.''

136. APONIUS, *Explanation of the Song of Songs* 4, 25-26 (on Cant 2:11-12)

> Critical edition: B. de Uregille and L. Neyrand, *Aponii in Canticum canticorum expositio* (*CChr.SL* 19; Turnhout: Brepols, 1986) 100.

Little is known of Aponius. He probably lived in Italy in the early fifth century.

a. The theme Pascha and spring, usually developed in a lyrical and naturalistic key (see text 56, note d), is here reinterpreted in an ecclesial key. See also Zeno of Verona, tractate 1, 33 (*CC* 22, 84).

b. The ancient tradition of Pascha and passion survived for a long time. (See, for example, Priscillian, Tractate 46 *Of the Pascha*; tractate 6 on Exodus [*PLS* 2, 1452f.]; Paschasinus, letter 13, 2 [*PL* 54, 608A]; Ps-Ambrose, sermon 35, 1; Fulgentius of Ruspe, letter 14, 43). It also found its way into various liturgies. For the Mozarabic liturgy, see *Le Liber Ordinis en usage dans l'église wisigothique et mozarabe d'Espagne du cinquième au onzième siècle*, ed. Marius Férotin (Paris: Firmin-Didot, 1904) 527. For the Ambrosian and the Roman Rites, see the respective Easter prefaces, in which the Pascha is seen as ''the day on which Christ is sacrificed.''

c. There is an analogous synthesis of *pascha* and *passio* with *transitus* (''passing over'') in Augustine (text 126).

d. From now on eschatology is reduced to anagogy. (See text 43.)

137. PSEUDO-AUGUSTINE, Sermon Caillau-St. Yves 1, 30

> Edition: A. B. Caillau and B. Saint-Yves, *S. Augustini operum supplementum* (Paris, 1836) 1:49. Reprinted in *PLS* 2, 965.

The sermon may have been preached in the fifth century.

a. The author is one of the few to continue Jerome's interpretation: *pascha = phase = transcensus* (passing over''). See also Eusebius Gallicanus, homily 14: *On Pascha* 4, 1, and Pseudo–Augustine, text 121, note a.

b. One of the very rare patristic texts that explicitly link *pascha* and *transitus* ("passing over") to Christ's resurrection. See text 122 and Quintus Julius Hilarianus, *De ratione Paschae et mentis* 13 (*PL* 13, 1114B).

138. PSEUDO-AUGUSTINE, Sermon Caillau-St. Yves 1, 31

> Edition: A. B. Caillau and B. Saint-Yves, *S. Augustini operum supplementum* (Paris, 1836) 1:49. Reprinted in *PLS* 2, 965.

a. The author seems to revive Augustine's theory of the "congruence of both languages"; see text 127.

b. One way of reconciling the two opposed traditions of *pascha* as "passing over" and *pascha* as "passion."

139. PSEUDO-AMBROSE, Sermon 12: *On the Pascha*, 4

> Critical edition: P. Mercier, *XIV homélies du IXe siècle d'un auteur inconnu de l'Italie du Nord* (*SC* 161; Paris: Cerf, 1970) 220.

The homily dates from the ninth century.

a. The citation of John 13:1 indicates that the dominant influence is Augustine's. This is true of many late patristic authors. See Paschasinus, *Letter to Leo* 13, 2 (*PL* 54, 608A); Isidore of Seville, *Etymologies* 6, 17, 11; and, for the Middle Ages, Rupert of Deutz, *On the Divine Offices* 6, 26 (*CChr.CM* 7, 207ff.).

b. The author unites the three dimensions of Pascha: the typological (the passage from Egypt to the Promised Land); the Christological (the passage of Christ from this world to the Father); and the ecclesiological. This last is understood morally, in the manner of Ambrose (passage from vices to virtue) rather than mystically, in the manner of Augustine (passage from death to life).

140. RUPERT OF DEUTZ, *On the Divine Offices* 6, 26

> Critical edition: R. Haacke, *CChr.CM* 7 (Turnhout: Brepols, 1967) 207.

Rupert of Deutz (ca. 1070–1129, or perhaps 1135), theologian and abbot. Rupert taught at Liège and Siegburg before becoming abbot of the Benedictine monastery at Deutz near Cologne about 1120. The work excerpted here is an explanation of the Church year.

a. Beginning from the fifth century (see text 116, § 38), *pascha* began, ever more exclusively, to mean "the Sunday of the Resurrection" or "Easter Sunday." See Pseudo-Cyril of Alexandria, *Prologus paschae* 5 (written in Spain in the seventh century; ed. Krusch, 1, 338): ". . . the Pascha of the Lord, which is the feast of the Resurrection."

b. The same criticism of the identification of Pascha with Easter Sunday to the neglect of the passion is found in Greek authors; see text 84.

141. SICARD OF CREMONA, *Mitrale* 6, 15

Edition: *PL* 213, 343.

Sicard, bishop of Cremona (1160–1215) was a historian, canonist, and liturgist. The work excerpted here is a moralizing and allegorical interpretation of places, ceremonies, and vestments. It sheds considerable light on the liturgical practices of the Middle Ages.

a. Sicard lists here one version of the four senses of Scripture. The teaching that Scripture has four senses is found as early as Augustine (see *On the Usefulness of Belief* 3, 5–9; *Unfinished Work on the Literal Interpretation of Genesis* 2, 5; *Literal Interpretation of Genesis* 1, 1, 1 Trans.). Each of the terms that Sicard uses is borrowed from Greek. *Historia* means "narrative." *Allegoria* means "allegory" and applied the text to the hearers' faith. *Tropologia* means "figurative expression," here used of the moral sense. *Anagogia*, which means "lifting up," was taken to refer to the way the text applied to the last things.

b. In this passage we have one of the most complete syntheses of the patristic interpretation of Pascha. For the close accord with the doctrine of the fourfold sense of Scripture, see Henri de Lubac, *Exégèse médiévale* 1, 1 (Paris 1959) 156. It is noteworthy that by this time the passage from vice to virtue is measured by relation to the sacrament of confession and penance.

Sigla for Periodicals, Series,
and Reference Works

ACO	*Acta Conciliorum Oecumenicorum*
ACW	*Ancient Christian Writers*
ALW	*Archiv für Liturgiewissenschaft*
AnBib	*Analecta Biblica*
ANFa	*Ante-Nicene Fathers*
ASNU	*Acta Seminarii Neotestamentici Upsalensis*
AUSS	*Andrews University Seminary Studies*
BHH	*Biblisch-historisches Handwörterbuch*
Bib	*Biblica*
BKV	*Bibliothek der Kirchenväter*
BVC	*Bible et Vie chrétienne*
ByZ	*Byzantinische Zeitschrift*
BZ	*Biblische Zeitschrift*
BZAW	*Beihefte zur Zeitschrift für die Neutestament-liche Wissenschaft*
CChr.CM	*Corpus Christianorum, continuatio medievalis*
CChr.SG	*Corpus Christianorum, series graeca*
CChr.SL	*Corpus Christianorum, series latina*
CHR	*The Catholic Historical Review*
CSCO/arm	*Corpus scriptorum Christianorum orientalium, Scriptores armeniaci*
CSCO/iber	*Corpus scriptorum Christianorum orientalium, Scriptores iberici*
CSCO/syr	*Corpus scriptorum Christianorum orientalium, Scriptores syri*
CSEL	*Corpus scriptorum ecclesiasticorum latinorum*
DACL	*Dictionnaire d'archéologie chrétienne et de liturgie*
DBS	*Dictionnaire de la Bible, Supplément*
DSp	*Dictionnaire de spiritualité ascétique et mystique*
DThC	*Dictionnaire de théologie catholique*

EL	*Ephemerides liturgicae*
EOr	*Echos d'Orient*
GCS	*Die griechischen christlichen Schriftsteller der ersten (drei) Jahrhunderte*
HThR	*Harvard Theological Review*
JBL	*Journal of Biblical Literature*
JLH	*Jahrbuch für Liturgik und Hymnologie*
JLW	*Jahrbuch für Liturgiewissenschaft*
JThS	*Journal of Theological Studies*
LCL	*Loeb Classical Library*
LebZeug	*Lebendiges Zeugnis*
LeDiv	*Lectio Divina*
LiZs	*Liturgische Zeitschrift*
LO	*Lex Orandi*
LWQF	*Liturgiewissenschaftliche Quellen und Forschungen*
MD	*La Maison-Dieu*
NPNF	*A Select Library of Nicene and Post-Nicene Fathers of the Christian Church, 1st and 2nd series*
NTS	*New Testament Studies*
OrSyr	*L'Orient syrien*
OrChr(R)	*Orientalia christiana*
ParOr	*Parole de l'Orient*
PG	*Patrologiae cursus completus, series graeca*
PGL	*Patristic Greek Lexicon*
PL	*Patrologiae cursus completus, series latina*
PLS	*Patrologiae latinae supplementum*
PO	*Patrologia orientalis*
QLP	*Questions liturgiques et paroissiales*
RAC	*Reallexikon für Antike und Christentum*
RB	*Revue biblique*
RdQ	*Revue de Qumran*
RE	*Realencyklopädie für protestantische Theologie und Kirche*
REByz	*Revue des études byzantines*
RET	*Revista Española de Teologia*
RevSR	*Revue des sciences religieuses*
RHE	*Revue d'histoire ecclésiastique*
RHPhR	*Revue d'histoire et de philosophie religieuses*
RivL	*Rivista Liturgica*
RQH	*Revue des questions historiques*
RSLR	*Rivista di storia e letteratura religiosa*

RSR	*Recherches de science religieuse*
SC	*Sources chrétiennes*
ScC	*La Scuola Cattolica*
SE	*Sacris Erudiri*
StANT	*Studien zum Alten und Neuen Testament*
StPat	*Studia Patavina*
StPatr	*Studia Patristica*
StT	*Studi e Testi*
StTh	*Studia Theologica*
TDNT	*Theological Dictionary of the New Testament*
TDOT	*Theological Dictionary of the Old Testament*
ThQ	*Theologische Quartalschrift*
ThZ	*Theologische Zeitschrift*
TU	*Texte und Untersuchungen zur Geschichte der altchristlichen Literatur*
VigChr	*Vigiliae christianae*
VT	*Vetus Testamentum*
ZKG	*Zeitschrift für Kirchengeschichte*
ZKTh	*Zeitschrift für katholische Theologie*
ZNW	*Zeitschrift für die neutestamentliche Wissenschaft und die Kunde des Urchristentums;* later: *und die Kunde der älteren Kirche*
ZThK	*Zeitschrift für Theologie und Kirche*
ZWTh	*Zeitschrift für wissenschaftliche Theologie*

Abbreviations of the Books of the Bible

Acts	Acts of the Apostles
Amos	Amos
Bar	Baruch
1 Chr	1 Chronicles
2 Chr	2 Chronicles
Col	Colossians
1 Cor	1 Corinthians
2 Cor	2 Corinthians
Dan	Daniel
Deut	Deuteronomy
Eph	Ephesians
Esth	Esther
Exod	Exodus
Ezek	Ezekiel
Ezra	Ezra
Gal	Galatians
Gen	Genesis
Hab	Habakkuk
Hag	Haggai (Aggaeus)
Heb	Hebrews
Hos	Hosea
Isa	Isaiah
Jas	James
Jdt	Judith
Jer	Jeremiah
Judg	Judges
Joel	Joel
John	John
1 John	1 John
2 John	2 John
3 John	3 John

Job	Job
Jonah	Jonah
Josh	Joshua
Jude	Jude
1 Kgs	1 Kings
2 Kgs	2 Kings
Lam	Lamentations
Lev	Leviticus
Luke	Luke
1 Macc	1 Maccabees
2 Macc	2 Maccabees
Mal	Malachi
Mic	Micah
Mark	Mark
Matt	Matthew
Nah	Nahum
Neh	Nehemiah
Num	Numbers
Obad	Obadiah (Abdias)
1 Pet	1 Peter
2 Pet	2 Peter
Phil	Philippians
Phlm	Philemon
Prov	Proverbs
Ps (Pss)	Psalms
Qoh/Eccl	Qohelet (Ecclesiastes)
Rev	Revelation
Rom	Romans
Ruth	Ruth
1 Sam	1 Samuel
2 Sam	2 Samuel
Sir	Sirach (Ecclesiasticus)
Cant	Song of Songs
1 Thess	1 Thessalonians
2 Thess	2 Thessalonians
1 Tim	1 Timothy
2 Tim	2 Timothy
Titus	Titus
Tob	Tobit (Tobias)
Zech	Zechariah
Zeph	Zephaniah (Sophonias)

Bibliography

A. THE PASCHA AND LENT

Arbesmann, Rudolf. "Fasttage." *RAC* 7 (1969) 500–524.

Arnold, Franz X. "Regenerative Erneuerung der Osterpredigt im Geist des christlichen Altertums." *Paschatis Sollemnia* (Jungmann-Festschrift). Eds. Balthasar Fischer and Johannes Wagner, 305–313. Freiburg: Herder, 1959.

Auf der Maur, Hansjörg. *Die Osterhomilien des Asterios Sophistes als Quelle für die Geschichte der Osterfeier.* Trierer theologische Studien 19. Trier: Paulinus-Verlag, 1967.

Balthasar, Hans Urs von. "Mysterium Paschale." *Mysterium Salutis.* Eds. Johannes Feiner and Magnus Löhrer, III/2, 133–326. Einsiedeln: Benziger, 1969.

Barnard, Leslie W. "The Epistle of Barnabas—A Paschal Homily?" *VigChr* 15 (1961) 8–22.

Bastiaensen, A. A. R. *Observations sur le vocabulaire liturgique dans l'Itinéraire d'Égérie.* Latinitas christianorum primaeva 17. Nijmegen: Dekker & Van de Vegt, 1962.

Baumstark, Anton. *Nocturna Laus. Typen frühchristlicher Vigilienfeier und ihr Fortleben vor allem im römischen und monastischen Ritus. LWQF* 32. Münster: Aschendorff, 1957; 2nd ed. 1967.

_____. *Comparative Liturgy.* Revised by Bernard Botte. Trans. by F. L. Cross. London: Mowbray, 1958.

Baus, Karl. "Ostern in der Verkündigung des heiligen Augustinus." *Paschatis Sollemnia* (Jungmann-Festschrift). Eds. Balthasar Fischer and Johannes Wagner, 57–67. Freiburg: Herder, 1959.

Benoît, André. *Le baptême chrétien au IIe siècle.* Paris: Presses Universitaires de France, 1953.

Benoit-Castelli, Georges. "Le 'Praeconium paschale.'" *EL* 67 (1–953) 309–334.

Berger, Rupert. "Ostern und Weihnachten: Zum Grundgefüge des Kirchenjahres." *ALW* 8/1 (1963) 1–20.

Betz, Johannes. *Die Eucharistie in der Zeit der griechischen Väter*. I/1, *Die Aktualpräsenz der Person und des Heilswerkes Jesu im Abendmahl nach der vorephesinischen griechischen Patristik*. Freiburg: Herder, 1955.

_____. "Vom Pascha-Mysterium." *Vom Mysterium unseres Pascha* = LebZeug 1965, 3 (Paderborn, 1965) 73–100.

Bieder, Werner. *Die Vorstellung von der Höllenfahrt Jesu Christi*. Abhandlungen zur Theologie des Alten und Neuen Testaments, 19. Zurich: Zwingli-Verlag, 1949.

Bonnard, Pierre E. "Les Pâques et la Pâque." *Lumière et Vie* (Lyon) 14 (1965) 8–18.

Bonner, Campbell. "The Homily on the Passion by Melito, Bishop of Sardis." *Mélanges Franz Cumont* = *Annuaire de l'Institut de Philologie et d'Histoire orientales et slaves* 4 (1936) 107–119.

_____. "Two Problems in Melito's Homily on the Passion." *HThR* 31 (1938) 175–190.

_____. "A Supplementary Note on the Opening of Melito's Homily." *HThR* 36 (1943) 317–319.

Botte, Bernard. "La question pascale: Pâque du vendredi ou Pâque du dimanche?" *MD 41 (1955) 84–95.*

_____. *"Pascha."* OrSyr 8 (1963) 213–226.

Bouyer, Louis. *The Paschal Mystery: Meditations on the Last Three Days of Holy Week*. Trans. by Mary Benoit. Chicago: Regnery, 1950.

Bowman, John. *The Gospel of Mark: The New Christian Jewish Passover Haggadah*. Studia Post-Biblica, 8. Leiden: Brill, 1965.

Brightman, Frank E. "The Quartodeciman Question." *JThS* 25 (1923–1924) 254–270.

Brox, Norbert. "Tendenzen und Parteilichkeiten im Osterfeststreit des zweiten Jahrhunderts." *ZKG* 83 (1972) 291–324.

Cadman, William H. "The Christian Pascha and the Day of the Crucifixion—Nisan 14 or 15?" *StPatr* 5 (= *TU* 80; 1962) 8–16.

Callewaert, Camille. "La synaxe eucharistique à Jérusalem, berceau du dimanche." *Ephemerides theologicae Lovanienses* 15 (1938) 34–73.

_____. "La durée et le caractère du carème ancien dans l'Église latine." *Collationes Brugenses* 18 (1913) 90–108, 311–323, 455–463; 19 (1914–1919) 193–206, 263–272; 20 (1920) 112–128, 200–204. Reprinted in *Sacris Erudiri. Fragmenta liturgica collecta a monachis S. Petri de Aldenburgo in Steenbrugge ne pereant*, 449–506. Steenbrugge: Abbatia S. Petri, 1940; 2nd ed. 1960.

Campenhausen, Hans Freiherr von. "Ostertermin oder Osterfasten? Zum Verständnis des Irenäusbriefs an Viktor (Euseb. Hist. Eccl. 5,24,12-17)." *VigChr* 28 (1974) 114–138.

Cantalamessa, Raniero. "La Pasqua ritorno alle origini nell'omelia pasquale dello Pseudo-Ippolito." *ScC* 95 (1967) 339–368.

──────────. *L'omelia "In s. Pascha" dello Pseudo-Ippolito di Roma. Ricerche sulla teologia dell'Asia Minore nella seconda metà del II secolo.* Milan: Vita e Pensiero, 1967.

──────────. " 'Ratio Paschae': La controversia sul significato della Pasqua nell'Ambrosiaster, in Girolamo e in Agostino." *Aevum* 44 (1970) 219–241.

──────────. "Questioni melitoniane." *RSLR* 6 (1970) 245–267.

──────────. *La Pasqua della nostra salvezza. Le tradizioni pasquali della Bibbia e della primitiva Chiesa.* Turin: Marietti, 1971.

──────────. *I più antichi testi pasquali della Chiesa. Le omelie di Melitone di Sardi e dell'Anonimo Quartodecimano e altri testi del II secolo.* Introduzione, traduzione e commentario. Rome: Edizioni Liturgiche, 1972.

──────────. "Les homélies pascales de Méliton de Sardes et du Pseudo-Hippolyte et les Extraits de Théodote." *EPEKTASIS: Mélanges patristiques J. Daniélou.* Ed. Jacques Fontaine and Charles Kannengiesser, 263–271. Paris: Beauchesne, 1972.

Capelle, Bernard. "L'*Exultet* pascal, oeuvre de saint Ambroise." *Miscellanea Giovanni Mercati* 1:219–246. *StT* 121. Vatican City: Biblioteca Apostolica Vaticana, 1946.

Carmignac, Jean. "Comment Jésus et ses contemporains pouvaient-ils célébrer la Pâque à une date non officielle?" *RdQ* 5 (1964) 59–79.

Casel, Odo. "Art und Sinn der ältesten christlichen Osterfeier." *JLW* 14 (1934) 1–78. = *La fête de Pâques dans l'Église des Pères.* Tr. by J. C. Didier. *LO* 37. Paris: Cerf, 1963.

──────────. "Der österliche Lichtgesang der Kirche." *LiZs* 4 (1931–1932) 179–191.

Cattaneo, E. "Lo sviluppo del calendario intorno al mistero pasquale." *RivLi* 57 (1970) 257–272.

Chavasse, Antoine. "Le cycle pascal." In *Église en prière. Introduction à la liturgie.* Ed. Aimé-Georges Martimort, 694–726. Tournai: Desclée, 1961. = "Der Osterkreis." *Handbuch der Liturgiewissenschaft.* Ed. A.-G. Martimort, 2:230–263. Freiburg: Herder, 1965.

Chenderlin, Fritz. "Distributed Observance of the Passover—A Hypothesis." *Bib* 56 (1975) 369–393.

──────────. "Distributed Observance of the Passover—A Preliminary Test of the Hypothesis." *Bib* 57 (1976) 1–24.

Christou, Panagiotou. "To ergon tou Melitonos Peri Pascha kai he akolouthia tou Pathous" = "Les écrits de Méliton sur la Pâque et l'Office de la Passion." *Kleronomia* 1 (1969) 65–78.

Chupungco, Anscar J. *The Cosmic Elements of the Christian Passover.* Studia Anselmiana, 72; Analecta Liturgica, 3. Rome: Editrice Anselmiana, 1977.

Comeau, Marie. "Les prédications pascales de saint Augustin." *RSR* 23 (1933) 257–282.

Corgnali, Duilio. *Il mistero pasquale in Cromazio di Aquileia.* Udine: La Nuova Base, 1979.

Corssen, Peter. "Das Osterfest." *Neue Jahrbücher für das klassische Altertum* 39 (1907) 170–189.

Cross, Frank Leslie. *I. Peter, A Paschal Liturgy.* London: Mowbray, 1954.

Czerwik, Stanislaus. *Homilia paschalis apud Patres usque ad saeculum quintum. Investigatio liturgico-pastoralis.* Rome: Anselmianum, 1961.

Dalmais, Irénée-Henri. "Pâques." *DSp* 12 (1983) 171–182.

Daniélou, Jean. "Traversée de la mer Rouge et baptême aux premiers siècles." *RSR* 33 (1946) 402–430.

——————. *From Shadows to Reality: Studies in the Biblical Typology of the Fathers.* Trans. Wulstan Hibberd. London: Burns & Oates, 1960.

——————. "Le symbolisme du jour de Pâques." *Dieu Vivant* 18 (1951) 43–56.

——————. *The Bible and the Liturgy.* University of Notre Dame Liturgical Studies, 3. Notre Dame: University of Notre Dame Press, 1956.

——————. "Baptême, Pâque, Eucharistie." *Communion solennelle et profession de foi: Vanves, 4–7 Avril 1951*, 117–133. LO 14. Paris: Cerf, 1952.

——————. "Catéchèse pascale et retour au paradis." *MD* 45 (1956) 99–119.

——————. "L'état du Christ dans la mort d'après Grégoire de Nysse." Historisches Jahrbuch 77 (1958) 63–72.

——————. "Figure et événement chez Méliton de Sardes." *Neotestamentica et Patristica* (Freundesgabe Oscar Cullmann) 282–292. Supplements to NT, 6. Leiden: Brill, 1962.

Daunoy, Fernand. "La question pascale au concile de Nicée." *EOr* 28 (1925) 424–445.

Dockx, S. "Le récit du repas pascal: Marc 14, 17–26." *Bib* 46 (1965) 445–453.

Dölger, F. J. "Der Durchzug durch das Rote Meer als Sinnbild der christlichen Taufe." *Antike und Christentum* 2 (1930) 63–69.

Drews, Paul. *"Passah, altkirchliches, liturgisch." RE* 14 (1904) 734–750.

Drumbl, Johann. "Die Improperien in der lateinischen Liturgie." *ALW* 15 (1973) 68-100.

Duchesne, Louis. "La question de la Pâque au Concile de Nicée." *RQH* 28 (1880) 5-42.

Dugmore, Clifford W. *The Influence of the Synagogue upon the Divine Office.* London: Oxford University Press, 1944. 2nd ed. London: Faith Press, 1964.

_____. "A Note on the Quartodecimans." *StPatr* 4 (= *TU* 79; 1961) 411-421.

_____. "Lord's Day and Easter." *Neotestamentica et Patristica* (Freundesgabe Oscar Cullmann) 272-281. Supplements to NT, 6. Leiden: Brill, 1962.

Fedrizzi, P. "Il mistero Pasquale nel messaggio Apostolico e nel ministero dell'unzione." *StPat* 13 (1966) 243-255.

Feneberg, Rupert. *Christliche Passafeier und Abendmahl. Eine biblisch-hermeneutische Untersuchung der neutestamentlichen Einsetzungsberichte. StANT* 27. Munich: Kösel, 1971.

Fischer, Balthasar. "Vom einen Pascha-Triduum zum Doppel-Triduum der heutigen Rubriken." *Paschatis Sollemnia* (Jungmann-Festschrift). Eds. Balthasar Fischer and Johannes Wagner, 146-156. Freiburg: Herder, 1959.

Fischer, Bonifatius. "Ambrosius der Verfasser des österlichen Exultet?" *ALW* 2 (1952) 61-74.

Fotheringham, David Ross. *The Date of Easter and Other Christian Festivals.* London: S.P.C.K., 1928.

Frank, Hieronymus. "Die Paschavigil als Ende der Quadragesima und ihr Festinhalt bei Augustinus." *ALW* 9/1 (1965) 1-27.

Fritz, G. "Pâques, les controverses pascales." *DThC* 11 (1932) 1948-1970.

Füglister, Notker. *Die Heilsbedeutung des Pascha. StANT* 8. Munich: Kösel, 1963.

Funk, Franz Xaver. "Die Entwicklung des Osterfastens." F. X. Funk, *Kirchengeschichtliche Abhandlungen und Untersuchungen,* 1:241-278. Paderborn: Schöningh, 1897.

Furlani, G. "Il mistero Pasquale nell'Epistola agli Ebrei." *StPat* 13 (1966) 236-242.

Gamber, Klaus. "Die ältesten Eucharistiegebete der lateinischen Osterliturgie." *Paschatis Sollemnia* (Jungmann-Festschrift). Eds. Balthasar Fischer and Johannes Wagner, 159-178. Freiburg: Herder, 1959.

Gärtner, Bertil Edgar. *John 6 and the Jewish Passover.* Coniectanea neotestamentica 17. Lund: Gleerup, 1959.

_____. "Eukaristien och paskalammet." *Välsignelsens kalk,*

ed. Eric Segelberg, 27-38. Saltsjoebaden: Bokfoerlaget Kyrkligt Forum, 1962.

Gaster, Theodor H. *Passover: Its History and Traditions.* New York: H. Schuman, 1949. 2nd ed. 1958.

Geraty, Lawrence T. "The Pascha and the Origin of Sunday Observance." *AUSS* 3 (1965) 85-96.

Gibert y Tarruell, Jordi. "El significado de la expresión 'Pascha' en la liturgía hispánica." *EL* 91 (1977) 3-31.

Goppelt, Leonhard. *Typos: The Typological Interpretation of the Old Testament in the New.* Trans. Donald H. Madvig. Grand Rapids: Eerdmans, 1982.

Greiff, Anton. *Das älteste Paschari­tuale der Kirche, Did 1-10, und das Johannesevangelium.* Johanneische Studien, 1. Paderborn: Schöningh, 1929.

Grelot, Pierre. "Études sur le Papyrus Pascal d'Elephantine." *VT* 4 (1954) 349-384.

Grelot, Pierre and Pierron, J. *The Paschal Feast in the Bible.* The Living Word, 3. Baltimore: Helicon, 1966.

Gribomont, Jean. "Les hymnes de saint Éphrem sur la Pâque." *Mélanges Mgr Pierre Dib = Melto* 3 (1967) 147-182.

_____. "Le triomphe de Pâques d'après S. Éphrem." *ParOr* 4 (1973) 147-189.

_____. "La tradition liturgique des Hymnes pascales de S. Éphrem." *ParOr* 4 (1973) 191-246.

Grillmeier, Alois. "Das Erbe der Söhne Adams in der Homilia de Passione Melitos, Bischof von Sardes." *Scholastik* 20-24 (1949) 481-502. Reprinted as "'Das Erbe der Söhne Adams' in der Pascha-homilie Melitons." Alois Grillmeier, *Mit ihm und in ihm,* 2nd ed., 175-197. Freiburg: Herder, 1975.

_____. "Der Gottessohn im Totenreich." *ZKTh* 71 (1949) 1-53, 184-203. Reprinted in Alois Grillmeier, *Mit ihm und in ihm,* 2nd ed., 76-174. Freiburg: Herder, 1975.

_____. "Die Wirkung des Heilshandelns Gottes in Christus." *Mysterium Salutis.* Eds. Johannes Feiner and Magnus Löhrer, 3:327-392. Einsiedeln: Benziger, 1969.

Grossi, Vittorino. "La Pasqua quartodecimana e il significato della croce nel II secolo." *Augustinianum* 16 (1976) 557-571.

Grumel, Venance. "Le problème de la date pascale aux IIIe et IVe siècles. L'origine du conflit: le nouveau cadre du comput juif." *REByz* 18 (1960) 163-178.

_____. "La date de l'équinox vernal dans le canon pascal d'Anatole de Laodicée." *Mélanges Eugène Tisserant,* 2:217-240. *StT* 232. Vatican City: Biblioteca Apostolica Vaticana, 1964.

Gry, L. "La date de la Parousie d'après l'Epistula Apostolorum." *RB* 49 (1940) 86–97.

Haag, Herbert. "Pâque." *DBS* 6 (1960) 1120–1149.

—————. *Vom alten zum neuen Pascha. Geschichte und Theologie des Osterfestes.* Stuttgarter Bibelstudien, 49. Stuttgart: KBW-Verlag, 1971.

—————. "Das christliche Pascha." *ThQ* 150 (1970) 289–298.

Hahn, Ferdinand. "Die alttestamentlichen Motive in der urchristlichen Abendmahlsüberlieferung." *Evangelische Theologie* 27 (1967) 337–374.

Hall, Stuart George. "The Melito Papyri." *JThS* n.s. 19 (1968) 476–508.

—————. "Melito, Peri Pascha 1 and 2: Text and Interpretation." *Kyriakon. Festschrift Johannes Quasten.* Eds. Patrick Granfield and Josef A. Jungmann, 1:236–248. Münster: Aschendorff, 1970.

—————. "Melito in the Light of the Passover Haggadah." *JThS* n.s. 22 (1971) 29–46.

Halton, Thomas. "Stylistic Devices in Melito, Peri Pascha." *Kyriakon. Festschrift Johannes Quasten.* Eds. Patrick Granfield and Josef A. Jungmann, 1:249–255. Münster: Aschendorff, 1970.

Hamman, Adalbert, ed. *The Paschal Mystery: Ancient Liturgies and Patristic Texts.* Trans. Thomas Halton. Staten Island: Alba House, 1969.

Henninger, Joseph. *Les fêtes de printemps chez les sémites et la Pâque israélite.* Paris: Gabalda, 1975.

Hertzberg, Hans Wilhelm. "Zum samaritanischen Passah." *Sammlung und Sendung* (Heinrich Rendtorff-Festschrift). Ed. Joachim Heubach, 130–136. Berlin: Christlicher Zeitschriftenverlag, 1958. Reprinted in Hans Wilhelm Hertzberg, *Beiträge zur Traditionsgeschichte und Theologie des Alten Testaments*, 126–133. Göttingen: Vandenhoeck & Ruprecht, 1962.

Hilgenfeld, Adolf. *Der Paschastreit der alten Kirche nach seiner Bedeutung für die Kirchengeschichte und für die Evangelienforschung.* Halle: Pfeffer, 1860.

Hilgert, Earle. "The Jubilees Calendar and the Origin of Sunday Observance." *AUSS* 1 (1963) 44–51.

Hofmann, Fritz. "Die Osterbotschaft in den Predigten Papst Leos des Grossen." *Paschatis Sollemnia* (Jungmann-Festschrift). Eds. Balthasar Fischer and Johannes Wagner, 76–86. Freiburg: Herder, 1959.

Holl, Karl. "Ein Bruchstück aus einem bisher unbekannten Brief des Epiphanius." *Festgabe für Adolf Jülicher*, 159–189. Tübingen: Mohr, 1927. Reprinted in Karl Holl, *Gesammelte Aufsätze zur Kirchengeschichte* 2, *Der Osten*, 204–224. Tübingen: Mohr, 1928.

Howard, J. K. "Passover and Eucharist in the Fourth Gospel." *Scottish Journal of Theology* 20 (1967) 329–337.

Hruby, Kurt. "La Pâque juive au temps du Christ à la lumière des documents de la littérature rabbinique." *OrSyr* 6 (1961) 81–94.

Huber, Wolfgang. *Passah und Ostern. Untersuchungen zur Osterfeier der alten Kirche.* Beihefte zur Zeitschrift für die neutestamentliche Wissenschaft 35. Berlin: Töpelmann, 1969.

Huglo, Michel. "L'auteur de l'Exultet pascal." *VigChr* 7 (1953) 79–88.

Hyldahl, Niels. "Zum Titel *Peri Pascha* bei Meliton." *StTh* 19 (1965) 55–67.

Jankowski, A. "Eucharystia jako 'nasza Pascha' (1 Kor 5, 7) w teologii biblijnej Nowego Testamentu." *Ruch biblijny i liturgiczny* 28 (1975) 89–100.

Jaubert, Annie. *The Date of the Last Supper.* Trans. Isaac Rafferty. New York: Alba House, 1965.

——————. "Une discussion patristique sur la chronologie de la passion." *RSR* 54 (1966) 407–410.

Jeremias, Joachim. *Die Passahfeier der Samaritaner und ihre Bedeutung für das Verständnis der alttestamentlichen Passahüberlieferung. BZAW* 59. Giessen: Töpelmann, 1932.

——————. "*Pascha.*" *TDNT* 5 (1967) 896–904.

——————. *The Eucharistic Words of Jesus.* Trans. from the 3rd German ed. by Norman Perrin. London: SCM; New York: Scribners, 1966.

——————. "Der Opfertod Jesu Christi." *Jesus und seine Botschaft,* 78–92. Stuttgart: Calwer, 1976.

Jossua, Jean-Pierre. *Le salut. Incarnation ou mystère pascal chez les Pères de l'Église de saint Irénée à saint Léon le Grand.* Paris: Cerf, 1968.

Jounel, Pierre. "The Easter Cycle." *The Church at Prayer: An Introduction to the Liturgy,* new ed., 4, *The Liturgy and Time.* Trans. Matthew J. O'Connell, 33–76. Collegeville: The Liturgical Press, 1986.

Kannengiesser, Charles. "Le mystère pascal du Christ mort et resuscité selon Jean Chrysostome et Augustin." *Jean Chrysostom et Augustin,* Actes du Colloque de Chantilly, 22–24 sept. 1974. Ed. Charles Kannengiesser, 241–246. Paris: Beauchesne, 1975.

——————. "Le mystère pascal du Christ mort et resuscité selon Athanase d'Alexandrie." *RSR* 63 (1975) 407–442.

Kirchgässner, Alfons. "Ostern das christliche Neujahrsfest." *Paschatis Sollemnia* (Jungmann-Festschrift). Eds. Balthasar Fischer and Johannes Wagner, 49–56. Freiburg: Herder, 1959.

Klein, Michael L. *The Fragment-Targums of the Pentateuch according to their Extant Sources. AnBib* 76. Rome: Biblical Institute Press, 1980.

_____. *Genizah Manuscripts of the Palestinian Targum to the Pentateuch.* Cincinnati: Hebrew Union College, 1986.

Koch, Hugo. "Pascha in der ältesten Kirche." *ZWTh* 55 (1914) 289–313.

_____. "Petrus und Paulus im zweiten Osterfeierstreit." *ZNW* 19 (1919–1920) 174–179.

_____. "Die *Tessarakoste* in can. V. von Nicäa (325)." *ZKG* 54 (1925) 481–488.

Kretschmar, Georg. "Christliches Passah im 2. Jahrhundert und die Ausbildung der christlichen Theologie." *Judéo-christianisme. Recherches historiques et théologiques offertes en hommage au cardinal Jean Daniélou,* 287–323. Paris: Beauchesne, 1972 = *RSR* 60 (1972) 287–323.

Kroll, Josef. *Gott und Hölle. Der Mythos vom Descensuskampfe.* Studien der Bibliothek Warburg, 20. Leipzig and Berlin: Teubner, 1932; repr. Darmstadt, 1963.

Krusch, Bruno. *Studien zur christlich-mittelalterlichen Chronologie.* Der 84 jährige Ostercyclus und siene Quellen. Leipzig: Veit, 1880.

Kutsch, Ernst. "Erwägungen zur Geschichte der Passahfeier und des Massot-festes." *ZThK* 55 (1958) 1–35.

Lambot, Cyrille. "Les sermons de saint Augustin pour les fêtes de Pâques. Tradition manuscrite." *Mélanges en l'honneur de Mgr Michel Andrieu,* 263–278. Strasbourg: Palais Universitaire, 1957.

_____. "Les sermons de saint Augustin pour les fêtes de Pâques: Liturgie et archéologie." *RevSR* 30 (1956) 230–240.

_____. "Une série pascale de sermons de saint Augustin sur les jours de la création." *Mélanges Christine Mohrmann,* 213–221. Utrecht: Spectrum, 1963.

Lampe, Geoffrey W. H. "The Reasonableness of Typology." *Essays on Typology* by G. W. H. Lampe and K. J. Woollcombe, 9–38. Studies in Biblical Theology, 22. London: SCM, 1957.

_____. "*Pascha*." *PGL* 1046–1049.

La Piana, George. "The Roman Church at the End of the Second Century." *HThR* 18 (1925) 201–277.

Leaney, Alfred R. C. "I Peter and the Passover: An Interpretation." *NTS* 10 (1963–1964) 238–250.

Leclercq, Henri. "Pâques." *DACL* 13 (1938) 1521–1574.

_____. "Tessaracosté—Carème ou Ascension?" *DACL* 15 (1953) 2056–2059.

Le Déaut, Roger. *La nuit pascale. Essai sur la signification de la Pâque juive à partir du Targum d'Exode XII, 42.* AnBib 22. Rome: Institut Biblique Pontifical, 1963.

_____. "Pâque juive et Pâque chrétienne." *BVC* 62 (1965) 14–26.

Le Déaut, Roger, and Joseph Lécuyer. "Exode." *DSp* 4 (1961) 1957–1995.

Lefort, L. T. "A propos des Festales de S. Athanase." *Le Muséon* 67 (1954) 43–50.

Leonardi, G. "La Pasqua ebraica precristiana." *StPat* 13 (1966) 226–235.

Lohse, Bernhard. *Das Passafest der Quartadecimaner.* Beiträge zur Förderung christlicher Theologie, 2nd series, 54. Gütersloh: Bertelsmann, 1953.

Loi, Vincenzo. "Il 25 marzo data pasquale e la cronologia giovannea della passione in età patristica." *EL* 85 (1971) 48–69.

——————. "La tipologia dell'agnello pasquale e l'attesa escatologica in età patristica." *Salesianum* 33 (1971) 187–204.

Lundberg, Per. *La typologie baptismale dans l'ancienne église. ASNU* 10. Uppsala: Lundeqvist; Leipzig: A. Lorentz, 1942.

Martin, Charles. "Un *Peri tou Pascha* de S. Hippolyte retrouvé?" *RSR* 16 (1926) 148–165.

Merendino, Pius. *Paschale Sacramentum. Eine Untersuchung über die Osterkatechese des hl. Athanasius von Alexandrien in ihrer Beziehung zu den frühchristlichen exegetisch-theologischen Überlieferungen. LWQF* 42. Münster: Aschendorff, 1965.

Michels, Th. "Das Frühlingssymbol in österlicher Liturgie, Rede und Dichtung des christlichen Altertums." *JLW* 6 (1926) 1–15.

Mohrmann, Christine. "Exultent divina mysteria." *EL* 66 (1952) 274–281.

——————. "Pascha, Passio, Transitus." *EL* 66 (1952) 37–52. Reprinted in C. Mohrmann, *Études sur le latin des chrétiens, 1, Le latin des chrétiens,* 2nd ed., 205–222 Rome: Edizioni di storia e letteratura, 1961.

——————. "Le conflit pascal au IIe siècle: note philologique." *VigChr* 16 (1962) 154–171.

Morris, L. L. "The Passover in Rabbinic Literature." *Australian Biblical Review* 4 (1954–1956) 59–76.

Nautin, Pierre. "L'homélie de Méliton sur la Passion." *RHE* 44 (1949) 429–438.

——————. *Le dossier d'Hippolyte et de Méliton.* Patristica, 1. Paris: Cerf, 1953.

——————. *Lettres et écrivains chrétiens des IIe et IIIe siècles.* Patristica, 2. Paris: Cerf, 1961.

Neunheuser, Burkhard. "Pasqua." *Dizionerio di Spiritualità* 2 (1976) 1401–1405.

Nikolasch, F. *Das Lamm als Christussymbol in den Schriften der Väter.* Wiener Beiträge zur Theologie, 3. Wien: Herder, 1963.

Noé, V. "*Sacramentum paschale:* la cinquantena pasquale in S. Leone M." *Rivista Liturgica* 49 (1962) 101–106.

Ortiz de Urbina, Ignacio. "La Pasqua nel pensiero teologico primitivo." *Orientalia christiana periodica* 36 (1970) 444–453.

Pascual, J. A. "El misterio pascual según san León Magno." *RET* 24 (1964) 299–319.

Pattaro, G. "Il mistero pasquale nella catechesi dei Padri." *StPat* 13 (1966) 256–276.

Peri, V. "Lo stato degli studi intorno all'origine della Quaresima." *Aevum* 34 (1960) 525–555.

_____. "La cronologia delle lettere festali di sant'Atanasio e la Quaresima." *Aevum* 35 (1961) 28–86.

_____. "La data della Pasqua. Nota sull'origine e lo sviluppo della questione pasquale tra le chiese cristiane." *Vetera Christianorum* 13 (1976) 319–348.

Perler, Othmar. *Ein Hymnus zur Ostervigil von Meliton?* Paradosis, 15. Freiburg (Switzerland): Éditions Universitaires, 1960.

_____. "Recherches sur le 'Peri Pascha' de Méliton." *RSR* 51 (1963) 407–421.

_____. "Typologie der Leiden des Herrn in Melitons Peri Pascha." *Kyriakon. Festschrift Johannes Quasten.* Eds. Patrick Granfield and Josef A. Jungmann, 1:256–265. Münster: Aschendorff, 1970.

Poque, Suzanne. "Les lectures liturgiques de l'octave pascale à Hippone d'après les Traités de saint Augustin sur la première épître de S. Jean." *RB* 74 (1964) 217–241.

Preuschen, Erwin. "Passah, altkirchliches und Passahstreitigkeiten." *RE* 14 (1904) 725–734.

Priotto, Michelangelo. *La prima pasqua in Sapienza 18, 5–25. Rilettura e attualizzazione.* Supplementi alla Rivista Biblica [Italiana], 15. Bologna: Ed. Dehoniane, 1987.

Puech, H.-Ch. "Audianer." *RAC* 1 (1950) 910–915.

Puniet, Pierre de. "St. Augustin et l'alleluja pascal." *QLP* 15 (1930) 85–96.

Quasten, Johannes. "Die Ostervigil im Testamentum Domini." *Paschatis Sollemnia* (Jungmann-Festschrift). Eds. Balthasar Fischer and Johannes Wagner, 87–95. Freiburg: Herder, 1959.

Rahner, Hugo. "Österliche Frühlingslyrik bei Kyrillos von Alexandreia." *Paschatis Sollemnia* (Jungmann-Festschrift). Eds. Balthasar Fischer and Johannes Wagner, 68–75. Freiburg: Herder, 1959.

Rahner, Karl. "Dogmatische Fragen zur Osterfrömmigkeit." *Paschatis Sollemnia* (Jungmann-Festschrift). Eds. Balthasar Fischer and Johannes Wagner, 1–12. Freiburg: Herder, 1959.

Rengstorf, Karl-Heinrich. "Ostern im Zeugnis der ältesten Gemeinde

Jesu." *In dieser österlichen Zeit*, ed. Hans-Jürgen Schultz, 191–96. Hamburg: Furche-Verlag, 1955.

Renoux, Athanase. *Le codex arménien Jérusalem 121*. Vol. I, *Introduction aux origines de la liturgie Hiérosolymitaine, lumières nouvelles.* Vol. II, *Édition comparée du texte et de deux autres manuscrits. Introduction, textes, traduction et notes. PO* 35/1, 36/2. Turnhout: Brepols, 1969, 1971.

Renoux, Charles. "Le Triduum Pascal dans le rite arménien et les hymnes de la Grande Semaine." *EL* 94 (1980) 323–72.

Richard, Cl. *Il est notre Pâque. La gratuité du salut en Jésus-Christ.* Paris: Cerf, 1980.

Richard, Marcel. "La question pascale au IIe siècle." *OrSyr* 6 (1961) 179–212.

———. "Une homélie monarchienne sur la Pâque." *StPatr* 3 (= TU 78; 1961) 273–289.

———. "La lettre de Saint Irénée au Pape Victor." *ZNW* 56 (1965) 260–282.

Richardson, Cyril C. "The Quartodecimans and the Synoptic Chronology." *HThR* 33 (1940) 177–190.

———. "A New Solution to the Quartodeciman Riddle." *JThS* n.s. 24 (1973) 74–84.

Righetti, Mario. *Manuale di Storia liturgica.* Milan: Ancora. Vol. 2, 2nd ed., 1955.

Römer, G. "Die Liturgie des Karfreitags." *ZKTh* 77 (1955) 39–93.

Rordorf, Willi. "Zum Ursprung des Osterfestes am Sonntag." *ThZ* 18 (1962) 167–189.

Ros Garmendía, S. *La Pascua en el Antiguo Testamento. Estudio de los textos pascuales del A.T. a la luz . . . de la Tradición.* Biblica Victoriensia, 3. Vitoria: Eset, 1978.

Rost, Leonhard, and Gerhard Sevenster. "Passa." *BHH* 3 (1966) 1396–1398.

Roth, A. "Pascha und Hinübergang durch Glaube, Hoffnung und Liebe (Augustinus, Brief 55 an Januarius)." *Mélanges Christine Mohrmann, Nouveau Recueil*, 96–107. Utrecht/Anvers: Spectrum, 1973.

Sauser, Ekkart. Das Paschamysterium in den sogenannten frühchristlichen Passionssarkophagen." *Kyriakon: Festschrift Johannes Quasten.* Eds. Patrick Granfield and Josef A. Jungmann, 2:654–662. Münster: Aschendorff, 1970.

Schildenberger, Johannes. "Der Gedächtnischarakter des alt- und neutestamentlichen Pascha." *Opfer Christi und Opfer der Kirche*, ed. Burkhard Neunheuser, 75–97. Düsseldorff: Patmos, 1960.

Schmid, Joseph. *Die Osterfestfrage auf dem ersten allgemeinen Konzil von Nicäa.* Theologische Studien der Leo-Gesellschaft, 13. Vienna: Mayer, 1905.

_____. *Die Osterfestberechnung in der abendländischen Kirche vom 1. allgemeinen Konzil zu Nicaea bis zum Ende des 8. Jahrhunderts.* Strassburger Theologische Studien, 9/1. Freiburg: Herder, 1907.

Schmidt, Carl, ed. and trans. *Gespräche Jesu mit seinen Jüngern nach der Auferstehung. Ein katholisch-apostolisches Sendschreiben des 2. Jahrhunderts. TU* 43. Leipzig: Hinrichs, 1919, repr. Hildesheim: Olms, 1967.

Schmidt, Hermann. "Paschalibus initiati mysteriis." *Gregorianum* 39 (1958) 463-480.

Schuberth, D. "Über Ursprung und Sinn der Osterkerze." *JLH* 12 (1967) 94-100.

Schulz, Hans-Joachim. "Die 'Höllenfahrt' als 'Anastasis': Eine Untersuchung über Eigenart und dogmengeschichtliche Voraussetzungen byzantinischer Osterfrömmigkeit." *ZKTh* 81 (1959) 1-66.

Schümmer, J. *Die altchristliche Fastenpraxis mit besonderer Berücksichtigung der Schriften Tertullians. LWQF* 27. Münster: Aschendorff, 1933.

Schürmann, Heinz. "Die Anfänge der christlichen Osterfeier." *ThQ* 131 (1951) 414-425. Repr. in Heinz Schürmann, *Ursprung und Gestalt,* 199-206. Düsseldorf: Patmos, 1970.

_____. "Vorgang und Sinngehalt der urchristlichen Osterfeier (Zu: Bernhard Lohse, *Das Paschafest der Quartadecimaner*)." Heinz Schürmann, *Ursprung und Gestalt,* 207-209. Düsseldorf: Patmos, 1970.

Schütz, W. " 'Was habe ich dir getan, mein Volk?' Die Wurzeln der Karfreitagsimproperien in der alten Kirche." *JLH* 13 (1968) 1-38.

Schwartz, Eduard. "Die Osterbriefe." *Nachrichten der königlichen Gesellschaft der Wissenschaften zu Göttingen, philosophisch-historische Klasse* (1904) 333-356. Repr. in Eduard Schwartz, *Gesammelte Schriften* 3:1-29. Berlin: de Gruyter, 1959.

_____. *Christliche und jüdische Ostertafeln.* Abhandlungen der Gesellschaft der Wissenschaften zu Göttingen, philologisch-historische Klasse, n.s 8, 6. Berlin: Weidmann, 1905.

_____. "Osterbetrachtungen." *ZNW* 7 (1906) 1-33. Repr. in Eduard Schwartz, *Gesammelte Schriften,* 5:1-41. Berlin: de Gruyter, 1963.

_____. "Zur Kirchengeschichte des vierten Jahrhunderts: I. Athanasius' Osterbriefe." *ZNW* 34 (1935) 129-137. Repr. in Eduard Schwartz, *Gesammelte Schriften* 4:1-11. Berlin: de Gruyter, 1960.

Segal, Judah Benzion. *The Hebrew Passover from the Earliest Times to A.D. 70*. London Oriental Series, 12. New York: Oxford University Press, 1963.

Sevenster, Gerhard. "Passalamm." *BHH* 3 (1966) 1398–99.

Shepherd, Massey H. *The Paschal Liturgy and the Apocalypse*. London: Lutterworth Press, 1960.

Sisti, A. "La Pasqua dei cristiani (Note su 1 Cor 5, 6-8)." *Euntes Docete* 28 (1975) 395–411.

Soos, Marie-Bernard de. *Le mystère liturgique d'après saint Léon le Grand*. *LWQF* 34. Münster: Aschendorff, 1958.

Souvay, Charles L. "The Paschal Controversy under Pope Victor I." *CHR* 15 (1929–1930) 43–62.

Stanley, David M. "St. John and the Paschal Mystery." *Worship* 33 (1959) 293–301. Repr. in *Contemporary New Testament Studies*, ed. M. Rosalie Ryan, 343–349. Collegeville: The Liturgical Press, 1965.

Strand, Kenneth A. "John as Quartodeciman: a Reappraisal." *JBL* 84 (1965) 251–258.

_____. "Another Look at 'Lord's Day' in the Early Church and in Rev 1:10." *NTS* 13 (1966–1967) 174–181.

Strobel, August. "Passa-Symbolik und Passa-Wunder in Act 12, 3ff." *NTS* 4 (1957–1958) 210–215.

_____. "Die Passa-Erwartung als urchristliches Problem in Lc 17, 20f." *ZNW* 49 (1958) 157–196.

_____. "Die 'bösen Buben' der syrischen Ostervigil." *ZKG* 69 (1958) 113–114.

_____. *Untersuchungen zum eschatologischen Verzögerungsproblem auf Grund der spätjüdisch-urchristlichen Geschichte von Habakuk 2, 2ff*. Supplements to NT, 2. Leiden: Brill, 1961.

_____. "In dieser Nacht (Luk 17,34). Zu einer älteren Form der Erwartung in Luk 17,20-37." *ZThK* 58 (1961) 16–29.

_____. "Zu Lk 17,20f." *BZ* n.s. 7 (1963) 111–113.

_____. "Die Osterberechnung des Aristides. Eine Berichtigung." *ZNW* 55 (1964) 131–132.

_____. *Ursprung und Geschichte des frühchristlichen Osterkalenders*. *TU* 121. Berlin: Akademie-Verlag, 1977.

_____. *Texte zur Geschichte des frühchristlichen Osterkalenders*. *LWQF* 64. Münster: Aschendorff, 1984.

Thibaut, Jean-Baptiste. *Ordre des offices de la Semaine Sainte à Jérusalem du IVe au Xe siècle*. Études de liturgie et de topographie palestiniennes. Paris: Maison de la bonne presse, 1926.

Thornton, T. C. G. "I Peter—a Paschal Liturgy?" *JThS* n.s. 12 (1961) 14–26.

Vandenbroucke, François. "Les origines de l'octave pascale." *QLP* 27 (1946) 133-149.

Van den Veken, B. J. "De primordiis liturgiae paschalis." *SE* 13 (1962) 461-501.

_____. "De sensu Paschatis in saeculo secundo et Epistula Apostolorum." *SE* 14 (1963) 5-33.

Van Esbroeck, Michel. "Le traité sur la Pâque de Méliton de Sardes en géorgien." *Le Muséon* 84 (1971) 373-394.

Van Goudoever, J. *Biblical Calendars*. 2nd ed. Leiden: Brill, 1961.

Van Unnik, Willem Cornelis. "Een merkwaardige formulering van de verlossing in de Paschahomilie van Melito van Sardes." *Ex auditu Verbi. Theologische opesteleen aangeboden aan G. C. Berkouwer*, 297-311. Kampen: Kok, 1965.

Vignolo, Roberto. "Storia della salvezza nel Peri Pascha di Melitone di Sardi." *ScC* 99 (1971) 3-26.

Vorgrimmler, Herbert. "War die altchristliche Ostervigil eine ununterbrochene Feier?" *ZKTh* 74 (1952) 464-472.

_____. "Vorfragen zur Theologie des Karsamstags." *Paschatis Sollemnia* (Jungmann-Festschrift). Eds. Balthasar Fischer and Johannes Wagner, 13-22. Freiburg: Herder, 1959.

Weitzel, C. L. *Die christliche Passafeier der ersten drei Jahhunderte*. Pforzheim: Flammer und Hoffmann, 1848.

Weller, Philip T. *The Easter Sermons of St. Augustine*. Catholic University Studies in Sacred Theology, 2nd ser., 87. Washington: Catholic University of America Press, 1955.

Wessel, Klaus. "Durchzug durch das Rote Meer." *RAC* 4 (1959) 370-389.

Wilhelm, P. "Auferstehung Christi." *Lexikon der christlichen Ikonographie* (1968) 1:201-218. Rome and Freiburg: Herder, 1968.

Zernov, N. "Eusebius and the Paschal Controversy at the End of the Second Century." *Church Quarterly Review* 116 (1933) 24-41.

Ziener, Georg. "Johannesevangelium und urchristliche Passafeier." *Biblische Zeitschrift* n.s. 2 (1958) 263-274.

Zimmermann, H. "Die Eucharistie als das Paschamahl des NT." *Vom Mysterium unseres Pascha = LebZeug* 3 (1965) 38-48.

Zuntz, G. "On the Opening Sentence of Melito's Paschal Homily." *HThR* 36 (1943) 299-315.

_____. "Melito—Syriac?" *VigChr* 6 (1952) 193-201.

Zwinggi, A. "Die Osternacht bei Augustinus." *Liturgisches Jahrbuch* 20 (1970) 4-10.

B. THE PENTECOST AND THE ASCENSION

Aalen, Sverre. "Pfingsten." *BHH* 3 (1966) 1440–1441.

Boeckh, Jürgen. "Die Entwicklung der altkirchlichen Pentecoste." *JLH* 5 (1960) 1–45.

Cabié, Robert. *La Pentecôte. L'évolution de la cinquantaine pascale au cours des cinq premiers siècles.* Tournai: Desclée, 1965.

Cantinat, J. "La Pentecôte." *BVC* 86 (1969) 57–69.

Davies, John Gordon. "The Perigrinatio Egeriae and the Ascension." *VigChr* 8 (1954) 93–100.

_____. *He Ascended into Heaven: A Study in the History of Doctrine.* London: Lutterworth Press, 1958.

Dekkers, E. "De datum der 'Peregrinatio Egeriae' en het Feest van Ons Heer Hemelvaart." *SE* 1 (1948) 181–205.

Delcor, M. "Das Bundesfest in Qumran und das Pfingstfest." *Bibel und Leben* 4 (1963) 188–204.

_____. "Pentecôte." *DBS* 7 (1966) 858–879.

Devos, Paul. "Égérie à Bethléem: le 40e jour après Pâques à Jérusalem, en 383." *Analecta Bollandiana* 86 (1968) 87–108.

Goetzmann, J. "La Pentecôte, prémices de la nouvelle création." *BVC* 27 (1959) 59–69.

Haag, Herbert. "Das liturgische Leben der Qumrangemeinde." *ALW* 10 (1967) 78–109.

Heisenberg, Aug. "Zur Feier von Weihnachten und Himmelfahrt im alten Jerusalem." *ByZ* 24 (1923–1924) 329–335.

Holzmeister, Urban. "Der Tag der Himmelfahrt des Herrn." *ZKTh* 55 (1931) 44–82.

Hruby, Kurt. "Shavu'ot ou la Pentecôte." *OrSyr* 8 (1963) 395–412.

_____. "La fête de la Pentecôte dans la tradition juive." *BVC* 63 (1965) 46–64.

Jaubert, Annie. "La notion d'alliance dans le judaïsme aux abords de l'ère chrétienne." *Patristica Sorbonensia* 6 (1963) 101–106.

Kraus, Hans-Joachim. *Gottesdienst in Israel.* 2nd ed. Munich: Kaiser, 1962.

Kretschmar, Georg. "Himmelfahrt und Pfingsten." *ZKG* 66 (1954–1955) 209–253.

Kutsch, Ernst. "Der Kalender des Jubiläenbuches und das Alte und das Neue Testament." *VT* 11 (1961) 39–47.

Kutsch, Ernst, and others. "Feste und Feiern." *Religion in Geschichte und Gegenwart* 2 (1958) 910–924.

Larrañaga, Victorien. *L'Ascension de Notre-Seigneur dans le Nouveau Testament.* Trans. J. Cazaux. Rome: Institut Biblique Pontifical, 1938.

Le Déaut, Roger. "Pentecôte et tradition juive." *Assemblées du Seigneur* 51 (1963) 22–38.

Leaney, Alfred R. C. *The Rule of Qumran and its Meaning: Introduction, Translation, and Commentary.* London: SCM; Philadelphia: Westminster, 1966.

Lohse, Eduard. *"Pentêkostê." TDNT* 6 (1968) 44–53.

Maertens, Thierry. *C'est fête en l'honneur de Yahvé.* Paris: Desclée de Brouwer, 1961.

Martin-Achard, Robert. *Essai biblique sur les fêtes d'Israël.* Geneva: Labor et Fides, 1974.

Noack, Bent. "The Day of Pentecost in Jubilees, Qumran, and Acts." *Annual of the Swedish Theological Institute in Jerusalem* 1 (1962) 73–95.

Potin, Jean. *La fête juive de la Pentecôte: étude des textes liturgiques.* 2 vols. *Lectio Divina* 65, a–b. Paris: Cerf, 1971.

Rétif, André. "Le mystère de la Pentecôte." *Vie Spirituelle* 84 (1951) 451–465.

Salaville, Sévérien. "La *Tessarakosté* du Ve canon de Nicée (325)." *EOr* 13 (1910) 65–72.

_____. "*Tessarakosté*, Ascension et Pentecôte au IVe siècle." *EOr* 32 (1929) 257–271.

Scripture Index

NEW TESTAMENT

Author Index

Subject Index